COMPARISON OF ASIAN INTERNATIONAL ARBITRATION RULES

Prepared by:

THE INTERNATIONAL ARBITRATION GROUP
OF
SIMPSON THACHER & BARTLETT LLP

John J. Kerr, Jr.
Peter C. Thomas
Robert H. Smit
Elizabeth A. Fuerstman

Juris Publishing

2003

ISBN 1-929446-50-0

Manufactured in the United States of America.

FOREWORD

The International Arbitration Group of Simpson Thacher & Bartlett LLP published its first chart comparing leading sets of international arbitration rules in 1998. In response to the positive feedback and demand we received to that chart, we published an updated second edition of that chart in 2002, and compiled this chart comparing the leading sets of Asian international arbitration rules.

Our International Arbitration Group uses this chart extensively, as it does the original chart, as an internal reference tool in connection with at least four different areas of our international arbitration practice. First, we regularly use the charts in assisting clients in selecting arbitration rules and drafting arbitration provisions for their international commercial contracts. For example, when a client wants to include a provision governing a specific procedural issue in an arbitration clause, the charts provide easy reference to the different provisions used in the leading sets of international arbitration rules. Second, the charts serve a similar function in connection with the advice we have provided to foreign governments in preparing their national legislation concerning international arbitration. Third, the charts assist us in developing arguments on procedural issues in connection with our representation of clients in international arbitration proceedings. Finally, members of our International Arbitration Group frequently refer to the charts in preparing articles for academic periodicals or conferences on international arbitration. By publishing these charts, we hope to share these benefits with users of international arbitration, practitioners, legislators and academics alike.

One of the most difficult tasks in compiling this chart was deciding which sets of Asian international arbitration rules to include in the chart in light of space and formatting limitations. We ultimately considered various factors in deciding which sets of rules to include in the chart. The China International Economic and Trade Arbitration Commission ("CIETAC"), Hong Kong International Arbitration Centre ("HKIAC"), Japan Commercial Arbitration Association ("JCAA"), Korean Commercial Arbitration Board ("KCAB"), and Singapore International Arbitration Centre ("SIAC") rules were included as leading sets of *institutional* Asian international arbitration rules. Other Asian institutional arbitration rules are not included simply for reasons of manageability and space. The arbitration rules of the United Nations Commission on International Trade ("UNCITRAL") were included as the preeminent set of *ad hoc* international arbitration rules, which are frequently used by parties in Asia as well as by Asian arbitration organizations, such as the HKIAC, as the basis for their institutional arbitration rules.

The structure of this chart follows the structure of the second edition of our chart on international arbitration rules, in part, to facilitate the use of the two charts together. Like the second edition of the chart on international arbitration rules, this chart contains an index of topics with page references to assist in locating subjects in the rules, and the full texts of the sets of arbitration rules are included in an appendix for ease of reference.

Compiling this chart was a challenging process, primarily because the various sets of international arbitration rules deal with specific procedural issues very differently. This chart was conceived and its compilation supervised by Robert Smit, but it never would have been completed without the extraordinary efforts of the members of our International Arbitration Group and the many associates and paralegals -- in particular Liz Fuerstman, Ryan Kane and Evelyn Scaramella -- who worked so hard creating the finished product. We also would like to express our deepest appreciation to Vratislav Pechota of Columbia

University's Parker School of Foreign and Comparative Law, with whom we very much enjoyed collaborating on the project.

TABLE OF CONTENTS

COMPARISON OF

Asian International Arbitration Rules

of

CIETAC, HKIAC, JCAA, KCAB, SIAC, and UNCITRAL

A Chart of Parallel Provisions

MODEL CLAUSE

INSTITUTIONAL					AD HOC
CIETAC ARBITRATION RULES (2000)	HKIAC ARBITRATION RULES (1985)	JCAA ARBITRATION RULES (1997)	KCAB ARBITRATION RULES (2000)	SIAC ARBITRATION RULES (1997)	UNCITRAL ARBITRATION RULES (1976)
Model Arbitration Clause "Any dispute arising from or in connection with this Contract shall be submitted China International Economic and Trade Arbitration Commission arbitration which shall be conducted in accordance with the Commission's arbitration rules in effect at the time of applying for arbitration. The arbitral award is final and binding upon both parties."	**Model Clauses** The Centre has adopted model clauses which those interested may wish to include in future contracts: a. "Any dispute, controversy, or claim arising out of or relating to this contract, or the breach, termination or invalidity thereof, shall be settled by arbitration in Hong Kong in accordance with the UNCITRAL Arbitration Rules in force at the date of this contract." b. "The appointing authority shall be the Hong Kong International Arbitration Centre." c. "Any such arbitration shall be administered by the Hong Kong International Arbitration Centre in accordance with its 'Procedures for Arbitration."	**Standard Arbitration Clause** All disputes, controversies or differences which may arise between the parties hereto, out of or in relation to or in connection with this Agreement shall be finally settled by arbitration in (name of city), Japan in accordance with the Commercial Arbitration Rules of The Japan Commercial Arbitration Association. The award rendered by the arbitrator(s) shall be final and binding upon the parties hereto.		**Model Clause** "Any dispute arising out of or in connection with this contract, including any question regarding its existence, validity or termination, shall be referred to and finally resolved by arbitration in [Singapore] in accordance with the Arbitration Rules of Singapore International Arbitration Centre ("SIAC Rules") for the time being in force which rules are deemed to be incorporated by reference to this clause." Parties may add: "The Tribunal shall consist of ________ arbitrator(s) to be appointed by the Chairman of SIAC." "The governing law of this contract shall be the substantive law of ________." "The language of the arbitration shall be ________."	"Any dispute, controversy or claim arising out of or relating to this contract, or the breach, termination or invalidity thereof, shall be settled by arbitration in accordance with the UNCITRAL Arbitration Rules as at present in force." Note - Parties may wish to consider adding: "(a) The appointing authority shall be… (name of institution or person);" "(b) The number of arbitrators shall be… (one or three);" "(c) The place of arbitration shall be… (town or country);" "(d) The language(s) to be used in the arbitral proceedings shall be…"

ARBITRATION CLAUSE
Model Clause

Institutional					Ad Hoc
CIETAC ARBITRATION RULES (2000)	HKIAC ARBITRATION RULES (1985)	JCAA ARBITRATION RULES (1997)	KCAB ARBITRATION RULES (2000)	SIAC ARBITRATION RULES (1997)	UNCITRAL ARBITRATION RULES (1976)
	d. "The parties agree to exclude any right of application or appeal to the Hong Kong Courts in connection with any question of law arising in the course of the arbitration or with respect to any award made." e. "The language(s) to be used in the arbitral proceedings shall be _________"				

ARBITRATION CLAUSE

Effect of Arbitration Clause/Application of Rules

Institutional					Ad Hoc
CIETAC ARBITRATION RULES (2000)	**HKIAC ARBITRATION RULES (1985)**	**JCAA ARBITRATION RULES (1997)**	**KCAB ARBITRATION RULES (2000)**	**SIAC ARBITRATION RULES (1997)**	**UNCITRAL ARBITRATION RULES (1976)**
Article 3 The Arbitration Commission will, upon the written application by one of the parties, accept a case in accordance with the arbitration agreement concluded between the parties, either before or after the occurrence of the dispute, in which it is provided that disputes are to be submitted to the Arbitration Commission for arbitration. An arbitration agreement means an arbitration clause in a contract concluded between the parties or any other form of written agreement providing for settlement of dispute by arbitration. **Article 7** If the parties agree to submit their dispute to the Arbitration Commission for arbitration, it will be taken that they have agreed to the case being arbitrated under	**Article 1 - Scope of Application** 1. Where the parties to a contract have agreed in writing that disputes in relation to that contract shall be referred to arbitration under the UNCITRAL Arbitration Rules, then such disputes shall be settled in accordance with these Rules subject to such modification as the parties may agree in writing. 2. These Rules shall govern the arbitration except that where any of these Rules is in conflict with a provision of the law applicable to the arbitration from which the parties cannot derogate, that provision shall prevail.	**Rule 2 - Application of These Rules** 1. These Rules shall apply where the parties have agreed to submit their dispute to arbitration under the Rules of the Association or simply arbitration at the Association (hereinafter the “arbitration agreement”). 2. These Rules shall apply if the parties agree, in writing, during the course of arbitral proceedings provided for in Rule 1, Paragraph 2, to conduct such arbitral proceedings pursuant to these Rules. In the case of such an agreement, the arbitral proceedings already conducted shall remain valid. **Rule 3 - Interpretation of These Rules** If any question arises concerning the interpretation of these Rules, the Association's	**Article 9 - Agreement of Parties** The parties shall be deemed to have made the provisions of the arbitration procedures of these Rules a part of their agreement whenever, in the submission of existing disputes or in a contract containing an arbitration clause, they have provided for arbitration by the KCAB or under these Rules. **Article 51 - Interpretation and Application of Rules** (1) The Tribunal in charge of the case shall interpret and apply these Rules insofar as they relate to the specific case.	**Preamble** Where any agreement, submission or reference provides for arbitration under the Arbitration Rules of Singapore International Arbitration Centre (“Centre”), the parties thereto shall be taken to have agreed that the arbitration shall be conducted in accordance with the following Rules, or such amended Rules as the Centre may have adopted to take effect before the commencement of the arbitration (see Rule 3.3), subject to such modifications as the parties may agree in writing. **Rule 1 - Scope of Application and Interpretation** 1.1 These Rules shall govern the arbitration save that, where any of these Rules is in conflict with a provision of the applicable law of the arbitration from which the parties cannot	**Article 1 - Scope of Application** 1. Where the parties to a contract have agreed in writing that disputes in relation to that contract shall be referred to arbitration under the UNCITRAL Arbitration Rules, then such disputes shall be settled in accordance with these Rules subject to such modification as the parties may agree in writing. 2. These Rules shall govern the arbitration except that where any of these Rules is in conflict with a provision of the law applicable to the arbitration from which the parties cannot derogate, that provision shall prevail.

INSTITUTIONAL					AD HOC
CIETAC ARBITRATION RULES (2000)	HKIAC ARBITRATION RULES (1985)	JCAA ARBITRATION RULES (1997)	KCAB ARBITRATION RULES (2000)	SIAC ARBITRATION RULES (1997)	UNCITRAL ARBITRATION RULES (1976)
these Rules. However, if the parties have agreed otherwise, and subject to consent by the Arbitration Commission, the parties' agreement will prevail.		interpretation shall prevail; provided that the interpretation of an arbitral tribunal shall, after such interpretation is made, prevail over that of the Association in the arbitration case before such tribunal. **Rule 4 - Arbitration Agreement** 2. When the parties have entered into an arbitration agreement, these Rules shall be deemed incorporated in such agreement; provided that the parties may agree otherwise to the extent that such agreement does not violate the spirit of these Rules.		derogate, that provision shall prevail. ***See also* Rule 34(2)-(3) at A-100.**	

NOTICE OR REQUEST FOR ARBITRATION

INSTITUTIONAL					AD HOC
CIETAC ARBITRATION RULES (2000)	HKIAC ARBITRATION RULES (1985)	JCAA ARBITRATION RULES (1997)	KCAB ARBITRATION RULES (2000)	SIAC ARBITRATION RULES (1997)	UNCITRAL ARBITRATION RULES (1976)
Article 13 The arbitration proceedings will commence from the date on which the Notice of Arbitration is issued by the Arbitration Commission or its Sub - Commissions. **Article 14** A Claimant submitting an Application for Arbitration must: (1) Submit an Application for Arbitration in writing, which shall, *inter alia*, contain: (a) the names and addresses of the Claimant and the Respondent, including the zip code, telephone, telex, fax, and cable numbers or any other means of electronic telecommunications, if any; (b) the arbitration agreement relied upon by the Claimant;	**Article 3 - Notice of Arbitration** 1. The party initiating recourse to arbitration (hereinafter called the "claimant") shall give to the other party (hereinafter called the "respondent") a notice of arbitration. 2. Arbitral proceedings shall be deemed to commence on the date on which the notice of arbitration is received by the respondent. 3. The notice of arbitration shall include the following: (a) A demand that the dispute be referred to arbitration; (b) The names and addresses of the parties; (c) A reference to the arbitration clause or the separate arbitration agreement that is invoked; (d) A reference to the contract out of or in relation to which the dispute arises;	**Rule 12 - Request for Arbitration** 1. To request the initiation of arbitral proceedings, the claimant shall submit to the Association a written request for arbitration setting forth the following: (1) a demand that the dispute be referred to arbitration under these Rules; (2) a reference to the arbitration agreement that is invoked; (3) the full personal or corporate names of the parties and their addresses; (4) if the claimant is represented by an agent, the name and address of such agent; (5) the relief or remedy claimed; (6) a summary of the dispute; and (7) the basis for the claim and the manner or method of proof.	**Article 10 - Claim** (1) A person desiring to file a claim with the KCAB under these Rules shall submit the following documents to the Secretariat accompanied by the arbitration costs as provided in Chapter IX: a) A document certifying agreement on arbitration; b) A power of attorney, in case the claim is made by an agent. (2) The following matters shall be stated in the statement of claim: a) The full names of the parties and their addresses (in case of corporations, the full names and addresses of the representatives shall also be stated); b) In case the Claimant is represented by an agent, the full name and address of the agent;	**Rule 3 - Request for or Notification of Arbitration** 3.1 The party wishing to commence an arbitration under these Rules (hereinafter called the "Claimant") shall give to the other party (hereinafter called the "Respondent") a Notice of Arbitration which shall include or be accompanied by the following: (a) a demand that the dispute be referred to arbitration; (b) the names and addresses of the parties to the arbitration; (c) a reference to the arbitration clause or the separate arbitration agreement that is invoked; (d) a reference to the contract out of or in relation to which the dispute arises;	**Article 3 - Notice of Arbitration** 1. The party initiating recourse to arbitration (hereinafter called the "claimant") shall give to the other party (hereinafter called the "respondent") a notice of arbitration. 2. Arbitral proceedings shall be deemed to commence on the date on which the notice of arbitration is received by the respondent. 3. The notice of arbitration shall include the following: (a) A demand that the dispute be referred to arbitration; (b) The names and addresses of the parties; (c) A reference to the arbitration clause or the separate arbitration agreement that is invoked; (d) A reference to the contract out of or in relation to which the dispute arises;

INSTITUTIONAL					AD HOC
CIETAC ARBITRATION RULES (2000)	HKIAC ARBITRATION RULES (1985)	JCAA ARBITRATION RULES (1997)	KCAB ARBITRATION RULES (2000)	SIAC ARBITRATION RULES (1997)	UNCITRAL ARBITRATION RULES (1976)
(c) the facts of the case and the main points of dispute; and (d) the Claimant's claim and the facts and reasons on which his claim is based. The Application for Arbitration shall be signed by, and/or affixed with the seal of, the Claimant and/or the authorized agent of the Claimant. (2) Attach to the Application for Arbitration the relevant documentary evidence which supports the facts on which the Claimant's claim is based. (3) Pay an arbitration fee in advance to the Arbitration Commission according to the Arbitration Fee Schedule of the Arbitration Commission. **Article 15** Upon receipt of the Application for Arbitration and its attachments, if the secretariat of the	(e) The general nature of the claim and an indication of the amount involved, if any; (f) The relief or remedy sought; (g) A proposal as to the number of arbitrators (i.e. one or three), if the parties have not previously agreed thereon. 4. The notice of arbitration may also include: (a) The proposals for the appointments of a sole arbitrator and an appointing authority referred to in article 6, paragraph 1; (b) The notification of the appointment of an arbitrator referred to in article 7; (c) The statement of claim referred to in article 18. ***See also* Articles 6-7 at A-29-31 and Article 18 at A-33-34.**	2. The claimant shall submit to the Association, together with the written request for arbitration, a copy of the arbitration clause or the separate arbitration agreement containing the arbitration agreement provided for in (2) of the preceding Paragraph. 3. If the claimant is represented by an agent in the arbitral proceedings, such agent shall submit a power of attorney to the Association together with the written request for arbitration. 4. The claimant shall, when it requests the initiation of arbitral proceedings, pay the request fee and the administrative fee provided for in the Arbitration Fee Regulations of the Association. If the claimant fails to pay such request fee and/or administrative fee, the Association may treat the request for arbitration as if it	c) The purport of the claim; d) The grounds for the claim and the method of proof. **Article 11 - Acceptance and Notification of Statement of Claim** (1) The Secretariat shall, upon submission of a statement of claim, examine whether such claim is in conformity with the provisions of Article 10 and accept it upon confirmation of its conformity. (2) The Secretariat shall, upon acceptance of the statement of claim, give such notice to both parties. In this case, a copy of the statement of claim shall be served on the Respondent accompanied by such notice. ***See also* Articles 12-13 at A-68-69 and Article 38 at A-76.**	(e) a brief statement describing the nature and circumstances of the dispute and specifying the relief claimed; and (f) a statement of any matters on which the parties have previously agreed as to the conduct of the arbitration or with respect to which the Claimant wishes to make a proposal. 3.2 The Notice of Arbitration may also include: (a) the proposals for the appointment of a sole arbitrator and an appointing authority referred to in Rules 7.1 and 7.2, respectively; (b) the notification of appointment of an arbitrator referred to in Rule 8; and (c) the Statement of Case referred to in Rule 18.2. 3.3 The date of receipt of the Notice of Arbitration by the Registrar of the Centre shall be deemed to be	(e) The general nature of the claim and an indication of the amount involved, if any; (f) The relief or remedy sought; (g) A proposal as to the number of arbitrators (i.e. one or three), if the parties have not previously agreed thereon. 4. The notice of arbitration may also include: (a) The proposals for the appointments of a sole arbitrator and an appointing authority referred to in article 6, paragraph 1; (b) The notification of the appointment of an arbitrator referred to in article 7; (c) The statement of claim referred to in article 18. ***See also* Articles 6-7 at A-103-104 and Article 18 at A-107-108.**

INSTITUTIONAL					AD HOC
CIETAC ARBITRATION RULES (2000)	HKIAC ARBITRATION RULES (1985)	JCAA ARBITRATION RULES (1997)	KCAB ARBITRATION RULES (2000)	SIAC ARBITRATION RULES (1997)	UNCITRAL ARBITRATION RULES (1976)
Arbitration Commission, after examination, finds that the Claimant has not yet completed the formalities required for arbitration, it will request the Claimant to complete them. If it finds that the Claimant has completed such formalities, the secretariat should promptly send to the Respondent a Notice of Arbitration, together with one copy each of the Claimant's Application for Arbitration and its attachments as well as the Arbitration Rules, the Panel of Arbitrators and the Arbitration Fee Schedule of the Arbitration Commission. At the same time, the Notice of Arbitration, the Arbitration Rules, the Panel of Arbitrators and Arbitration Fee Schedule should be sent to the Claimant as well. The secretariat of the Arbitration Commission, after sending the Notice of Arbitration to the		had not been made and return the written request for arbitration to the claimant with notification to such effect. 5. Arbitral proceedings shall be deemed to be initiated on the date on which the Association receives the written request for arbitration. **Rule 13 - Acceptance and Notification of Request for Arbitration** 1. The Association, upon confirmation that the request for arbitration has been made in conformity with the provisions of Paragraphs 1 through 3 of the preceding Rule, shall notify, without delay, the claimant and the respondent of the acceptance of the request for arbitration. Copies of the written request for arbitration and the arbitration agreement shall be attached to the notice sent to the respondent. 2. The Association shall designate one of		the date on which the arbitration has commenced. 3.4 The Claimant shall file with the Registrar a copy of the Notice of Arbitration served on the Respondent. 3.5 If the parties have agreed on an appointing authority other than the Chairman, they shall inform the Registrar of the name of that authority.	

INSTITUTIONAL					AD HOC
CIETAC ARBITRATION RULES (2000)	**HKIAC ARBITRATION RULES (1985)**	**JCAA ARBITRATION RULES (1997)**	**KCAB ARBITRATION RULES (2000)**	**SIAC ARBITRATION RULES (1997)**	**UNCITRAL ARBITRATION RULES (1976)**
Claimant and Respondent, shall appoint one of its staff-members to take charge of procedural administration of the case.		its offices as the secretariat in charge of administrative services and give notice thereof to each party when the Association notifies the parties of the acceptance of the request for arbitration provided for in the preceding Paragraph. **Rule 19 - Withdrawal of Request for Arbitration** 1. The claimant may, within thirty (30) days after the initiation of arbitral proceedings and before the appointment of any arbitrator, withdraw its request for arbitration upon written notice. 2. Except as provided in the preceding Paragraph, the claimant may withdraw its request for arbitration only with the written consent of the respondent. 3. Withdrawal of the request for arbitration shall become effective when the written notice of withdrawal and, in the case provided for in the			

INSTITUTIONAL					AD HOC
CIETAC ARBITRATION RULES (2000)	HKIAC ARBITRATION RULES (1985)	JCAA ARBITRATION RULES (1997)	KCAB ARBITRATION RULES (2000)	SIAC ARBITRATION RULES (1997)	UNCITRAL ARBITRATION RULES (1976)
		preceding Paragraph, the respondent's written consent thereto reach the Association. ***See also* Rule 14 at A-47 and Rule 41 at A-56**.			

COMMENCEMENT OF ARBITRATION

ANSWER AND COUNTERCLAIMS/REPLY

INSTITUTIONAL					AD HOC
CIETAC ARBITRATION RULES (2000)	HKIAC ARBITRATION RULES (1985)	JCAA ARBITRATION RULES (1997)	KCAB ARBITRATION RULES (2000)	SIAC ARBITRATION RULES (1997)	UNCITRAL ARBITRATION RULES (1976)
Article 17 The Respondent shall, within 45 days from the date of receipt of the Notice of Arbitration, submit his written defense and relevant documentary evidence to the secretariat of the Arbitration Commission. **Article 18** The Respondent shall, at the latest within 60 days from the date of receipt of the Notice of Arbitration, file with the secretariat of the Arbitration Commission his counterclaim in writing, if any. The arbitration tribunal may extend that time limit if it deems that there are justified reasons. When filing a counterclaim, the Respondent must state in his written statement of counterclaim his specific claim and facts and reasons upon which his claim is based, and attach to his written statement	**Article 19 - Statement of Defence** 1. Within a period of time to be determined by the arbitral tribunal, the respondent shall communicate his statement of defence in writing to the claimant and to each of the arbitrators. 2. The statement of defence shall reply to the particulars (b), (c) and (d) of the statement of claim (article 18, para. 2). The respondent may annex to his statement the documents on which he relies for his defence or may add a reference to the documents or other evidence he will submit. 3. In his statement of defence, or at a later stage in the arbitral proceedings if the arbitral tribunal decides that the delay was justified under the circumstances, the respondent may make a counter-claim arising out of the same contract or rely on a	**Rule 15 - Answer** 1. The respondent shall, within four (4) weeks from the Basic Date, submit to the Association a written answer setting forth the following: (1) the full personal or corporate names of the parties and their addresses; (2) if the respondent is represented by an agent, the name and address of such agent; (3) confirmation or denial of the claims; (4) a summary of the dispute; and (5) the basis for the answer and the manner or method of proof. 2. If the respondent is represented by an agent in the arbitral proceedings, such agent shall submit a power of attorney to the Association together with the written answer. 3. Subsequent to submission of the	**Article 12 - Defence** (1) The Respondent may, within 15 days in case of Domestic Arbitration and within 30 days in case of International Arbitration from the date of receipt of the notice in accordance with Paragraph (2) of Article 11 (hereinafter referred to as "Basic Date"), file a defence with the same Secretariat by submitting the following documents: a) A statement of defence; b) The original or reproduced copy of documentary evidence, if any, proving the grounds stated in the said defence; c) A power of attorney, in case the said defence is made by an agent. (2) The following matters shall be stated in the statement of defence provided in a) of Paragraph (1):	**Rule 4 - Response by Respondent** 4.1 For the purpose of facilitating the appointment of arbitrators, within fourteen (14) days of receipt of the Notice of Arbitration, the Respondent may send to the Claimant a Response, in which case, it shall contain: (a) a confirmation or denial of all or part of the claims; (b) a brief statement of the nature and circumstances of any envisaged counterclaims; and (c) a comment in response to any statements contained in the Notice of Arbitration, as called for under Rule 3.1 paragraph (f), on matters relating to the conduct of the arbitration. 4.2 The Response may also include - (a) a comment in response to any proposal for the	**Article 19 - Statement of Defence** 1. Within a period of time to be determined by the arbitral tribunal, the respondent shall communicate his statement of defence in writing to the claimant and to each of the arbitrators. 2. The statement of defence shall reply to the particulars (b), (c) and (d) of the statement of claim (article 18, para. 2). The respondent may annex to his statement the documents on which he relies for his defence or may add a reference to the documents or other evidence he will submit. 3. In his statement of defence, or at a later stage in the arbitral proceedings if the arbitral tribunal decides that the delay was justified under the circumstances, the respondent may make a counter-claim arising out of the same contract or rely on a

INSTITUTIONAL					AD HOC
CIETAC ARBITRATION RULES (2000)	HKIAC ARBITRATION RULES (1985)	JCAA ARBITRATION RULES (1997)	KCAB ARBITRATION RULES (2000)	SIAC ARBITRATION RULES (1997)	UNCITRAL ARBITRATION RULES (1976)
of counterclaim any relevant documentary evidence. When filing a counterclaim, the Respondent must pay an arbitration fee in advance according to the Arbitration Fee Schedule of the Arbitration Commission.	claim arising out of the same contract for the purpose of a set-off. 4. The provisions of article 18, paragraph 2, shall apply to a counter-claim and a claim relied on for the purpose of a set-off.	written answer, the Association shall send, without delay, a copy thereof to the other party or parties and, if an arbitrator has or arbitrators have been appointed, to such arbitrator or arbitrators. 4. If the written answer contains a counterclaim, the provisions of the following Rule shall apply to such counterclaim. **Rule 16 - Counterclaim** 1. The respondent may, only within six (6) weeks from the Basic Date, submit a counterclaim that is related to the claimant's claim(s) and covered by the same arbitration agreement. The arbitral tribunal shall examine any such counterclaim together with the claimant's claim(s). 2. The provisions of Rules 12, 13 and 15 shall apply *mutatis mutandis* to any counterclaim provided	a) The full names of the parties and their addresses(in case of corporations, the full names and their addresses including the full names of representatives and their addresses shall also be stated); b) In case the Respondent is represented by an agent, the full name and address of the agent; c) The purport of the defence; d) The grounds for the defence and the method of proof. (3) The Secretariat shall, upon receipt of the statement of defence, examine whether such defence is in conformity with the provision of Paragraph (2) of this Article, and upon confirmation of its conformity, accept it. (4) The Secretariat shall, upon acceptance of the statement of defence, give notice to the	appointments of a sole arbitrator and for an appointing authority; and (b) the notification of the appointment of an arbitrator referred to in Rule 8. 4.3 The Respondent shall send a copy of any Response to the Registrar and shall confirm to the Registrar that copies have been served on the other party. 4.4 Failure to send a Response shall not preclude the Respondent from denying the claim or from setting out a counterclaim in its Statement of Defence.	claim arising out of the same contract for the purpose of a set-off. 4. The provisions of article 18, paragraph 2, shall apply to a counter-claim and a claim relied on for the purpose of a set-off.

INSTITUTIONAL					AD HOC
CIETAC ARBITRATION RULES (2000)	HKIAC ARBITRATION RULES (1985)	JCAA ARBITRATION RULES (1997)	KCAB ARBITRATION RULES (2000)	SIAC ARBITRATION RULES (1997)	UNCITRAL ARBITRATION RULES (1976)
		for in the preceding Paragraph.	same effect to both parties. In this case, a copy of the said defence shall be served on the Claimant. (5) If no statement of defence is filed within the period provided in Paragraph (1) hereinabove, the Respondent is considered to have dismissed the claim. **Article 14 - Counterclaim** (1) The Respondent may submit a counterclaim at any time during the arbitral proceeding. However, if a counterclaim is filed late in the proceeding and has an undue effect on the other party or delays the completion of the proceeding, then the Tribunal may, pursuant to the other party's request or at its own discretion, deny filing of such counterclaim. (2) The proceedings of the Respondent's counterclaim shall be annexed to the		

INSTITUTIONAL					AD HOC
CIETAC ARBITRATION RULES (2000)	HKIAC ARBITRATION RULES (1985)	JCAA ARBITRATION RULES (1997)	KCAB ARBITRATION RULES (2000)	SIAC ARBITRATION RULES (1997)	UNCITRAL ARBITRATION RULES (1976)
			Claimant's request for arbitration. (3) The provisions of Article 10 through Article 13 shall apply *mutatis mutandis* to the acceptance of a counterclaim, its notice and the answer thereto. ***See also* Articles 15–16 at A-69.**		

COMMENCEMENT OF ARBITRATION
REGISTRATION FEE/ADVANCE ON COSTS

INSTITUTIONAL					AD HOC
CIETAC ARBITRATION RULES (2000)	HKIAC ARBITRATION RULES (1985)	JCAA ARBITRATION RULES (1997)	KCAB ARBITRATION RULES (2000)	SIAC ARBITRATION RULES (1997)	UNCITRAL ARBITRATION RULES (1976)
Article 14 A Claimant submitting an Application for Arbitration must: (3) Pay an arbitration fee in advance to the Arbitration Commission according to the Arbitration Fee Schedule of the Arbitration Commission. ***See also* Article 18 at A-8.**	**Article 41 - Deposit of Costs** 1. The arbitral tribunal, on its establishment, may request each party to deposit an equal amount as an advance for the costs referred to in article 38, paragraphs (a), (b) and (c). 2. During the course of the arbitral proceedings the arbitral tribunal may request supplementary deposits from the parties. 3. If an appointing authority has been agreed upon by the parties or designated by the Secretary-General of the Permanent Court of Arbitration at The Hague, and when a party so requests and the appointing authority consents to perform the function, the arbitral tribunal shall fix the amounts of any deposits or supplementary deposits only after consultation with the appointing authority which may make any	**Rule 12 - Request for Arbitration** 4. The claimant shall, when it requests the initiation of arbitral proceedings, pay the request fee and the administrative fee provided for in the Arbitration Fee Regulations of the Association. If the claimant fails to pay such request fee and/or administrative fee, the Association may treat the request for arbitration as if it had not been made and return the written request for arbitration to the claimant with notification to such effect. **Rule 67 - Payment to the Association** 1. The parties shall pay to the Association, in the manner and within the period of time determined by the arbitral tribunal, a sum of money fixed by it to cover the hearing fee, the hearing schedule alteration fee, the arbitrators' remuneration and necessary expenses	**Article 62 - Fees** (1) The fees shall be deposited in advance by the Claimant and divided into the administrative fee and the hearing date rescheduling fee; provided the Tribunal changes the date of hearing on its own initiative, the hearing date rescheduling fee will not be assessed. (2) In case the amount of claim is reduced by the change in the claim according to the provisions of Article 16, any differences in the administrative fee shall not be refunded. (3) The actual rate and the method of deposit, or the ratio and the method of refunds, for the fees shall be determined by the attached Fee Schedule. Fees not specified in the attached Fee Schedule shall be decided by the KCAB. **Article 63 - Expenses** (1) All the expenses required for arbitration	**Rule 27 - Deposits and Security** 27.1 The Registrar or the Tribunal (at any time after it has been constituted) may direct each party to deposit an equal amount with the Centre as an advance of the costs referred to in Rule 30. 27.2 During the course of the arbitration proceedings the Registrar or the Tribunal may request supplementary deposits from the parties. 27.3 The Tribunal shall have the power to order any party to provide security for the legal or other costs of any other party by way of deposit or bank guarantee or in any other manner the Tribunal thinks fit. 27.4 Without prejudice to the right of any party to apply to a competent court for pre-award conservatory measures, the Tribunal shall also have the power to	**Article 41 - Deposit of Costs** 1. The arbitral tribunal, on its establishment, may request each party to deposit an equal amount as an advance for the costs referred to in article 38, paragraphs (a), (b) and (c). 2. During the course of the arbitral proceedings the arbitral tribunal may request supplementary deposits from the parties. 3. If an appointing authority has been agreed upon by the parties or designated by the Secretary-General of the Permanent Court of Arbitration at The Hague, and when a party so requests and the appointing authority consents to perform the function, the arbitral tribunal shall fix the amounts of any deposits or supplementary deposits only after consultation with the appointing authority which may make any

INSTITUTIONAL					AD HOC
CIETAC ARBITRATION RULES (2000)	HKIAC ARBITRATION RULES (1985)	JCAA ARBITRATION RULES (1997)	KCAB ARBITRATION RULES (2000)	SIAC ARBITRATION RULES (1997)	UNCITRAL ARBITRATION RULES (1976)
	comments to the arbitral tribunal which it deems appropriate concerning the amount of such deposits and supplementary deposits. 4. If the required deposits are not paid in full within thirty days after the receipt of the request, the arbitral tribunal shall so inform the parties in order that one or another of them may make the required payment. If such payment is not made, the arbitral tribunal may order the suspension or termination of the arbitral proceedings. 5. After the award has been made, the arbitral tribunal shall render an accounting to the parties of the deposits received and return any unexpended balance to the parties. ***See also* Appointment Fee Schedule at A-25 and HKIAC As Appointing Authority: Advisory Comments**	incurred during the proceedings. 2. If a party fails to make payment as provided for in the preceding Paragraph, the arbitral tribunal may suspend or terminate the arbitral proceedings unless the other party makes such payment on behalf of the first party. 3. If, subsequent to termination of the arbitral proceedings, the total sum of money paid under the provisions of Paragraph 1 exceeds the total sum of the administrative fee and other fees and expenses determined by the arbitral tribunal under the provisions of Rule 49, Paragraph 3 and the hearing schedule alteration fee, the Association shall refund the difference to either or both of the parties. ***See also* Rule 65 at A-62.**	including the expenses of the arbitrators and Clerk, the expenses of any proofs produced, the expenses of witness or expert witness, the expenses of inspection, interpretation or translation, tape record, stenographic record or all transcripts thereof shall be deposited in advance by the party ordering such services. (2) The expenses in Paragraph (1) if they accrued from such services as requested by the Tribunal, shall be deposited in advance by the Claimant unless otherwise specified. **Article 64 - Allowances for Arbitrators** The allowances for the arbitrators fixed by the KCAB shall be deposited in advance by the Claimant. **Article 65 - Method of Deposits, etc.** (1) The Claimant shall deposit in advance to	order any party to provide security for all or part of any amount in dispute in the arbitration. 27.5 In the event that orders under Rules 27.1, 27.2, 27.3 or 27.4 are not complied with, the Tribunal may refuse to hear the claims or counterclaims by the non-complying party, although it may proceed to determine claims or counterclaims by complying parties.	comments to the arbitral tribunal which it deems appropriate concerning the amount of such deposits and supplementary deposits. 4. If the required deposits are not paid in full within thirty days after the receipt of the request, the arbitral tribunal shall so inform the parties in order that one or another of them may make the required payment. If such payment is not made, the arbitral tribunal may order the suspension or termination of the arbitral proceedings. 5. After the award has been made, the arbitral tribunal shall render an accounting to the parties of the deposits received and return any unexpended balance to the parties.

INSTITUTIONAL					AD HOC
CIETAC ARBITRATION RULES (2000)	HKIAC ARBITRATION RULES (1985)	JCAA ARBITRATION RULES (1997)	KCAB ARBITRATION RULES (2000)	SIAC ARBITRATION RULES (1997)	UNCITRAL ARBITRATION RULES (1976)
	Regarding Deposits at A-25, and HKIAC As Arbitration Administrator: Deposits at A-26.		the Secretariat at the time of the request the specified costs of arbitration provided in Article 62 through Article 64 in such currency as the Secretariat deems necessary. (2) In case such sums of advance payment provided in Paragraph (1) are deemed insufficient, the Secretariat may demand of the Claimant any additional sums of deposit. If the Claimant fails to pay in advance such deposits as provided in Paragraph (1) and (2) herein or the Respondent does not pay in lieu of the Claimant, the Tribunal may terminate the proceedings on its own decision. (3) The Secretariat shall prepare an Accounting Statement of the deposits when the hearing is closed, and the Balance Statement when the arbitral award is made. After delivery of the arbitral award		

INSTITUTIONAL					AD HOC
CIETAC ARBITRATION RULES (2000)	HKIAC ARBITRATION RULES (1985)	JCAA ARBITRATION RULES (1997)	KCAB ARBITRATION RULES (2000)	SIAC ARBITRATION RULES (1997)	UNCITRAL ARBITRATION RULES (1976)
			enclosed with the Balance Statement, the Secretariat shall refund any balance to the parties concerned. ***See also* Article 28 at A-74 and Article 30 at A-74.**		

CONSTITUTION OF THE ARBITRAL TRIBUNAL
NUMBER OF ARBITRATORS

INSTITUTIONAL					AD HOC
CIETAC ARBITRATION RULES (2000)	HKIAC ARBITRATION RULES (1985)	JCAA ARBITRATION RULES (1997)	KCAB ARBITRATION RULES (2000)	SIAC ARBITRATION RULES (1997)	UNCITRAL ARBITRATION RULES (1976)
	Article 5 - Number of Arbitrators If the parties have not previously agreed on the number of arbitrators (i.e. one or three), and if within fifteen days after the receipt by the respondent of the notice of arbitration the parties have not agreed that there shall be only one arbitrator, three arbitrators shall be appointed.	**Rule 21 - Agreement of Parties** 1. The parties may, by written agreement, appoint one or more arbitrators or determine the number, the method or the period of time (or all of the above) of appointment of the arbitrators. 2. The parties shall notify the Association, within, at the latest, three (3) weeks from the Basic Date, of the contents of an agreement provided for in the preceding Paragraph. **Rule 22 - Appointment of Arbitrators where the Parties have Determined the Method of Appointment** 4. If the parties have not entered into an agreement provided for in the latter part of Paragraph 1 of the preceding Rule with respect to the number of arbitrators, such number shall be determined pursuant	**Article 23 - Number of Arbitrators** If the number of arbitrators is specified in the arbitration agreement, the disputes shall be heard and determined by the same number of arbitrators as so specified; if, however, there has been no agreement as such, the number of the arbitrators shall be determined as 1 or 3 by the Secretariat.	**Rule 6 - Number of Arbitrators** A sole arbitrator shall be appointed unless the parties have agreed otherwise.	**Article 5 - Number of Arbitrators** If the parties have not previously agreed on the number of arbitrators (i.e. one or three), and if within fifteen days after the receipt by the respondent of the notice of arbitration the parties have not agreed that there shall be only one arbitrator, three arbitrators shall be appointed.

INSTITUTIONAL					AD HOC
CIETAC ARBITRATION RULES (2000)	HKIAC ARBITRATION RULES (1985)	JCAA ARBITRATION RULES (1997)	KCAB ARBITRATION RULES (2000)	SIAC ARBITRATION RULES (1997)	UNCITRAL ARBITRATION RULES (1976)
		to the provisions of the following Rule. **Rule 23 - Number of Arbitrators** If the parties fail to notify the Association, within three (3) weeks from the Basic Date, of their agreement with respect to the number of arbitrators, such number shall be one (1); provided that if either party requests in writing, within four (4) weeks from the Basic Date, that such number be three (3) and the Association determines that such request is appropriate, such number shall be three (3). ***See also* Rule 26(3) at A-51.**			

CONSTITUTION OF THE ARBITRAL TRIBUNAL
NATIONALITY/QUALIFICATIONS OF ARBITRATORS

INSTITUTIONAL					AD HOC
CIETAC ARBITRATION RULES (2000)	HKIAC ARBITRATION RULES (1985)	JCAA ARBITRATION RULES (1997)	KCAB ARBITRATION RULES (2000)	SIAC ARBITRATION RULES (1997)	UNCITRAL ARBITRATION RULES (1976)
Article 10 The Arbitration Commission establishes a Panel of Arbitrators. The arbitrators are selected and appointed by the Arbitration Commission from among Chinese and foreign persons with professional knowledge and practical experience in the fields of law, economics and trade, science and technology, etc.	**Article 6 - Appointment of Arbitrators** 4. In making the appointment, the appointing authority shall have regard to such considerations as are likely to secure the appointment of an independent and impartial arbitrator and shall take into account as well the advisability of appointing an arbitrator of a nationality other than the nationalities of the parties. ***See also* Article 8.2 at A-31.**	**Rule 20 - Qualification of Arbitrators** No person having a beneficial interest in the case under arbitration shall be an arbitrator. **Rule 24 - Appointment of Arbitrator - Single Arbitrator** 3. If the Association is to appoint an arbitrator pursuant to the provisions of the preceding Paragraph, the Association shall give due consideration to a written request, submitted by either party within one (1) week from the date on which it is determined that the Association shall make such appointment, that a person of a different nationality from those of the parties be appointed as such arbitrator. **Rule 25 - Appointment of Arbitrators - More than One Arbitrator** 5. If the Association is	**Article 19 - Qualifications of Arbitrator** No person shall serve as an arbitrator if he has any legal or financial interest in the outcome of the arbitration, provided, however, that the parties can appoint such person as an arbitrator notwithstanding their knowledge of disqualification by mutual agreement in writing. **Article 22 - Restriction on Appointment of Arbitrators** In regards to arbitrator(s) to be appointed by the Secretariat, if the parties are nationals of different countries and/or are domiciled in different countries, the sole arbitrator or the presiding arbitrator shall, upon the request of either party, be appointed from among the nationals of a country other than that of any of the parties. However, the request	**Rule 11 - Independence and Impartiality of Arbitrators** 11.1 In making an appointment under these Rules, the Chairman shall have due regard to any qualifications required of the arbitrator by the agreement of the parties and to such considerations as are likely to secure the appointment of an independent and impartial arbitrator and where the parties are of different nationalities, shall also take into account the advisability of appointing an arbitrator of a nationality other than those of the parties. 11.2 Any Arbitrator (whether or not appointed by the parties) conducting an arbitration under these Rules shall be and remain at all times independent and impartial, and shall not act as advocate for any party.	**Article 6 - Appointment of Arbitrators** 4. In making the appointment, the appointing authority shall have regard to such considerations as are likely to secure the appointment of an independent and impartial arbitrator and shall take into account as well the advisability of appointing an arbitrator of a nationality other than the nationalities of the parties. ***See also* Article 8.2 at A-105.**

INSTITUTIONAL					AD HOC
CIETAC ARBITRATION RULES (2000)	HKIAC ARBITRATION RULES (1985)	JCAA ARBITRATION RULES (1997)	KCAB ARBITRATION RULES (2000)	SIAC ARBITRATION RULES (1997)	UNCITRAL ARBITRATION RULES (1976)
		to make the appointment under the provisions of the preceding Paragraph, the provisions of Paragraph 3 of the preceding Rule shall apply *mutatis mutandis*. ***See also* Rule 28 at A-52.**	for appointment of arbitrators provided in this Article shall be filed with the Secretariat no later than the return of the list of candidates provided in Paragraph (2) of Article 21.	***See also* Rule 10 at A-89-90.**	

CONSTITUTION OF THE ARBITRAL TRIBUNAL

DISCLOSURE BY ARBITRATORS

INSTITUTIONAL					AD HOC
CIETAC ARBITRATION RULES (2000)	**HKIAC ARBITRATION RULES (1985)**	**JCAA ARBITRATION RULES (1997)**	**KCAB ARBITRATION RULES (2000)**	**SIAC ARBITRATION RULES (1997)**	**UNCITRAL ARBITRATION RULES (1976)**
Article 28 Any appointed arbitrator having a personal interest in the case shall himself disclose such circumstances to the Arbitration Commission and request a withdrawal from his office.	**Article 9 - Challenge of Arbitrators** A prospective arbitrator shall disclose to those who approach him in connexion with his possible appointment any circumstances likely to give rise to justifiable doubts as to his impartiality or independence. An arbitrator, once appointed or chosen, shall disclose such circumstances to the parties unless they have already been informed by him of these circumstances. **The HKIAC as Appointing Authority: Challenge of Arbitrators** Arbitrators appointed by the HKIAC are required to confirm their independence and impartiality. Where a decision is required by the appointing authority under the Rules on any challenge of an arbitrator, such decision is made on behalf of the HKIAC by	**Rule 20 - Qualification of Arbitrators** No person having a beneficial interest in the case under arbitration shall be an arbitrator.	**Article 25 - Disclosure by Arbitrator of Disqualifications** (1) Upon being notified of his appointment as an arbitrator, he shall immediately disclose in writing to the Secretariat any and all circumstances which might cause reasonable question about his fairness or independence. (2) Upon receipt of such disclosure of information as prescribed in Paragraph (1), the Secretariat shall immediately disclose it to both the Tribunal and the parties. If either party wishes to raise any objection to the appointment of such arbitrator(s), he or she shall make the challenge within 15 days from the date of the establishment of the Tribunal or from the date when the party making the challenge was informed of those circumstances provided in Paragraph (1) of this Article. But,	**Rule 11 - Independence and Impartiality of Arbitrators** 11.3 A prospective arbitrator shall disclose to those who approach him in connection with his possible appointment, any circumstances likely to give rise to justifiable doubts as to his impartiality or independence. 11.4 An arbitrator, once appointed or chosen, shall disclose any such circumstance (referred to in Rule 11.3 above) to all parties, not already been informed by him, of these circumstances.	**Article 9 - Challenge of Arbitrators** A prospective arbitrator shall disclose to those who approach him in connexion with his possible appointment any circumstances likely to give rise to justifiable doubts as to his impartiality or independence. An arbitrator, once appointed or chosen, shall disclose such circumstances to the parties unless they have already been informed by him of these circumstances.

INSTITUTIONAL					AD HOC
CIETAC ARBITRATION RULES (2000)	HKIAC ARBITRATION RULES (1985)	JCAA ARBITRATION RULES (1997)	KCAB ARBITRATION RULES (2000)	SIAC ARBITRATION RULES (1997)	UNCITRAL ARBITRATION RULES (1976)
	the Court of Appointment.		if either party does not submit any objection within the above period, he can not submit any objection to the qualification of such arbitrator(s) on the same grounds. (3) If either party submits an objection to the appointment of such questioned arbitrator(s) on the ground of notified reason, the vacancy thus created shall be filled in the same method as provided in Article 26.		

CONSTITUTION OF THE ARBITRAL TRIBUNAL

APPOINTMENT OF ARBITRATORS

INSTITUTIONAL					AD HOC
CIETAC ARBITRATION RULES (2000)	HKIAC ARBITRATION RULES (1985)	JCAA ARBITRATION RULES (1997)	KCAB ARBITRATION RULES (2000)	SIAC ARBITRATION RULES (1997)	UNCITRAL ARBITRATION RULES (1976)
Article 16 The Claimant and the Respondent shall, within 20 days as from the date of receipt of the Notice of Arbitration, each appoint an arbitrator from among the Panel of Arbitrators of the Arbitration Commission or authorize the Chairman of the Arbitration Commission to make such appointment. **Article 24** Each of the parties shall appoint one arbitrator from among the Panel of Arbitrators of the Arbitration Commission or entrust the Chairman of the Arbitration Commission to make such appointment. A third arbitrator shall be jointly appointed by the parties or appointed by the Chairman of the Arbitration Commission upon the parties' joint authorization.	**Article 6 - Appointment of Arbitrators** 1. If a sole arbitrator is to be appointed, either party may propose to the other: (a) The names of one or more persons, one of whom would serve as the sole arbitrator; and (b) If no appointing authority has been agreed upon by the parties, the name or names of one or more institutions or persons, one of whom would serve as appointing authority. 2. If within thirty days after receipt by a party of a proposal made in accordance with paragraph 1 the parties have not reached agreement on the choice of a sole arbitrator, the sole arbitrator shall be appointed by the appointing authority agreed upon by the parties. If no appointing authority has been agreed upon by the parties, or if the	**Rule 5 - Arbitral Tribunal** 1. Arbitration under these Rules shall be conducted by an arbitral tribunal composed of one or more arbitrators who have been appointed pursuant to the provisions of Rules 20 through 26 (including the application *mutatis mutandis* of Rule 26 under the provisions of Rule 41, Paragraph 2), Rule 29 and Rule 57. 2. If the arbitral tribunal is composed of more than one arbitrator, the arbitrators may, after all of them have been appointed, agree upon and appoint a presiding arbitrator from among themselves. **Rule 8 - Panel of Arbitrators** The Association shall prepare and maintain a panel of arbitrators to facilitate the appointment or arbitrators.	**Article 20 - Appointment by Agreement of Parties** (1) If, in the agreement of the parties, mention is specifically made of the names of the arbitrators or the method of appointment thereof (inclusive of a presiding arbitrator who shall act as chairman, also inclusive thereof as provided in the following provisions), the arbitrator(s) shall be appointed in accordance therewith. (2) If the arbitrators are to be appointed pursuant to the agreement of the parties provided in Paragraph (2) of Article 12, it shall be done in accordance with the following subparagraphs: a) When the parties have directly appointed arbitrator(s), a document stating the full name(s), address(es) and occupation(s) of the arbitrator(s) together with his/their written	**Rule 7 - Appointment of Sole Arbitrator** 7.1 If a sole arbitrator is to be appointed, either party may propose to the other, the names of one or more persons, one of whom would serve as the sole arbitrator. 7.2 If within twenty-one (21) days after receipt by a party of a proposal made in accordance with Rule 7.1 the parties have not reached agreement on the choice of a sole arbitrator, the sole arbitrator shall be appointed by the appointing authority agreed upon by the parties, and if no appointing authority has been agreed upon by the parties, or if the appointing authority agreed upon refuses to act or fails to appoint the arbitrator within twenty-one (21) days of the receipt of a party's request thereof, the Chairman shall appoint the arbitrator as soon as practicable.	**Article 6 - Appointment of Arbitrators** 1. If a sole arbitrator is to be appointed, either party may propose to the other: (a) The names of one or more persons, one of whom would serve as the sole arbitrator; and (b) If no appointing authority has been agreed upon by the parties, the name or names of one or more institutions or persons, one of whom would serve as appointing authority. 2. If within thirty days after receipt by a party of a proposal made in accordance with paragraph 1 the parties have not reached agreement on the choice of a sole arbitrator, the sole arbitrator shall be appointed by the appointing authority agreed upon by the parties. If no appointing authority has been agreed upon by the parties, or if the

Appointment of Arbitrators

Institutional					Ad Hoc
CIETAC ARBITRATION RULES (2000)	**HKIAC ARBITRATION RULES (1985)**	**JCAA ARBITRATION RULES (1997)**	**KCAB ARBITRATION RULES (2000)**	**SIAC ARBITRATION RULES (1997)**	**UNCITRAL ARBITRATION RULES (1976)**
In case the two parties fail to jointly appoint a third arbitrator or fail to jointly entrust the Chairman of the Arbitration Commission to appoint a third arbitrator within 20 days from the date on which the Respondent receives the Notice of Arbitration, the third arbitrator will be appointed by the Chairman of the Arbitration Commission. The third arbitrator will act as the presiding arbitrator. The presiding arbitrator and the two appointed arbitrators will jointly form an arbitration tribunal to jointly hear the case. **Article 25** The Claimant and the Respondent may jointly appoint or jointly authorize the Chairman of the Arbitration Commission to appoint a sole arbitrator to form an arbitration tribunal to hear the case alone.	appointing authority agreed upon refuses to act or fails to appoint the arbitrator within sixty days of the receipt of a party's request therefor, either party may request the Secretary-General of the Permanent Court of Arbitration at The Hague to designate an appointing authority. 3. The appointing authority shall, at the request of one of the parties, appoint the sole arbitrator as promptly as possible. In making the appointment the appointing authority shall use the following list-procedure, unless both parties agree that the list-procedure should not be used or unless the appointing authority determines in its discretion that the use of the list-procedure is not appropriate for the case: (a) At the request of one of the parties the appointing authority shall communicate to both parties an identical list containing	**Rule 21 - Agreement of Parties** 1. The parties may, by written agreement, appoint one or more arbitrators or determine the number, the method or the period of time (or all of the above) of appointment of the arbitrators. 2. The parties shall notify the Association, within, at the latest, three (3) weeks from the Basic Date, of the contents of an agreement provided for in the preceding Paragraph. **Rule 22 - Appointment of Arbitrators where the Parties have Determined the Method of Appointment** 1. If the parties have entered into an agreement provided for in the latter part of Paragraph 1 of the preceding Rule, an arbitrator shall be appointed pursuant to such agreement.	acceptance of assuming appointment shall be submitted to the Secretariat within 15 days from the Basic Date in case of Domestic Arbitration and within 30 days from the Basic Date in case of International Arbitration; b) The Secretariat shall, upon the request of any appointing party, submit a Panel of Arbitrators of the KCAB; c) If the agreement of the parties specifies a period of time within which arbitrator(s) shall be appointed, and any party fails to make the appointment thereunder within the fixed period, the Secretariat shall appoint the arbitrator(s); d) If a time period for appointing arbitrator(s) is not specified in the agreement, the Secretariat shall immediately notify the parties to make the appointment of arbitrator(s), and if within 15 days in case	7.3 If either party does not wish to propose the names of one or more persons to serve as the sole arbitrator, either party may request the Chairman to appoint the sole arbitrator. The Chairman shall as soon as practicable appoint the sole arbitrator upon the receipt of such a request. 7.4 A decision on a matter entrusted by Rule 7.2 and 7.3 to the Chairman shall not be subject to appeal. **Rule 8 - Appointment of Three Arbitrators** 8.1 If three arbitrators are to be appointed, each party shall appoint one arbitrator. The two arbitrators thus appointed shall choose the third arbitrator who will act as the presiding arbitrator of the tribunal. 8.2 If within twenty-one (21) days after the receipt of a party's notification of the appointment of an	appointing authority agreed upon refuses to act or fails to appoint the arbitrator within sixty days of the receipt of a party's request therefor, either party may request the Secretary-General of the Permanent Court of Arbitration at The Hague to designate an appointing authority. 3. The appointing authority shall, at the request of one of the parties, appoint the sole arbitrator as promptly as possible. In making the appointment the appointing authority shall use the following list-procedure, unless both parties agree that the list-procedure should not be used or unless the appointing authority determines in its discretion that the use of the list-procedure is not appropriate for the case: (a) At the request of one of the parties the appointing authority shall communicate to both parties an identical list containing

CONSTITUTION OF THE ARBITRAL TRIBUNAL

APPOINTMENT OF ARBITRATORS

INSTITUTIONAL					AD HOC
CIETAC ARBITRATION RULES (2000)	HKIAC ARBITRATION RULES (1985)	JCAA ARBITRATION RULES (1997)	KCAB ARBITRATION RULES (2000)	SIAC ARBITRATION RULES (1997)	UNCITRAL ARBITRATION RULES (1976)
If both parties agree to having a sole arbitrator to hear their case but are unable to agree on the choice of such a sole arbitrator within 20 days from the date on which the Respondent receives the Notice of Arbitration, the Chairman of the Arbitration Commission will make the appointment. **Article 26** If the Claimant or the Respondent fails to appoint or authorize the Chairman of the Arbitration Commission to appoint an arbitrator according to Article 16 of these Rules, the Chairman of the Arbitration Commission will appoint an arbitrator for the Claimant or the Respondent. **Article 27** Where there are two or more Claimants and/or Respondents involved in an arbitration case, the Claimants' side and/or	at least three names; (b) Within fifteen days after the receipt of this list, each party may return the list to the appointing authority after having deleted the name or names to which he objects and numbered the remaining names on the list in the order of his preference; (c) After the expiration of the above period of time the appointing authority shall appoint the sole arbitrator from among the names approved on the lists returned to it and in accordance with the order of preference indicated by the parties; (d) If for any reason the appointment cannot be made according to this procedure, the appointing authority may exercise its discretion in appointing the sole arbitrator.	2. If one or both of the parties fails or fail to notify the Association of the appointment of an arbitrator, as provided for in the preceding Paragraph, within the period of time for appointment agreed upon by the parties or, if the parties have not agreed upon such period of time, within four (4) weeks from the earlier of the date on which the notice provided for in Paragraph 2 of the preceding Rule reaches the Association or the date provided for in the same Paragraph, the Association shall appoint such arbitrator. If the Association is to make such an appointment, it shall respect, to the extent possible, the contents of the agreement provided for in Paragraph 1 of the preceding Rule. 3. If the Association appoints an arbitrator under the provisions of the preceding Paragraph, the provisions of Rule 24, Paragraph 3 shall	of Domestic Arbitration and within 30 days in case of International Arbitration thereafter such arbitrator has not been appointed thereunder, the Secretariat shall appoint the arbitrator(s); e) In case arbitrators appointed by the parties in accordance with parties' mutual agreement are mandated to appoint the other arbitrator(s), and the parties do not fix the period of appointment for the other arbitrator or arbitrators do not appoint the other arbitrator within the period of appointment, the Secretariat shall notify arbitrators appointed by the parties to make an appointment of the other arbitrator and if within 15 days in case of Domestic Arbitration and within 30 days in case of International Arbitration thereafter such arbitrator has not been appointed thereunder, the Secretariat shall appoint such	arbitrator, the other party has not notified the first party of the arbitrator he has appointed: (a) the first party may request the appointing authority previously designated by the parties to appoint the arbitrator; or (b) if no such authority has been previously designated by the parties, or if the appointing authority previously designated refuses to act or fails to appoint the arbitrator within twenty-one (21) days after receipt of a party's request thereof, the first party may request the Chairman to appoint the second arbitrator. 8.3 If within twenty-one (21) days after the appointment of the second arbitrator the two arbitrators have not agreed on the choice of the presiding arbitrator, the presiding arbitrator shall be appointed by an appointing authority or by the Chairman if	at least three names; (b) Within fifteen days after the receipt of this list, each party may return the list to the appointing authority after having deleted the name or names to which he objects and numbered the remaining names on the list in the order of his preference; (c) After the expiration of the above period of time the appointing authority shall appoint the sole arbitrator from among the names approved on the lists returned to it and in accordance with the order of preference indicated by the parties; (d) If for any reason the appointment cannot be made according to this procedure, the appointing authority may exercise its discretion in appointing the sole arbitrator.

APPOINTMENT OF ARBITRATORS

INSTITUTIONAL					AD HOC
CIETAC ARBITRATION RULES (2000)	**HKIAC ARBITRATION RULES (1985)**	**JCAA ARBITRATION RULES (1997)**	**KCAB ARBITRATION RULES (2000)**	**SIAC ARBITRATION RULES (1997)**	**UNCITRAL ARBITRATION RULES (1976)**
the Respondents' side each shall, through consultation, appoint or entrust the Chairman of the Arbitration Commission to appoint one arbitrator from among the Panel of Arbitrators of the Arbitration Commission. If the Claimants' side or the Respondents' side fails to make such appointment or entrustment within 20 days as from the date on which the Respondents' side receives the Notice of Arbitration, the appointment will be made by the Chairman of the Arbitration Commission.	**Article 7 - Appointment of Arbitrators** 1. If three arbitrators are to be appointed, each party shall appoint one arbitrator. The two arbitrators thus appointed shall choose the third arbitrator who will act as the presiding arbitrator of the tribunal. 2. If within thirty days after the receipt of a party's notification of the appointment of an arbitrator the other party has not notified the first party of the arbitrator he has appointed: (a) The first party may request the appointing authority previously designated by the parties to appoint the second arbitrator; or (b) If no such authority has been previously designated by the parties, or if the appointing authority previously designated refuses to act or fails to appoint the arbitrator within thirty	apply *mutatis mutandis*. 4. If the parties have not entered into an agreement provided for in the latter part of Paragraph 1 of the preceding Rule with respect to the number of arbitrators, such number shall be determined pursuant to the provisions of the following Rule. **Rule 24 - Appointment of Arbitrator - Single Arbitrator** 1. If the number of arbitrators is one (1) under the agreement provided for in Rule 21 or the provisions of the preceding Rule, the parties shall agree upon and appoint an arbitrator. 2. If the parties fail to notify the Association of the appointment of an arbitrator provided for in the preceding Paragraph within four (4) weeks from the date when the notice provided for in Rule 21, Paragraph 2 reaches the	arbitrator. (3) If the parties have not appointed arbitrator(s) or have not provided the method of appointment as provided in Paragraph (1) of this Article, or if the Secretariat appoints an arbitrator(s) in accordance with c) and d) of Paragraph (2) of this Article, an arbitrator(s) shall be appointed by the Secretariat applying Article 21 *mutatis mutandis*. **Article 21 - Appointment by Secretariat** (1) If, after the acceptance of a claim, there is no hope of settlement by conciliation or such conciliation proves unsuccessful as provided in Article 18, the Secretariat shall without delay furnish both parties with a list of several candidate arbitrators by choosing from among the Panel of Arbitrators.	no appointing authority has been previously designated by the parties or, if the appointing authority previously designated refuses to act within the prescribed time, in the same way as a sole arbitrator would be appointed under Rule 7. 8.4 A decision on a matter entrusted by Rule 8.2 or 8.3 to the Chairman shall not be subject to appeal. **Rule 9 - Multi-party Appointment of Arbitrator(s)** 9.1 If there are three or more parties in the arbitration, the parties shall endeavour to agree on the procedure for appointing the arbitrator(s) and if within twenty-one (21) days of the receipt of the Notice of Arbitration, the parties have not reached an agreement on the procedure for appointing the arbitrator(s), the arbitrator(s) shall be appointed by the	**Article 7 - Appointment of Arbitrators** 1. If three arbitrators are to be appointed, each party shall appoint one arbitrator. The two arbitrators thus appointed shall choose the third arbitrator who will act as the presiding arbitrator of the tribunal. 2. If within thirty days after the receipt of a party's notification of the appointment of an arbitrator the other party has not notified the first party of the arbitrator he has appointed: (a) The first party may request the appointing authority previously designated by the parties to appoint the second arbitrator; or (b) If no such authority has been previously designated by the parties, or if the appointing authority previously designated refuses to act or fails to appoint the arbitrator within thirty

INSTITUTIONAL					AD HOC
CIETAC ARBITRATION RULES (2000)	**HKIAC ARBITRATION RULES (1985)**	**JCAA ARBITRATION RULES (1997)**	**KCAB ARBITRATION RULES (2000)**	**SIAC ARBITRATION RULES (1997)**	**UNCITRAL ARBITRATION RULES (1976)**
	days after receipt of a party's request therefor, the first party may request the Secretary-General of the Permanent Court of Arbitration at The Hague to designate the appointing authority. The first party may then request the appointing authority so designated to appoint the second arbitrator. In either case, the appointing authority may exercise its discretion in appointing the arbitrator. 3. If within thirty days after the appointment of the second arbitrator the two arbitrators have not agreed on the choice of the presiding arbitrator, the presiding arbitrator shall be appointed by an appointing authority in the same way as a sole arbitrator would be appointed under article 6.	Association if the number of arbitrators fixed under an agreement provided for in Rule 21 is one (1) or the last day of the third week immediately following the Basic Date if the number of arbitrators fixed under the provisions of the preceding Rule is one (1), the Association shall appoint such arbitrator. If the Association is to make such an appointment, it shall respect, to the extent possible, the contents of an agreement, if one exists, provided for in Rule 21, Paragraph 1. 3. If the Association is to appoint an arbitrator pursuant to the provisions of the preceding Paragraph, the Association shall give due consideration to a written request, submitted by either party within one (1) week from the date on which it is determined that the Association shall make such appointment, that a person of a different nationality from those	(2) Within 15 days from the date of receipt of the list in case of Domestic Arbitration, and within 30 days from the date of receipt of the list in case of International Arbitration, each party shall return to the Secretariat the list of such candidates as provided in Paragraph (1) after marking by number the order of his preference of the names of the candidates in the respective columns of the said list for a presiding arbitrator and the other arbitrators. If a party or parties fail to return the list within the above period, all of the candidates shall be deemed to be of the same preference and if more than two candidates are marked on the same order of preference or no particular order of preference is marked on candidate(s) or if the name(s) to which each party objects has been deleted, then the KCAB shall adjust the order of preference giving due	Chairman as soon as practicable after the receipt of a party's request to the Chairman. 9.2 A decision on a matter entrusted by Rule 9.1 to the Chairman shall not be subject to appeal. **Rule 10 - Information to be Furnished to the Appointing Authority** 10.1 When an appointing authority is requested to appoint an arbitrator pursuant to Rule 7 or 8, the party which makes the request shall send to the appointing authority a copy of the Notice of Arbitration, a copy of the contract out of or in relation to which the dispute has arisen and a copy of the arbitration agreement if it is not contained in the contract. The appointment authority may require from either party such information as it deems necessary to fulfill its function.	days after receipt of a party's request therefor, the first party may request the Secretary-General of the Permanent Court of Arbitration at The Hague to designate the appointing authority. The first party may then request the appointing authority so designated to appoint the second arbitrator. In either case, the appointing authority may exercise its discretion in appointing the arbitrator. 3. If within thirty days after the appointment of the second arbitrator the two arbitrators have not agreed on the choice of the presiding arbitrator, the presiding arbitrator shall be appointed by an appointing authority in the same way as a sole arbitrator would be appointed under article 6.

APPOINTMENT OF ARBITRATORS

INSTITUTIONAL					AD HOC
CIETAC ARBITRATION RULES (2000)	**HKIAC ARBITRATION RULES (1985)**	**JCAA ARBITRATION RULES (1997)**	**KCAB ARBITRATION RULES (2000)**	**SIAC ARBITRATION RULES (1997)**	**UNCITRAL ARBITRATION RULES (1976)**
	Article 8 - Appointment of Arbitrators 1. When an appointing authority is requested to appoint an arbitrator pursuant to article 6 or article 7, the party which makes the request shall send to the appointing authority a copy of the notice of arbitration, a copy of the contract out of or in relation to which the dispute has arisen and a copy of the arbitration agreement if it is not contained in the contract. The appointing authority may require from either party such information as it deems necessary to fulfil its function. 2. Where the names of one or more persons are proposed for appointment as arbitrators, their full names, addresses and nationalities shall be indicated, together with a description of their qualifications. ***See also* HKIAC as Appointing Authority**	of the parties be appointed as such arbitrator. **Rule 25 - Appointment of Arbitrators - More than One** 1. If the parties agree under the provisions of Rule 21 that there shall be more than one arbitrator but not on the method of appointment or if the number of arbitrators is fixed at three (3) pursuant to the proviso of Rule 23, each party shall appoint the same number of arbitrators, the sum of which shall not exceed the number of arbitrators thus fixed, and if the number thus fixed is an odd number, the arbitrators appointed thereby shall appoint one (1) more arbitrator. 2. The parties shall appoint, within four (4) weeks from the date on which they have given notice under the provisions of Rule 21, Paragraph 2 or from the date on which the number of arbitrators	consideration to the opponent's order of preference. The remaining names on the list shall be given the following order of preference: more than two candidates who have been marked on the same order of preference; candidate(s) for whom no particular order of preference is marked; and candidates who have been deleted. (3) The Secretariat shall select the arbitrators in accordance with the designated order of the candidates provided in Paragraph (2) and shall invite the written acceptance of each such arbitrator to serve. However, in the event that there are two or more candidates occupying the same place in the designated order, the Secretariat shall appoint the arbitrators from among the candidates. (4) If the candidates acceptable to both parties refuse to serve or are unable to	10.2 Where the names of one or more persons are proposed for appointment as arbitrators, their full names, addresses and nationalities shall be indicated, together with a description of their qualifications. ***See also* Rule 34(4) at A-100.**	**Article 8 - Appointment of Arbitrators** 1. When an appointing authority is requested to appoint an arbitrator pursuant to article 6 or article 7, the party which makes the request shall send to the appointing authority a copy of the notice of arbitration, a copy of the contract out of or in relation to which the dispute has arisen and a copy of the arbitration agreement if it is not contained in the contract. The appointing authority may require from either party such information as it deems necessary to fulfil its function. 2. Where the names of one or more persons are proposed for appointment as arbitrators, their full names, addresses and nationalities shall be indicated, together with a description of their qualifications.

Institutional					Ad Hoc
CIETAC ARBITRATION RULES (2000)	HKIAC ARBITRATION RULES (1985)	JCAA ARBITRATION RULES (1997)	KCAB ARBITRATION RULES (2000)	SIAC ARBITRATION RULES (1997)	UNCITRAL ARBITRATION RULES (1976)
	at A-24.	is fixed at three (3) pursuant to the proviso of Rule 23, the same number of arbitrators which each party should appoint pursuant to the provisions of the preceding Paragraph. 3. If either party fails to appoint an arbitrator or arbitrators within the period of time provided for in the preceding Paragraph, the Association shall appoint such arbitrator or arbitrators. 4. If the number of arbitrators is odd and the arbitrators appointed by the parties or the arbitrators appointed pursuant to the provisions of the preceding Paragraph fail to appoint one (1) more arbitrator within three (3) weeks from the date on which the last of such arbitrators was appointed, the Association shall appoint such arbitrator. 5. If the Association is to make the appointment under the	perform their duties for any reasons, then candidates on the next order of preference on the candidate's list shall be appointed. If the list of candidates has been fully exhausted, then a new arbitrator shall be appointed pursuant to this Article. (5) When the Secretariat requests an acceptance to serve as arbitrator(s), it invites his/their attention to the requirements provided in Article 25 of these Rules and enclose a copy of these Rules. **Article 24 - Notice of Appointment of Arbitrators** If the arbitrators have been appointed pursuant to these Rules, the Secretariat shall without delay notify in writing all the arbitrator(s) and both parties of the full name(s), address(es) and occupation(s) of all the arbitrator(s). ***See also* Articles 4-5 at A-66 and Article 22**		

INSTITUTIONAL					AD HOC
CIETAC ARBITRATION RULES (2000)	HKIAC ARBITRATION RULES (1985)	JCAA ARBITRATION RULES (1997)	KCAB ARBITRATION RULES (2000)	SIAC ARBITRATION RULES (1997)	UNCITRAL ARBITRATION RULES (1976)
		provisions of the preceding Paragraph, the provisions of Paragraph 3 of the preceding Rule shall apply *mutatis mutandis*. **Rule 26 - Appointment of Arbitrators where Third Party Participates in Proceedings** 1. If, prior to the establishment of an arbitral tribunal, a third party participates or is allowed to participate in arbitral proceedings under the provisions of Rule 40, one or more arbitrators shall be appointed by agreement of the claimant, the respondent and such third party. 2. If the appointment of the number of arbitrators fixed by the agreement provided for in the preceding Paragraph has not been completed within three (3) weeks from the date on which such third party has participated in arbitral proceedings, the	**at A-72.**		

CONSTITUTION OF THE ARBITRAL TRIBUNAL

APPOINTMENT OF ARBITRATORS

INSTITUTIONAL					AD HOC
CIETAC ARBITRATION RULES (2000)	HKIAC ARBITRATION RULES (1985)	JCAA ARBITRATION RULES (1997)	KCAB ARBITRATION RULES (2000)	SIAC ARBITRATION RULES (1997)	UNCITRAL ARBITRATION RULES (1976)
		Association shall appoint the arbitrator(s) yet to be appointed. 3. If the number of arbitrators has not been agreed upon by the date fixed under the provisions of the preceding Paragraph, the Association shall appoint the number of arbitrator(s) determined by the Association. ***See also* Rule 5 at A-44-45, Rule 8 at A-45 and Rule 27 at A-51.**			

CHALLENGE OF ARBITRATORS

INSTITUTIONAL					AD HOC
CIETAC ARBITRATION RULES (2000)	HKIAC ARBITRATION RULES (1985)	JCAA ARBITRATION RULES (1997)	KCAB ARBITRATION RULES (2000)	SIAC ARBITRATION RULES (1997)	UNCITRAL ARBITRATION RULES (1976)
Article 29 Any party who has justified reasons to suspect the impartiality and independence of an appointed arbitrator may make a request in writing to the Arbitration Commission for that arbitrator's withdrawal. In the request, the facts and reasons on which the request is based shall be stated with the supporting evidence provided. A challenge against an arbitrator must be put forward in writing no later than the first oral hearing. If the grounds for the challenge come out or are made known after the first oral hearing, the challenge may nevertheless be raised before the conclusion of the last hearing. **Article 30** The Chairman of the Arbitration Commission shall decide whether an arbitrator should be withdrawn.	**Article 10 - Challenge of Arbitrators** 1. Any arbitrator may be challenged if circumstances exist that give rise to justifiable doubts as to the arbitrator's impartiality or independence. 2. A party may challenge the arbitrator appointed by him only for reasons of which he becomes aware after the appointment has been made. **Article 11 - Challenge of Arbitrators** 1. A party who intends to challenge an arbitrator shall send notice of his challenge within fifteen days after the appointment of the challenged arbitrator has been notified to the challenging party or within fifteen days after the circumstances mentioned in articles 9 and 10 became known to that party. 2. The challenge shall be notified to the other		**Article 25 - Disclosure by Arbitrator of Disqualifications** (1) Upon being notified of his appointment as an arbitrator, he shall immediately disclose in writing to the Secretariat any and all circumstances which might cause reasonable question about his fairness or independence. (2) Upon receipt of such disclosure of information as prescribed in Paragraph (1), the Secretariat shall immediately disclose it to both the Tribunal and the parties. If either party wishes to raise any objection to the appointment of such arbitrator(s), he or she shall make the challenge within 15 days from the date of the establishment of the Tribunal or from the date when the party making the challenge was informed of those circumstances provided in Paragraph (1) of this Article. But,	**Rule 12 - Challenge of Arbitrators** 12.1 Any arbitrator may be challenged if circumstances exist that give rise to justifiable doubts as to the arbitrator's impartiality or independence. 12.2 A party may challenge the arbitrator appointed by him only for reasons of which he becomes aware after the appointment has been made. **Rule 13 - Notice of Challenge** 13.1 A party who intends to challenge an arbitrator shall send notice of his challenge within fourteen (14) days after the appointment of the challenged arbitrator has been notified to the challenging party or within fourteen (14) days after the circumstances mentioned in Rule 12.1 or 12.2 became known to that party. 13.2 The challenge shall be notified to the	**Article 10 - Challenge of Arbitrators** 1. Any arbitrator may be challenged if circumstances exist that give rise to justifiable doubts as to the arbitrator's impartiality or independence. 2. A party may challenge the arbitrator appointed by him only for reasons of which he becomes aware after the appointment has been made. **Article 11 - Challenge of Arbitrators** 1. A party who intends to challenge an arbitrator shall send notice of his challenge within fifteen days after the appointment of the challenged arbitrator has been notified to the challenging party or within fifteen days after the circumstances mentioned in articles 9 and 10 became known to that party. 2. The challenge shall be notified to the other

CONSTITUTION OF THE ARBITRAL TRIBUNAL
CHALLENGE OF ARBITRATORS

INSTITUTIONAL					AD HOC
CIETAC ARBITRATION RULES (2000)	HKIAC ARBITRATION RULES (1985)	JCAA ARBITRATION RULES (1997)	KCAB ARBITRATION RULES (2000)	SIAC ARBITRATION RULES (1997)	UNCITRAL ARBITRATION RULES (1976)
Before any decision is made by the Chairman of the Arbitration Commission, the challenged arbitrator shall continue to perform the duties of an arbitrator.	party, to the arbitrator who is challenged and to the other members of the arbitral tribunal. The notification shall be in writing and shall state the reasons for the challenge. 3. When an arbitrator has been challenged by one party, the other party may agree to the challenge. The arbitrator may also, after the challenge, withdraw from his office. In neither case does this imply acceptance of the validity of the grounds for the challenge. In both cases the procedure provided in article 6 or 7 shall be used in full for the appointment of the substitute arbitrator, even if during the process of appointing the challenged arbitrator a party had failed to exercise his right to appoint or to participate in the appointment. **Article 12 - Challenge of Arbitrators** 1. If the other party does not agree to the		if either party does not submit any objection within the above period, he can not submit any objection to the qualification of such arbitrator(s) on the same grounds. (3) If either party submits an objection to the appointment of such questioned arbitrator(s) on the ground of notified reason, the vacancy thus created shall be filled in the same method as provided in Article 26.	other party, the arbitrator who is challenged and the other members of the Tribunal. The notification shall be in writing and shall state the reasons for the challenge. Upon receiving the notification of challenge by the Registrar, the arbitration shall be suspended until the challenge is resolved or decided upon. 13.3 When an arbitrator has been challenged by one party, the other party may agree to the challenge. The arbitrator may also, after the challenge, withdraw from his office. In neither case does this imply acceptance of the validity of the grounds for the challenge. In both cases, the procedure provided in Rule 7, 8 or 9 shall be used in full for the appointment of the substitute arbitrator, even if during the process of appointing the challenged arbitrator, a party had	party, to the arbitrator who is challenged and to the other members of the arbitral tribunal. The notification shall be in writing and shall state the reasons for the challenge. 3. When an arbitrator has been challenged by one party, the other party may agree to the challenge. The arbitrator may also, after the challenge, withdraw from his office. In neither case does this imply acceptance of the validity of the grounds for the challenge. In both cases the procedure provided in article 6 or 7 shall be used in full for the appointment of the substitute arbitrator, even if during the process of appointing the challenged arbitrator a party had failed to exercise his right to appoint or to participate in the appointment. **Article 12 - Challenge of Arbitrators** 1. If the other party does not agree to the

INSTITUTIONAL					AD HOC
CIETAC ARBITRATION RULES (2000)	HKIAC ARBITRATION RULES (1985)	JCAA ARBITRATION RULES (1997)	KCAB ARBITRATION RULES (2000)	SIAC ARBITRATION RULES (1997)	UNCITRAL ARBITRATION RULES (1976)
	challenge and the challenged arbitrator does not withdraw, the decision on the challenge will be made: (a) When the initial appointment was made by an appointing authority, by that authority; (b) When the initial appointment was not made by an appointing authority, but an appointing authority has been previously designated, by that authority; (c) In all other cases, by the appointing authority to be designated in accordance with the procedure for designating an appointing authority as provided for in article 6. 2. If the appointing authority sustains the challenge, a substitute arbitrator shall be appointed or chosen pursuant to the procedure applicable to the appointment or choice of an arbitrator			failed to exercise his right to appoint or to participate in the appointment. **Rule 14 - Decision on Challenge** 14.1 If the other party does not agree to the challenge and the challenged arbitrator does not withdraw, the decision on the challenge will be made: (a) when the initial appointment was made by an appointing authority, by that authority; and (b) in all other cases, by the Chairman whose decision shall be final and not be subject to appeal. 14.2 If the appointing authority or the Chairman, as the case may be, sustains the challenge, a substitute arbitrator shall be appointed or chosen pursuant to the procedure applicable to the appointment or choice of an arbitrator as provided in Rules 6 to 9 except that, when	challenge and the challenged arbitrator does not withdraw, the decision on the challenge will be made: (a) When the initial appointment was made by an appointing authority, by that authority; (b) When the initial appointment was not made by an appointing authority, but an appointing authority has been previously designated, by that authority; (c) In all other cases, by the appointing authority to be designated in accordance with the procedure for designating an appointing authority as provided for in article 6. 2. If the appointing authority sustains the challenge, a substitute arbitrator shall be appointed or chosen pursuant to the procedure applicable to the appointment or choice of an arbitrator

INSTITUTIONAL					AD HOC
CIETAC ARBITRATION RULES (2000)	HKIAC ARBITRATION RULES (1985)	JCAA ARBITRATION RULES (1997)	KCAB ARBITRATION RULES (2000)	SIAC ARBITRATION RULES (1997)	UNCITRAL ARBITRATION RULES (1976)
	as provided in articles 6 to 9 except that, when this procedure would call for the designation of an appointing authority, the appointment of the arbitrator shall be made by the appointing authority which decided on the challenge. **The HKIAC as Appointing Authority: Challenge of Arbitrators** Arbitrators appointed by the HKIAC are required to confirm their independence and impartiality. Where a decision is required by the appointing authority under the Rules on any challenge of an arbitrator, such decision is made on behalf of the HKIAC by the Court of Appointment.			this procedure would call for the designation of an appointing authority, the appointment of the arbitrator shall be made by the appointing authority which decided on the challenge.	as provided in articles 6 to 9 except that, when this procedure would call for the designation of an appointing authority, the appointment of the arbitrator shall be made by the appointing authority which decided on the challenge.

Replacement of Arbitrators

Institutional					Ad Hoc
CIETAC ARBITRATION RULES (2000)	**HKIAC ARBITRATION RULES (1985)**	**JCAA ARBITRATION RULES (1997)**	**KCAB ARBITRATION RULES (2000)**	**SIAC ARBITRATION RULES (1997)**	**UNCITRAL ARBITRATION RULES (1976)**
Article 31 If an arbitrator is unable to perform the duties owing to his/her withdrawal, demise, removal from the Panel of Arbitrators or any other reasons, a substitute arbitrator shall be appointed in accordance with the procedure pursuant to which the original arbitrator was appointed. After the appointment of the substitute arbitrator, the arbitration tribunal has discretion to decide whether to repeat the whole or a part of the previous procedures.	**Article 13 - Replacement of an Arbitrator** 1. In the event of the death or resignation of an arbitrator during the course of the arbitral proceedings, a substitute arbitrator shall be appointed or chosen pursuant to the procedure provided for in articles 6 to 9 that was applicable to the appointment or choice of the arbitrator being replaced. 2. In the event that an arbitrator fails to act or in the event of the *de jure* or *de facto* impossibility of his performing his functions, the procedure in respect of the challenge and replacement of an arbitrator as provided in the preceding articles shall apply. **Article 14 - Repetition of Hearings in the Event of the Replacement of an Arbitrator** If under articles 11 to 13 the sole or	**Rule 29 - Replacement of Arbitrator** 1. If an arbitrator resigns or dies, the Association shall, without delay, notify the parties and the remaining arbitrator(s) thereof. 2. If the arbitrator who resigns or dies is one appointed by a party or parties or the remaining arbitrators, the party or parties or the remaining arbitrators shall appoint a substitute arbitrator within three (3) weeks from the date on which such party or parties or such arbitrators receive the notice provided for in the preceding Paragraph. If the arbitrator who resigns or dies is one appointed by the Association, the Association shall appoint a substitute arbitrator within three (3) weeks from the date on which it learns of such resignation or death. 3. If such party or parties or arbitrators	**Article 26 - Vacancy of Arbitrator** (1) If an arbitrator must resign from the appointed Tribunal because of resignation, death or other causes, the party which appointed the arbitrator shall appoint and notify thereof accordingly, a new arbitrator to take his place in the same manner of appointment as for the vacating arbitrator concerned. If the arbitrator was an appointee of the Secretariat, then the appointment shall be made, and duly notified, pursuant to Paragraphs (3) and (4) of Article 21. (2) In case of Paragraph (1), unless the parties have agreed otherwise, if both parties submit the conclusions of the previous hearing to the new arbitrator(s) and the new arbitrator(s) do not raise objections thereto, the proceeding shall continue. However, if the parties request a	**Rule 15 - Replacement of An Arbitrator** 15.1 In the event of the death or resignation of an arbitrator during the course of the arbitral proceedings, a substitute arbitrator shall be appointed or chosen pursuant to the procedure provided for in Rules 7 to 11 that was applicable to the appointment or choice of the arbitrator being replaced. 15.2 In the event that an arbitrator refuses or fails to act or in the event of the *de jure* or *de facto* impossibility of his performing functions, the procedure in respect of the challenge and replacement of an arbitrator as provided in Rules 12 to 14 and 15.1 shall apply. **Rule 16 - Repetition of Hearings in the Event of the Replacement of an Arbitrator** If under Rules 13 to 15 the sole or presiding	**Article 13 - Replacement of an Arbitrator** 1. In the event of the death or resignation of an arbitrator during the course of the arbitral proceedings, a substitute arbitrator shall be appointed or chosen pursuant to the procedure provided for in articles 6 to 9 that was applicable to the appointment or choice of the arbitrator being replaced. 2. In the event that an arbitrator fails to act or in the event of the *de jure* or *de facto* impossibility of his performing his functions, the procedure in respect of the challenge and replacement of an arbitrator as provided in the preceding articles shall apply. **Article 14 - Repetition of Hearings in the Event of the Replacement of an Arbitrator** If under articles 11 to 13 the sole or

INSTITUTIONAL					AD HOC
CIETAC ARBITRATION RULES (2000)	**HKIAC ARBITRATION RULES (1985)**	**JCAA ARBITRATION RULES (1997)**	**KCAB ARBITRATION RULES (2000)**	**SIAC ARBITRATION RULES (1997)**	**UNCITRAL ARBITRATION RULES (1976)**
	presiding arbitrator is replaced, any hearings held previously shall be repeated; if any other arbitrator is replaced, such prior hearings may be repeated at the discretion of the arbitral tribunal. **The HKIAC as Appointing Authority: Replacement of Arbitrator** Replacement of an arbitrator is effected by the HKIAC in accordance with the Rules as necessary. ***See also* Article 12.2 at A-32.**	fails or fail to appoint a substitute arbitrator within the period of time provided for in the preceding Paragraph, the Association shall appoint such substitute arbitrator. **Rule 30 - Removal of Arbitrator** 1. The Association may remove any arbitrator who fails to perform its duties or unduly delays in the performance of its duties, or is legally or actually unable to perform its duties. 2. The provisions of Paragraph 2 of the preceding Rule shall apply *mutatis mutandis* to the appointment of a substitute arbitrator.	new hearing with regard to a witness from a previous hearing, the arbitrators must conduct the hearing. ***See also* Article 25 at A-73.**	arbitrator is replaced, any hearings held previously shall be repeated unless otherwise agreed to by the parties. If any other arbitrator is replaced, such prior hearings may be repeated at the discretion of the Tribunal.	presiding arbitrator is replaced, any hearings held previously shall be repeated; if any other arbitrator is replaced, such prior hearings may be repeated at the discretion of the arbitral tribunal. ***See also* Article 12.2 at A-106.**

TRUNCATED TRIBUNALS

INSTITUTIONAL					AD HOC
CIETAC ARBITRATION RULES (2000)	HKIAC ARBITRATION RULES (1985)	JCAA ARBITRATION RULES (1997)	KCAB ARBITRATION RULES (2000)	SIAC ARBITRATION RULES (1997)	UNCITRAL ARBITRATION RULES (1976)
Article 54 Where a case is heard by an arbitration tribunal composed of three arbitrators, the arbitral award shall be decided by the majority of the arbitrators and the minority opinion may be recorded and placed on file. When the arbitration tribunal cannot attain a majority opinion, the arbitral award shall be decided in accordance with the presiding arbitrator's opinion.	**Article 31 - Decisions** 1. When there are three arbitrators, any award or other decision of the arbitral tribunal shall be made by a majority of the arbitrators. **Article 32 - Form and Effect of the Award** 4. An award shall be signed by the arbitrators and it shall contain the date on which and the place where the award was made. Where there are three arbitrators and one of them fails to sign, the award shall state the reason for the absence of the signature.	**Rule 49 - Arbitral Award** 4. If there are more than one arbitrator and an arbitrator fails to sign and affix its seal to the arbitral award, the arbitral tribunal shall set forth the reasons for such failure in the arbitral award.	**Article 48 - The Award** (2) Where the Tribunal is composed of more than one arbitrator and less than a majority of arbitrators refuse to partake in the arbitration decision or do not participate in the arbitration decision without just cause, the award shall be made by the remaining majority of arbitrators.	**Rule 28 - The Award** 28.2 If any arbitrator refuses or fails to comply with the mandatory provisions of any applicable law relating to the making of the award, having been given a reasonable opportunity to do so, the remaining arbitrators shall proceed in his absence.	**Article 31 - Decisions** 1. When there are three arbitrators, any award or other decision of the arbitral tribunal shall be made by a majority of the arbitrators. **Article 32 - Form and Effect of the Award** 4. An award shall be signed by the arbitrators and it shall contain the date on which and the place where the award was made. Where there are three arbitrators and one of them fails to sign, the award shall state the reason for the absence of the signature.

COMPENSATION OF ARBITRATORS

INSTITUTIONAL					AD HOC
CIETAC ARBITRATION RULES (2000)	HKIAC ARBITRATION RULES (1985)	JCAA ARBITRATION RULES (1997)	KCAB ARBITRATION RULES (2000)	SIAC ARBITRATION RULES (1997)	UNCITRAL ARBITRATION RULES (1976)
Article 55 The arbitration tribunal shall state in the arbitral award the claims, the facts of the dispute, the reasons on which the arbitral award is based, the result of the arbitral award, the allocation of the arbitration costs, the date on which and the place at which the arbitral award is made. The facts of the dispute and the reasons on which the arbitral award is based may not be stated in the arbitral award if the parties have agreed not to state them in the arbitral award, or the arbitral award is made in accordance with the contents of the settlement agreement reached between the parties. **Article 58** The arbitration tribunal has the power to determine in the arbitral award the arbitration fee and other expenses to be paid by the parties to the Arbitration Commission.	**Article 39 - Costs** 1. The fees of the arbitral tribunal shall be reasonable in amount, taking into account the amount in dispute, the complexity of the subject-matter, the time spent by the arbitrators and any other relevant circumstances of the case. 2. If an appointing authority has been agreed upon by the parties or designated by the Secretary-General of the Permanent Court of Arbitration at The Hague, and if that authority has issued a schedule of fees for arbitrators in international cases which it administers, the arbitral tribunal in fixing its fees shall take that schedule of fees into account to the extent that it considers appropriate in the circumstances of the case. 3. If such appointing authority has not issued a schedule of fees for arbitrators in	**Rule 28 - Allocation of Expenses of Non-resident Arbitrator** 1. If a party has appointed an arbitrator who is not resident in Japan, such party shall bear the expenses required due to such arbitrator's non-residence; provided that the arbitral tribunal may allocate such expenses in a manner different therefrom. 2. If the Association has, or the arbitrators have, appointed an arbitrator who is not resident in Japan, the arbitral tribunal shall allocate such expenses in its arbitral award. **Rule 49 - Arbitral Award** 3. The arbitral tribunal shall set forth in the text of its arbitral award the total amount and the allocation of the administrative fee, the hearing fee, the necessary expenses incurred during the proceedings and the arbitrators'	**Article 64 - Allowances for Arbitrators** The allowances for the arbitrators fixed by the KCAB shall be deposited in advance by the Claimant.	**Rule 30 - Costs** 30.1 The costs of the arbitration shall be taxed by the Registrar or fixed by the Tribunal in its award. The term "costs of the arbitration" includes: (a) the fees of the Tribunal; (b) the travel and other expenses incurred by the arbitrators. **Rule 31 - Amount of Tribunal's Fees** 31.1 The fees of the Tribunal shall be reasonable in amount, taking into account the amount in dispute, the complexity of the subject-matter, the time spent by the arbitrators and any other relevant circumstances of the case. 31.2 If an appointing authority has been agreed upon by the parties or designated by the Chairman, and if that authority has issued a schedule of fees for arbitrators in international cases	**Article 39 - Costs** 1. The fees of the arbitral tribunal shall be reasonable in amount, taking into account the amount in dispute, the complexity of the subject-matter, the time spent by the arbitrators and any other relevant circumstances of the case. 2. If an appointing authority has been agreed upon by the parties or designated by the Secretary-General of the Permanent Court of Arbitration at The Hague, and if that authority has issued a schedule of fees for arbitrators in international cases which it administers, the arbitral tribunal in fixing its fees shall take that schedule of fees into account to the extent that it considers appropriate in the circumstances of the case. 3. If such appointing authority has not issued a schedule of fees for arbitrators in

INSTITUTIONAL					AD HOC
CIETAC ARBITRATION RULES (2000)	HKIAC ARBITRATION RULES (1985)	JCAA ARBITRATION RULES (1997)	KCAB ARBITRATION RULES (2000)	SIAC ARBITRATION RULES (1997)	UNCITRAL ARBITRATION RULES (1976)
Article 88 Apart from charging arbitration fees from the parties according to the arbitration Fee Schedule of the Arbitration Commission, the Arbitration Commission may collect from the parties other extra, reasonable and actual expenses including arbitrators' special remuneration and their travel and boarding expenses for dealing with the case, as well as the fees and expenses for experts, appraisers and interpreters appointed by the arbitration tribunal, etc. If a case is withdrawn after the parties have reached between themselves an amicable settlement or is concluded with an arbitral award made according to paragraph 4 of Article 44, the Arbitration Commission may charge a certain amount of fees from the parties in consideration of the	international cases, any party may at any time request the appointing authority to furnish a statement setting forth the basis for establishing fees which is customarily followed in international cases in which the authority appoints arbitrators. If the appointing authority consents to provide such a statement, the arbitral tribunal in fixing its fees shall take such information into account to the extent that it considers appropriate in the circumstances of the case. 4. In cases referred to in paragraphs 2 and 3, when a party so requests and the appointing authority consents to perform the function, the arbitral tribunal shall fix its fees only after consultation with the appointing authority which may make any comment it deems appropriate to the arbitral tribunal concerning the fees.	remuneration and shall, if there is a party who has deposited an amount of money less than the amount allocated in the text of the arbitral award, set forth an order to the effect that the balance shall be paid to the other party. **Rule 66 - Allocation of Remuneration for Arbitrators** The parties shall bear equally the cost of the remuneration fixed by the Association for the arbitrators; provided that the arbitral tribunal may, in view of the circumstances, allocate such cost in any other manner.		which it administers, the Tribunal in fixing its fees shall take that schedule of fees into account to the extent that it considers appropriate in the circumstances of the case. 31.3 If such appointing authority has not issued a schedule of fees for arbitrators in international cases, and if the parties fail to agree, an appropriate rate shall be determined by the Registrar and communicated in writing to the parties. 31.4 In all cases when a party so requests, the Tribunal shall fix its fees only after consultation with the Registrar who may advise the Tribunal concerning the fees.	international cases, any party may at any time request the appointing authority to furnish a statement setting forth the basis for establishing fees which is customarily followed in international cases in which the authority appoints arbitrators. If the appointing authority consents to provide such a statement, the arbitral tribunal in fixing its fees shall take such information into account to the extent that it considers appropriate in the circumstances of the case. 4. In cases referred to in paragraphs 2 and 3, when a party so requests and the appointing authority consents to perform the function, the arbitral tribunal shall fix its fees only after consultation with the appointing authority which may make any comment it deems appropriate to the arbitral tribunal concerning the fees.

INSTITUTIONAL					AD HOC
CIETAC ARBITRATION RULES (2000)	HKIAC ARBITRATION RULES (1985)	JCAA ARBITRATION RULES (1997)	KCAB ARBITRATION RULES (2000)	SIAC ARBITRATION RULES (1997)	UNCITRAL ARBITRATION RULES (1976)
quantity of work and the amount of the actual expenses incurred by the Arbitration Commission.	**The HKIAC as Appointing Authority: Assistance in Fixing Fees of Arbitrators** The fees for arbitrators appointed by the HKIAC are generally calculated by reference to work done by them in connection with the arbitration and are charged at rates appropriate to the particular circumstances of the case including its complexity and any special qualifications of the arbitrators. If the parties so wish the HKIAC will consult with the arbitral tribunal to establish the rates applicable to a particular case.				

CONSTITUTION OF THE ARBITRAL TRIBUNAL

COMMUNICATIONS BETWEEN PARTIES AND ARBITRATORS

INSTITUTIONAL					AD HOC
CIETAC ARBITRATION RULES (2000)	HKIAC ARBITRATION RULES (1985)	JCAA ARBITRATION RULES (1997)	KCAB ARBITRATION RULES (2000)	SIAC ARBITRATION RULES (1997)	UNCITRAL ARBITRATION RULES (1976)
Article 20 When submitting application for arbitration, written defense, statement of counterclaim, documentary evidence and other documents, the parties shall submit them in quintuplicate. If the number of the parties is more than two, additional copies shall be provided accordingly. If the arbitration tribunal is composed of only one arbitrator, the number of copies submitted may be reduced by two.	**Article 15 - General Provisions** 3. All documents or information supplied to the arbitral tribunal by one party shall at the same time be communicated by that party to the other party. **The HKIAC as Appointing Authority: Communications** Communications and notices between the parties and the arbitral tribunal in the course of arbitration proceedings (except at meetings and hearings) will be addressed through the HKIAC, and deemed received by the addressee when received by the HKIAC. When passed on by the HKIAC to a party such communications and notices will be sent to the address of that party contained in the Notice of Arbitration or such other address as may have been notified in writing to			**Rule 18 - Submission of Written Statements and Documents** 18.7 Copies of all statements referred to in this Rule shall be served on the Tribunal and the Registrar. **Rule 22 - Hearings** 22.7 All statements, documents or other information supplied to the Tribunal by one party shall be communicated to the other party. Also, any expert report or evidentiary document on which the Tribunal may rely in making its decision shall be communicated to the parties.	**Article 15 - General Provisions** 3. All documents or information supplied to the arbitral tribunal by one party shall at the same time be communicated by that party to the other party.

Institutional					Ad Hoc
CIETAC ARBITRATION RULES (2000)	HKIAC ARBITRATION RULES (1985)	JCAA ARBITRATION RULES (1997)	KCAB ARBITRATION RULES (2000)	SIAC ARBITRATION RULES (1997)	UNCITRAL ARBITRATION RULES (1976)
	the HKIAC by that party.				

INSTITUTIONAL					AD HOC
CIETAC ARBITRATION RULES (2000)	HKIAC ARBITRATION RULES (1985)	JCAA ARBITRATION RULES (1997)	KCAB ARBITRATION RULES (2000)	SIAC ARBITRATION RULES (1997)	UNCITRAL ARBITRATION RULES (1976)
				Rule 33 - Exclusion of Liability 33.1 Neither the Centre, any of its officers, employees or agents, nor any arbitrator shall be liable for: (a) negligence in respect of anything done or omitted to be done in the capacity of arbitrator or in connection with any arbitration conducted under these Rules; and (b) any mistake in law, fact or procedure made in the course of arbitral proceedings or in the making of an arbitral award. 33.2 Neither the Centre, any of its officers, employees or agents, nor any arbitrator shall be under any obligation to make any statement to any person about any matter concerning the arbitration, nor shall any party seek to make any arbitrator or any officer, member, servant or agent of the Centre, a witness in	

INSTITUTIONAL					AD HOC
CIETAC ARBITRATION RULES (2000)	HKIAC ARBITRATION RULES (1985)	JCAA ARBITRATION RULES (1997)	KCAB ARBITRATION RULES (2000)	SIAC ARBITRATION RULES (1997)	UNCITRAL ARBITRATION RULES (1976)
				any legal proceedings arising out of the arbitration whether before, during or after the arbitration.	

NOTICES AND COMMUNICATIONS/CALCULATIONS OF PERIODS OF TIME

INSTITUTIONAL					AD HOC
CIETAC ARBITRATION RULES (2000)	HKIAC ARBITRATION RULES (1985)	JCAA ARBITRATION RULES (1997)	KCAB ARBITRATION RULES (2000)	SIAC ARBITRATION RULES (1997)	UNCITRAL ARBITRATION RULES (1976)
Article 13 The arbitration proceedings will commence from the date on which the Notice of Arbitration is issued by the Arbitration Commission or its Sub-Commissions. **Article 86** All the arbitration documents, notices and materials may be sent to the parties and/or their arbitration agents in person, or by registered letter or express airmail, telefax, telex, cable or by any other means considered proper by the secretariat of the Arbitration Commission. **Article 87** Any written correspondence to the parties and/or their arbitration agents shall be taken to have been properly served if it is delivered to the addressee or delivered at his place of business, habitual residence or mailing	**Article 2 - Notice, Calculation of Periods of Time** 1. For the purposes of these Rules, any notice, including a notification, communication or proposal, is deemed to have been received if it is physically delivered to the addressee or if it is delivered at his habitual residence, place of business or mailing address, or, if none of these can be found after making reasonable inquiry, then at the addressee's last-known residence or place of business. Notice shall be deemed to have been received on the day it is so delivered. 2. For the purposes of calculating a period of time under these Rules, such period shall begin to run on the day following the day when a notice, notification, communication or proposal is received. If the last day of such period is an official	**Rule 11 - Means of Communication** Communication during arbitration under these Rules shall be by way of a document or other means of communication followed by a document. **Rule 12 - Request for Arbitration** 5. Arbitral proceedings shall be deemed to be initiated on the date on which the Association receives the written request for arbitration. **Rule 33 - Submission of Written Statements** 3. The arbitral tribunal shall confirm at hearings the receipt of the written statements submitted otherwise than at a hearing. **Rule 63 - Extension of Period of Time** 1. The parties may, by written agreement, extend any period of time provided for in these Rules, except for the period of time	**Article 47 - Extensions of Period** The parties may modify any period prescribed under these Rules by a mutual agreement in writing. The Tribunal for good cause may extend any period established by these Rules except the period for making an award. The Tribunal shall notify the parties through the Secretariat of any such extension and reasons therefor. ***See also* Article 39 at A-77 and Article 45 at A-78-79.**	**Rule 2 - Notice, Calculation of Periods of Time** 2.1 For the purposes of these Rules, any notice, including a notification, communication or proposal, shall be in writing and is deemed to have been received if it is physically delivered to the addressee or if it is delivered at his habitual residence, place of business or mailing address, or, if none of these can be found after making reasonable inquiry, then at the addressee's last-known residence or place of business. The notice shall be deemed to have been received on the day it is so delivered. 2.2 For the purposes of calculating any period of time under these Rules, such period shall begin to run on the day following the day when a notice, notification, communication or proposal is received. If the last day of such	**Article 2 - Notice, Calculation of Periods of Time** 1. For the purposes of these Rules, any notice, including a notification, communication or proposal, is deemed to have been received if it is physically delivered to the addressee or if it is delivered at his habitual residence, place of business or mailing address, or, if none of these can be found after making reasonable inquiry, then at the addressee's last-known residence or place of business. Notice shall be deemed to have been received on the day it is so delivered. 2. For the purposes of calculating a period of time under these Rules, such period shall begin to run on the day following the day when a notice, notification, communication or proposal is received. If the last day of such period is an official

INSTITUTIONAL					AD HOC
CIETAC ARBITRATION RULES (2000)	**HKIAC ARBITRATION RULES (1985)**	**JCAA ARBITRATION RULES (1997)**	**KCAB ARBITRATION RULES (2000)**	**SIAC ARBITRATION RULES (1997)**	**UNCITRAL ARBITRATION RULES (1976)**
address, or if, after reasonable inquiries, none of the aforesaid addresses can be found, the written correspondence is sent to the addressee's last known place of business, habitual residence or mailing address by registered letter or by any other means which provides a record of the attempt to deliver it. ***See also* Article 15 at A-7-8 and Article 20 at A-8.**	holiday or a non-business day at the residence or place of business of the addressee, the period is extended until the first business day which follows. Official holidays or non-business days occurring during the running of the period of time are included in calculating the period. **Article 15 - General Provisions** 3. All documents or information supplied to the arbitral tribunal by one party shall at the same time be communicated by that party to the other party. **Article 23 - Periods of Time** The periods of time fixed by the arbitral tribunal for the communication of written statements (including the statement of claim and statement of defence) should not exceed forty-five days. However, the arbitral tribunal may extend	provided for in Rule 10, Paragraph 1, Rule 15, Paragraph 1, Rule 16, Paragraph 1, Rule 19, Paragraph 1 and Rule 24, Paragraph 3 (including the application *mutatis mutandis* of the provisions or such Paragraph under the provisions of Rule 25, Paragraph 5). In the event of such an extension, the parties shall, without delay, notify the arbitral tribunal (or, hereinafter, for purposes of this Rule, the Association if the arbitral tribunal has not been established) thereof. 2. The arbitral tribunal may, if deemed necessary, extend any period of time provided for in these Rules (including a period of time determined by the arbitral tribunal) except for the period of time provided for in Rule 59. In the event of such an extension, the arbitral tribunal shall, without delay, notify the parties thereof. ***See also* Rule 13.1 at**		period is an official holiday at the residence or place of business of the addressee, the period is extended until the first business day which follows. Official holidays occurring during the running of the period of time are included in calculating the period. 2.3 Any written communication may be made by way of any form of electronic transmission effected to a business address of a party or to a facsimile number or e-mail address indicated in a party's letterhead and is deemed to have been received if it is so transmitted on the day of transmission. 2.4 The parties shall file with the Registrar a copy of any notice, including a notification, communication or proposal concerning the arbitral proceedings. **Rule 22 - Hearings** 22.7 All statements, documents or other	holiday or a non-business day at the residence or place of business of the addressee, the period is extended until the first business day which follows. Official holidays or non-business days occurring during the running of the period of time are included in calculating the period. **Article 15 - General Provisions** 3. All documents or information supplied to the arbitral tribunal by one party shall at the same time be communicated by that party to the other party. **Article 23 - Periods of Time** The periods of time fixed by the arbitral tribunal for the communication of written statements (including the statement of claim and statement of defence) should not exceed forty-five days. However, the arbitral tribunal may extend

INSTITUTIONAL					AD HOC
CIETAC ARBITRATION RULES (2000)	HKIAC ARBITRATION RULES (1985)	JCAA ARBITRATION RULES (1997)	KCAB ARBITRATION RULES (2000)	SIAC ARBITRATION RULES (1997)	UNCITRAL ARBITRATION RULES (1976)
	the time-limits if it concludes that an extension is justified. **HKIAC as Arbitration Administrator: Communications** Communications and notices between the parties and the arbitral tribunal in the course of arbitration proceedings (except at meetings and hearings) will be addressed through the HKIAC, and deemed received by the addressee when received by the HKIAC. When passed on by the HKIAC to a party such communications and notices will be sent to the address of that party contained in the Notice of Arbitration or such other address as may have been notified in writing to the HKIAC by that party.	**A-47.**		information supplied to the Tribunal by one party shall be communicated to the other party. Also, any expert report or evidentiary document on which the Tribunal may rely in making its decision shall be communicated to the parties. **Rule 25 - Additional Powers of the Tribunal** Unless the parties at any time agree otherwise, and subject to any mandatory limitations of any applicable law, the Tribunal shall have the power, on the application of any party or of its own motion, but in either case only after giving the parties a proper opportunity to state their views, to: (d) extend or abbreviate any time limits provided by these Rules or by its directions.	the time-limits if it concludes that an extension is justified.

GENERAL CONDITIONS
PLACE OF ARBITRATION

INSTITUTIONAL					AD HOC
CIETAC ARBITRATION RULES (2000)	HKIAC ARBITRATION RULES (1985)	JCAA ARBITRATION RULES (1997)	KCAB ARBITRATION RULES (2000)	SIAC ARBITRATION RULES (1997)	UNCITRAL ARBITRATION RULES (1976)
Article 12 The Parties may agree to have their dispute arbitrated by the Arbitration Commission in Beijing or by the Shenzhen Sub-Commission in Shenzhen or by the Shanghai Sub-Commission in Shanghai. In the absence of such an agreement, the Claimant will have option to submit the case to be arbitrated by the Arbitration Commission in Beijing or by the Shenzhen Sub-commission in Shenzhen or by the Shanghai Sub-Commission in Shanghai. When deciding on where the case should be arbitrated, the first choice should be final. In case of any dispute, the Arbitration Commission will make a decision accordingly. **Article 35** Where the parties have agreed on the place of arbitration, the	**Article 16 - Place of Arbitration** 1. Unless the parties have agreed upon the place where the arbitration is to be held, such place shall be determined by the arbitral tribunal, having regard to the circumstances of the arbitration. 2. The arbitral tribunal may determine the locale of the arbitration within the country agreed upon by the parties. It may hear witnesses and hold meetings for consultation among its members at any place it deems appropriate, having regard to the circumstances of the arbitration. 3. The arbitral tribunal may meet at any place it deems appropriate for the inspection of goods, other property or documents. The parties shall be given sufficient notice to enable them to be present at such inspection. 4. The award shall be	**Rule 32 - Hearings** 1. The date and place of hearings shall be decided by the arbitral tribunal upon consultation with the parties. If a hearing lasts more than one (1) day, it shall be held on consecutive days, to the extent possible. 2. After the date and place of hearing have been decided, the clerk in charge shall, without delay, notify the parties thereof. One notice shall suffice even if hearings are held on consecutive days.	**Article 17 - Fixing of Locale** The place of arbitration, in the absence of an agreement by the parties, shall be determined by the Secretariat considering the convenience of the parties and access to documentary evidence. **Article 27 - Time, Date and Place** (1) The Tribunal shall determine the time, date, place and manner of each arbitration hearing.	**Rule 19 - Place of Arbitration** 19.1 The parties may choose the place of arbitration. Failing such a choice, the place of arbitration shall be Singapore, unless the Tribunal determines in view of all the circumstances of the case that another place is more appropriate. 19.2 The Tribunal may hold hearings and meetings anywhere convenient, subject to the provisions of Rule 22.2 and provided that the award shall be made at the place of arbitration.	**Article 16 - Place of Arbitration** 1. Unless the parties have agreed upon the place where the arbitration is to be held, such place shall be determined by the arbitral tribunal, having regard to the circumstances of the arbitration. 2. The arbitral tribunal may determine the locale of the arbitration within the country agreed upon by the parties. It may hear witnesses and hold meetings for consultation among its members at any place it deems appropriate, having regard to the circumstances of the arbitration. 3. The arbitral tribunal may meet at any place it deems appropriate for the inspection of goods, other property or documents. The parties shall be given sufficient notice to enable them to be present at such inspection. 4. The award shall be

PLACE OF ARBITRATION

INSTITUTIONAL					AD HOC
CIETAC ARBITRATION RULES (2000)	HKIAC ARBITRATION RULES (1985)	JCAA ARBITRATION RULES (1997)	KCAB ARBITRATION RULES (2000)	SIAC ARBITRATION RULES (1997)	UNCITRAL ARBITRATION RULES (1976)
case shall be arbitrated in that place. Unless the parties agree otherwise, the cases accepted by the Arbitration Commission shall be heard in Beijing, or in other places with the approval of the Secretary-General of the Arbitration Commission. The cases accepted by a Sub-Commission of the Arbitration Commission shall be heard in the place where the Sub-Commission is located, or in other places with the approval of the Secretary-General of that Sub-Commission.	made at the place of arbitration.				made at the place of arbitration.

GENERAL CONDITIONS

LANGUAGE

INSTITUTIONAL					AD HOC
CIETAC ARBITRATION RULES (2000)	**HKIAC ARBITRATION RULES (1985)**	**JCAA ARBITRATION RULES (1997)**	**KCAB ARBITRATION RULES (2000)**	**SIAC ARBITRATION RULES (1997)**	**UNCITRAL ARBITRATION RULES (1976)**
Article 85 The Chinese language is the official language of the Arbitration Commission. If the parties have agreed otherwise, their agreement shall prevail. At the hearing, if the parties or their arbitration agents or witnesses require language interpretation, the secretariat of the Arbitration Commission may provide an interpreter for them. Or the parties may bring with them their own interpreter. The arbitration tribunal and/or the secretariat of the Arbitration Commission may, as considers necessary, request the parties to hand in the corresponding translation copies in Chinese language or other languages of the documents and evidential materials submitted by the parties.	**Article 17 - Language** 1. Subject to an agreement by the parties, the arbitral tribunal shall, promptly after its appointment, determine the language or languages to be used in the proceedings. This determination shall apply to the statement of claim, the statement of defence, and any further written statements and, if oral hearings take place, to the language or languages to be used in such hearings. 2. The arbitral tribunal may order that any documents annexed to the statement of claim or statement of defence, and any supplementary documents or exhibits submitted in the course of the proceedings, delivered in their original language, shall be accompanied by a translation into the language or languages agreed upon by the parties or determined by the arbitral tribunal.	**Rule 44 - Interpretation and Translation** 1. The clerk in charge shall, when the arbitral tribunal has so ordered or a party has so requested, arrange for interpreting. Such order or request shall, in principle, be made not less than three (3) weeks before the date when interpreting is required. 2. The provisions of Paragraph 3 of the preceding Rule shall apply *mutatis mutandis* to the cost of interpreting. 3. The provisions of the preceding two (2) Paragraphs shall apply mutatis mutandis to the translation of documents. **Rule 62 - Language** 1. The language or languages to be used in arbitral proceedings shall be Japanese or English or both. The arbitral tribunal shall, except where the parties have agreed such languages	**Article 29 - Presentation of Translation** Parties shall, upon request, present to the Secretariat or the Tribunal, translations of the written statements and evidentiary documents and/or other written materials which are requested by the Secretariat or the Tribunal. **Article 30 - Interpretation or Translation** (1) The Secretariat shall make necessary arrangements for the services of interpretation or translation upon the request of one or both parties or by order of the Tribunal. (2) The requesting party shall deposit an advance payment to the Secretariat of the expenses involved in such services described in Paragraph (1). (3) The expenses involved in the	**Rule 20 - Language of Arbitration** 20.1 Subject to any agreement by the parties, the Tribunal shall, promptly after its appointment, determine the language or languages to be used in the proceedings. This determination shall apply to the Statement of Case, the Statement of Defence, and any further written statements or other communications and, if oral hearings take place, to the language or languages to be used in such hearings. 20.2 If a document is drawn up in a language other than the language(s) of the arbitration, and no translation of such document is submitted by the party producing the document, the Tribunal, or if the Tribunal has not been established, the Registrar, may order that party to submit a translation in a form to be determined by the Tribunal or the Registrar	**Article 17 - Language** 1. Subject to an agreement by the parties, the arbitral tribunal shall, promptly after its appointment, determine the language or languages to be used in the proceedings. This determination shall apply to the statement of claim, the statement of defence, and any further written statements and, if oral hearings take place, to the language or languages to be used in such hearings. 2. The arbitral tribunal may order that any documents annexed to the statement of claim or statement of defence, and any supplementary documents or exhibits submitted in the course of the proceedings, delivered in their original language, shall be accompanied by a translation into the language or languages agreed upon by the parties or determined by the arbitral tribunal.

INSTITUTIONAL					AD HOC
CIETAC ARBITRATION RULES (2000)	HKIAC ARBITRATION RULES (1985)	JCAA ARBITRATION RULES (1997)	KCAB ARBITRATION RULES (2000)	SIAC ARBITRATION RULES (1997)	UNCITRAL ARBITRATION RULES (1976)
		determine, without delay, the language or languages to be used. The arbitral tribunal shall, in so determining, take into consideration whether interpreting or translating will be required and how the cost thereof should be allocated. 2. Arbitral proceedings conducted, prior to the determination of language or languages pursuant to the preceding Paragraph, in a language other than the language or languages so determined shall remain valid. The Association may, if such language is one other than Japanese or English, require the submission of Japanese or English translations. 3. If it is determined that both Japanese and English are to be the languages used during arbitral proceedings, either Japanese or English may be, at a party's option, used during all arbitral proceedings,	services provided in Paragraph (1) herein by order of the Tribunal shall be paid from the deposits made in advance by the party under Article 65. **Article 50 - Language** The Korean language shall be used in the arbitral proceedings unless otherwise agreed by the parties. In case there has been a request submitted by one of the parties or both, or there is among the arbitrators a person of nationality other than that of Korea, the arbitral award may be written in both Korean and English languages and both versions shall be the duly authenticated arbitral award. However, when a discrepancy in interpretation has arisen between the two versions, interpretation by the Korean language shall prevail.		

GENERAL CONDITIONS
LANGUAGE

INSTITUTIONAL					AD HOC
CIETAC ARBITRATION RULES (2000)	HKIAC ARBITRATION RULES (1985)	JCAA ARBITRATION RULES (1997)	KCAB ARBITRATION RULES (2000)	SIAC ARBITRATION RULES (1997)	UNCITRAL ARBITRATION RULES (1976)
		including hearings; provided that the arbitral award shall be written in Japanese and English, both versions of which shall be official, and if a discrepancy in interpretation arises between the two (2) versions, the interpretation of the Japanese version shall prevail.			

GENERAL CONDITIONS

Representation and Assistance

Institutional					Ad Hoc
CIETAC ARBITRATION RULES (2000)	HKIAC ARBITRATION RULES (1985)	JCAA ARBITRATION RULES (1997)	KCAB ARBITRATION RULES (2000)	SIAC ARBITRATION RULES (1997)	UNCITRAL ARBITRATION RULES (1976)
Article 22 The parties may authorize arbitration agents to deal with the matters relating to arbitration; the authorized arbitration agent must produce a Power of Attorney to the Arbitration Commission. Both Chinese and foreign citizens can be authorized to act as arbitration agents.	**Article 4 - Representation and Assistance** The parties may be represented or assisted by persons of their choice. The names and addresses of such persons must be communicated in writing to the other party; such communication must specify whether the appointment is being made for purposes of representation or assistance. ***See also* The HKIAC as Arbitration Administrator: Procedural Advice at A-26.**	**Rule 9 - Representation and Assistance** A party may be represented or assisted by any person of its choice in the proceedings under these Rules. Subsequent to such selection, the arbitral tribunal may, for good cause, reject a party's selection of such representative or assistant.	**Article 7 - Representation** Any party may, in taking proceedings under these Rules, be represented by a counsel or such other person as shall be recognized to be proper. However, the Tribunal reserves the right to prohibit such representation when it is deemed to be improper. ***See also* Article 10(2) at A-67 and Article 12(2) at A-68.**	**Rule 21 - Party Representatives** Any party may be represented by legal practitioners or any other representatives, subject to such proof of authority as the Tribunal may require.	**Article 4 - Representation and Assistance** The parties may be represented or assisted by persons of their choice. The names and addresses of such persons must be communicated in writing to the other party; such communication must specify whether the appointment is being made for purposes of representation or assistance.

GENERAL CONDITIONS
CONFIDENTIALITY/PRIVACY

INSTITUTIONAL					AD HOC
CIETAC ARBITRATION RULES (2000)	**HKIAC ARBITRATION RULES (1985)**	**JCAA ARBITRATION RULES (1997)**	**KCAB ARBITRATION RULES (2000)**	**SIAC ARBITRATION RULES (1997)**	**UNCITRAL ARBITRATION RULES (1976)**
Article 36 The arbitration tribunal shall not hear cases in open session. However, if both parties request that an open session hearing be held, the arbitration tribunal shall decide whether to do so or not. **Article 37** For cases heard in closed session, the parties, their arbitration agents, witnesses, arbitrators, experts consulted by the arbitration tribunal and appraisers appointed by the arbitration tribunal and the relevant staff-members of the secretariat of the Arbitration Commission shall not disclose to outsiders the substantive or procedural matters of the case.	**Article 25 - Evidence and Hearings** 4. Hearings shall be held *in camera* unless the parties agree otherwise. The arbitral tribunal may require the retirement of any witness or witnesses during the testimony of other witnesses. The arbitral tribunal is free to determine the manner in which witnesses are examined. **Article 32 - Form and Effect of Award** 5. The award may be made public only with the consent of both parties.	**Rule 42 - Closed Proceedings, Obligation of Confidentiality** 1. Arbitral proceedings and records thereof shall be closed to the public. 2. The arbitrators, the staff of the Association, the parties and their representatives or assistants shall not disclose facts related to arbitration cases or facts learned through arbitration cases; provided that disclosure may be made subject to the conditions provided in a consent of the arbitral tribunal.	**Article 8 - Closed Proceedings** The proceedings of the arbitration shall be kept confidential.	**Rule 22 - Hearings** 22.5 All meetings and hearings shall be in private unless the parties agree otherwise. **Rule 34 - General Provisions** 34.6 The parties and the Tribunal shall at all times treat all matters relating to the proceedings (including the existence of the proceedings) and the award as confidential. A party or any arbitrator shall not, without the prior written consent of the other party or the parties, as the case may be, disclose to a third party any such matter except: (a) for the purpose of making an application to any competent court; (b) for the purpose of making an application to the courts of any State to enforce the award; (c) pursuant to the order of a court of	**Article 25 - Evidence and Hearings** 4. Hearings shall be held *in camera* unless the parties agree otherwise. The arbitral tribunal may require the retirement of any witness or witnesses during the testimony of other witnesses. The arbitral tribunal is free to determine the manner in which witnesses are examined. **Article 32 - Form and Effect of Award** 5. The award may be made public only with the consent of both parties.

INSTITUTIONAL					AD HOC
CIETAC ARBITRATION RULES (2000)	HKIAC ARBITRATION RULES (1985)	JCAA ARBITRATION RULES (1997)	KCAB ARBITRATION RULES (2000)	SIAC ARBITRATION RULES (1997)	UNCITRAL ARBITRATION RULES (1976)
				competent jurisdiction; (d) in compliance with the provisions of the laws of any State which is binding on the party making the disclosure; or (e) in compliance with the request or requirement of any regulatory body or other authority which, if not binding, nonetheless would be observed customarily by the party making the disclosure.	

PRELIMINARY ISSUES

JURISDICTIONAL ISSUES

INSTITUTIONAL					AD HOC
CIETAC ARBITRATION RULES (2000)	HKIAC ARBITRATION RULES (1985)	JCAA ARBITRATION RULES (1997)	KCAB ARBITRATION RULES (2000)	SIAC ARBITRATION RULES (1997)	UNCITRAL ARBITRATION RULES (1976)
Article 4 The Arbitration Commission has the power to decide on the existence and validity of an arbitration agreement and on jurisdiction over an arbitration case. If the parties concerned dispute the validity of an arbitration agreement, with one party requesting the Arbitration Commission to make a decision and the other party requesting the people's court to make a ruling, the people's court will make such a ruling. **Article 6** Any objection to an arbitration agreement and/or the jurisdiction over an arbitration case shall be raised before the first hearing conducted by the arbitration tribunal. Where a case is examined on the basis of documents only, an objection to jurisdiction should be raised before submission of the first substantive	**Article 21 - Pleas as to the Jurisdiction of the Arbitral Tribunal** 1. The arbitral tribunal shall have the power to rule on objections that it has no jurisdiction, including any objections with respect to the existence or validity of the arbitration clause or of the separate arbitration agreement. 2. The arbitral tribunal shall have the power to determine the existence or the validity of the contract of which an arbitration clause forms a part. For the purposes of article 21, an arbitration clause which forms part of a contract and which provides for arbitration under these Rules shall be treated as an agreement independent of the other terms of the contract. A decision by the arbitral tribunal that the contract is null and void shall not entail *ipso jure* the invalidity of the arbitration clause.	**Rule 13 - Acceptance and Notification of Request for Arbitration** 1. The Association, upon confirmation that the request for arbitration has been made in conformity with the provisions of Paragraphs 1 through 3 of the preceding Rule, shall notify, without delay, the claimant and the respondent of the acceptance of the request for arbitration. Copies of the written request for arbitration and the arbitration agreement shall be attached to the notice sent to the respondent. 2. The Association shall designate one of its offices as the secretariat in charge of administrative services and give notice thereof to each party when the Association notifies the parties of the acceptance of the request for arbitration provided for in the preceding Paragraph.	**Article 11 - Acceptance and Notification of Statement of Claim** (1) The Secretariat shall, upon submission of a statement of claim, examine whether such claim is in conformity with the provisions of Article 10 and accept it upon confirmation of its conformity.	**Rule 26 - Jurisdiction of The Tribunal** 26.1 The Tribunal shall have the power to rule on its own jurisdiction, including any objections with respect to the existence, termination or validity of the arbitration agreement. For that purpose, an arbitration agreement which forms part of a contract shall be treated as an agreement independent of the other terms of the contract. A decision by the Tribunal that the contract is null and void shall not entail *ipso jure* the invalidity of the arbitration agreement. 26.2 A plea that the Tribunal does not have jurisdiction shall be raised not later than in the Statement of Defence. A plea that the Tribunal is exceeding the scope of its authority shall be raised promptly after the Tribunal has indicated its intention to decide on the	**Article 21 - Pleas as to the Jurisdiction of the Arbitral Tribunal** 1. The arbitral tribunal shall have the power to rule on objections that it has no jurisdiction, including any objections with respect to the existence or validity of the arbitration clause or of the separate arbitration agreement. 2. The arbitral tribunal shall have the power to determine the existence or the validity of the contract of which an arbitration clause forms a part. For the purposes of article 21, an arbitration clause which forms part of a contract and which provides for arbitration under these Rules shall be treated as an agreement independent of the other terms of the contract. A decision by the arbitral tribunal that the contract is null and void shall not entail *ipso jure* the invalidity of the arbitration clause.

INSTITUTIONAL					AD HOC
CIETAC ARBITRATION RULES (2000)	HKIAC ARBITRATION RULES (1985)	JCAA ARBITRATION RULES (1997)	KCAB ARBITRATION RULES (2000)	SIAC ARBITRATION RULES (1997)	UNCITRAL ARBITRATION RULES (1976)
defense. Any objection to an arbitration agreement and/or the jurisdiction over an arbitration case shall not affect the hearing of the case according to the arbitration procedures. ***See also* Articles 1-2 at A-4-5, and Article 89 at A-21.**	3. A plea that the arbitral tribunal does not have jurisdiction shall be raised not later than in the statement of defence or, with respect to a counter-claim, in the reply to the counter-claim. 4. In general, the arbitral tribunal should rule on a plea concerning its jurisdiction as a preliminary question. However, the arbitral tribunal may proceed with the arbitration and rule on such a plea in their final award			matter alleged to be beyond the scope of its authority. In either case the Tribunal may nevertheless admit a late plea under this Rule if it considers the delay justified. A party is not precluded from raising such a plea by the fact that he has appointed, or participated in the appointment of an arbitrator. 26.3 In addition to the jurisdiction to exercise the powers defined elsewhere in these Rules, the Tribunal shall have jurisdiction to determine any question of law arising in the arbitration; proceed with the arbitration notwithstanding the failure or refusal of any party to comply with these Rules or with the Tribunal's orders or directions, or to attend any meeting or hearing, but only after giving that party written notice that it intends to do so; and to receive and take into account such written or oral	3. A plea that the arbitral tribunal does not have jurisdiction shall be raised not later than in the statement of defence or, with respect to a counter-claim, in the reply to the counter-claim. 4. In general, the arbitral tribunal should rule on a plea concerning its jurisdiction as a preliminary question. However, the arbitral tribunal may proceed with the arbitration and rule on such a plea in their final award.

Institutional					Ad Hoc
CIETAC ARBITRATION RULES (2000)	**HKIAC ARBITRATION RULES (1985)**	**JCAA ARBITRATION RULES (1997)**	**KCAB ARBITRATION RULES (2000)**	**SIAC ARBITRATION RULES (1997)**	**UNCITRAL ARBITRATION RULES (1976)**
				evidence as it shall determine to be relevant, whether or not strictly admissible in law. 26.4 The Tribunal may rule on a plea referred to in Rule 26.2 above either as a preliminary question or in an award on the merits.	

INSTITUTIONAL					AD HOC
CIETAC ARBITRATION RULES (2000)	HKIAC ARBITRATION RULES (1985)	JCAA ARBITRATION RULES (1997)	KCAB ARBITRATION RULES (2000)	SIAC ARBITRATION RULES (1997)	UNCITRAL ARBITRATION RULES (1976)
			Article 52 - Scope of Award (1) The Tribunal may not only order the specific performance of a contract but may also grant any remedy and relief which is deemed just and equitable within the scope of the arbitration agreement of the parties.		

INSTITUTIONAL					AD HOC
CIETAC ARBITRATION RULES (2000)	HKIAC ARBITRATION RULES (1985)	JCAA ARBITRATION RULES (1997)	KCAB ARBITRATION RULES (2000)	SIAC ARBITRATION RULES (1997)	UNCITRAL ARBITRATION RULES (1976)
Article 53 The arbitration tribunal shall independently and impartially make its arbitral award on the basis of the facts, in accordance with the law and the terms of the contracts, with reference to international practices and in compliance with the principle of fairness and reasonableness.	**Article 33 - Applicable Law, *Amiable Compositeur*** 1. The arbitral tribunal shall apply the law designated by the parties as applicable to the substance of the dispute. Failing such designation by the parties, the arbitral tribunal shall apply the law determined by the conflict of laws rules which it considers applicable. 2. The arbitral tribunal shall decide as *amiable compositeur* or *ex aequo et bono* only if the parties have expressly authorized the arbitral tribunal to do so and if the law applicable to the arbitral procedure permits such arbitration. 3. In all cases, the arbitral tribunal shall decide in accordance with the terms of the contract and shall take into account the usages of the trade applicable to the transaction.			**Rule 17 - Conduct of the Proceedings** 17.2 In the absence of procedural rules agreed by the parties or contained herein, the Tribunal shall have the widest discretion allowed under such law as may be applicable to ensure the just, expeditious, economical, and final determination of the dispute. **Rule 25 - Additional Powers of the Tribunal** Unless the parties at any time agree otherwise, and subject to any mandatory limitations of any applicable law, the Tribunal shall have the power, on the application of any party or of its own motion, but in either case only after giving the parties a proper opportunity to state their views, to: (a) order the correction of any such contract or arbitration agreement, but only to the extent	**Article 33 - Applicable Law, *Amiable Compositeur*** 1. The arbitral tribunal shall apply the law designated by the parties as applicable to the substance of the dispute. Failing such designation by the parties, the arbitral tribunal shall apply the law determined by the conflict of laws rules which it considers applicable. 2. The arbitral tribunal shall decide as *amiable compositeur* or *ex aequo et bono* only if the parties have expressly authorized the arbitral tribunal to do so and if the law applicable to the arbitral procedure permits such arbitration. 3. In all cases, the arbitral tribunal shall decide in accordance with the terms of the contract and shall take into account the usages of the trade applicable to the transaction.

INSTITUTIONAL					AD HOC
CIETAC ARBITRATION RULES (2000)	HKIAC ARBITRATION RULES (1985)	JCAA ARBITRATION RULES (1997)	KCAB ARBITRATION RULES (2000)	SIAC ARBITRATION RULES (1997)	UNCITRAL ARBITRATION RULES (1976)
				required to rectify any mistake which it determines to be common to all the parties and then only if and to the extent to which the rules of law governing or applicable to the contract permit such correction. ***See also* Rule 28.2 at A-97.**	

ARBITRAL PROCEEDINGS

CONDUCT OF PROCEEDINGS GENERALLY/APPLICABLE PROCEDURAL LAW

INSTITUTIONAL					AD HOC
CIETAC ARBITRATION RULES (2000)	**HKIAC ARBITRATION RULES (1985)**	**JCAA ARBITRATION RULES (1997)**	**KCAB ARBITRATION RULES (2000)**	**SIAC ARBITRATION RULES (1997)**	**UNCITRAL ARBITRATION RULES (1976)**
Article 7 If the parties agree to submit their dispute to the Arbitration Commission for arbitration, it will be taken that they have agreed to the case being arbitrated under these Rules. However, if the parties have agreed otherwise, and subject to consent by the Arbitration Commission, the parties' agreement will prevail. ***See also* Article 11 at A-6.**	**Article 15 - General Provisions** 1. Subject to these Rules, the arbitral tribunal may conduct the arbitration in such manner as it considers appropriate, provided that the parties are treated with equality and that at any stage of the proceedings each party is given a full opportunity of presenting his case.	**Rule 31 - Supervision of Examination Proceedings** 1. The examination proceedings, including hearings, shall be conducted under the supervision of the arbitral tribunal. 2. The arbitral tribunal shall treat the parties equally and give each party sufficient opportunity to state and prove its case and present a defense against the other party's case. **Rule 39 - Assignment of Arbitrator's Authority** The arbitral tribunal may, when it deems it necessary and upon obtaining the consent of the parties, cause one or more of the arbitrators constituting the arbitral tribunal to examine witnesses, make verifications, conduct inspections or investigations under the provisions of Rule 34 or mediate a settlement.	**Article 9 - Agreement of Parties** The parties shall be deemed to have made the provisions of the arbitration procedures of these Rules a part of their agreement whenever, in the submission of existing disputes or in a contract containing an arbitration clause, they have provided for arbitration by the KCAB or under these Rules. **Article 35 - Proceedings of Hearing** (6) The Tribunal may vary the procedure when it may be deemed necessary but the Tribunal shall afford full and equal opportunity to both parties for the presentation of any materials or relevant evidence.	**Rule 17 - Conduct of the Proceedings** 17.1 The parties may agree on the arbitral procedure, and are encouraged to do so. 17.2 In the absence of procedural rules agreed by the parties or contained herein, the Tribunal shall have the widest discretion allowed under such law as may be applicable to ensure the just, expeditious, economical, and final determination of the dispute. **Rule 32 - Law of the Arbitration** If the place of arbitration is Singapore, the parties agree that the International Arbitration Act (Cap 143A) as amended from time to time is applicable. ***See also* Rule 17 at A-91, Rule 25 at A-95, and Rule 34(5) at A-100.**	**Article 15 - General Provisions** 1. Subject to these Rules, the arbitral tribunal may conduct the arbitration in such manner as it considers appropriate, provided that the parties are treated with equality and that at any stage of the proceedings each party is given a full opportunity of presenting his case.

Institutional					Ad Hoc
CIETAC ARBITRATION RULES (2000)	HKIAC ARBITRATION RULES (1985)	JCAA ARBITRATION RULES (1997)	KCAB ARBITRATION RULES (2000)	SIAC ARBITRATION RULES (1997)	UNCITRAL ARBITRATION RULES (1976)
		See also Rule 40 at A-55.			

INSTITUTIONAL					AD HOC
CIETAC ARBITRATION RULES (2000)	HKIAC ARBITRATION RULES (1985)	JCAA ARBITRATION RULES (1997)	KCAB ARBITRATION RULES (2000)	SIAC ARBITRATION RULES (1997)	UNCITRAL ARBITRATION RULES (1976)
	Article 31 - Decisions 2. In the case of questions of procedure, when there is no majority or when the arbitral tribunal so authorizes, the presiding arbitrator may decide on his own, subject to revision, if any, by the arbitral tribunal. ***See also* Article 31.1 at A-37.**		**Article 33 - Decisions of Tribunal** Whenever there is more than one arbitrator, simple majority rule shall apply for all decisions, including that of the arbitral awards, unless parties agree otherwise. However, if no majority rule is reached with regard to a procedural matter, then the presiding arbitrator shall decide. ***See also* Article 51 at A-80.**	**Rule 17 - Conduct of the Proceedings** 17.3 In the case of a three-member Tribunal, the presiding arbitrator may, after consulting the other arbitrators, make procedural rulings alone.	**Article 31 - Decisions** 2. In the case of questions of procedure, when there is no majority or when the arbitral tribunal so authorizes, the presiding arbitrator may decide on his own, subject to revision, if any, by the arbitral tribunal. ***See also* Article 31.1 at A-111.**

INSTITUTIONAL					AD HOC
CIETAC ARBITRATION RULES (2000)	HKIAC ARBITRATION RULES (1985)	JCAA ARBITRATION RULES (1997)	KCAB ARBITRATION RULES (2000)	SIAC ARBITRATION RULES (1997)	UNCITRAL ARBITRATION RULES (1976)
Article 64 Unless otherwise agreed by the parties, this Summary Procedure shall apply to any case in dispute where the amount of the claim totals not more than RMB 500,000 yuan, and to any case in dispute where the amount of the claim totals more than RMB 500,000 yuan provided that one party applies for arbitration under this Summary Procedure and the other party agrees in writing. **Article 65** When an application for arbitration is submitted to the Arbitration Commission, the secretariat of the Arbitration Commission shall, if such application is examined and found to be acceptable and qualified for application of the Summary Procedure, send a Notice of Arbitration immediately to the parties.		**Rule 52 - Application of Expedited Procedures** 1. In any case where the amount and economic value of the claimant's claim are not more than ¥20,000,000, arbitration shall be conducted under the provisions set forth in this Chapter; provided that the provisions set forth in this Chapter shall not apply to either of the following cases: (1) if the parties notify the Association, within two (2) weeks from the Basic Date provided for in Rule 54, of their agreement that they shall not submit their dispute to the Expedited Procedures; (2) if the parties notify the Association, within two (2) weeks from the Basic Date provided for in Rule 54, of their agreement that the number of arbitrators shall be more than one (1); or (3) if a counterclaim is submitted pursuant to	**Article 56 - Scope of Application** The Expedited Procedure shall be applied to an arbitration case where both parties have agreed to follow the procedures provided in this Chapter in a separate agreement or to a Domestic Arbitration case of which the claim amount is less than 20,000,000 won in the Korean currency. In case of Domestic Arbitration of which the claim amount is less than 20,000,000 won, the increase of the claim amount after the Basic Date shall not be considered. ***See also* Articles 57-60 at A-81-82.**	**Rule 25 - Additional Powers of the Tribunal** Unless the parties at any time agree otherwise, and subject to any mandatory limitations of any applicable law, the Tribunal shall have the power, on the application of any party or of its own motion, but in either case only after giving the parties a proper opportunity to state their views, to: (d) extend or abbreviate any time limits provided by these Rules or by its directions.	

INSTITUTIONAL					AD HOC
CIETAC ARBITRATION RULES (2000)	HKIAC ARBITRATION RULES (1985)	JCAA ARBITRATION RULES (1997)	KCAB ARBITRATION RULES (2000)	SIAC ARBITRATION RULES (1997)	UNCITRAL ARBITRATION RULES (1976)
Unless both parties have jointly appointed one sole arbitrator from among the Panel of Arbitrators of the Arbitration Commission, they shall jointly appoint or jointly entrust the Chairman of the Arbitration Commission to appoint one sole arbitrator within 15 days from the date on which the Notice of Arbitration is received by the Respondent. Should the parties fail to make such appointment or entrustment, the Chairman of the Arbitration Commission shall immediately appoint one sole arbitrator to form an arbitration tribunal to hear the case. ***See also* Articles 66-74 at A-17-18.**		the provisions set forth in Rule 55 and the amount and/or economic value of such counterclaim exceed ¥20,000,000. 2. The amount of interest and other fruits, compensation for damages, penalty for breach of contract and expenses incidental to a principal claim shall not be included in either the amount or the economic value of the claim provided for in the preceding Paragraph. 3. Where the economic value of a claim cannot be calculated or its calculation is extremely difficult, or where there is a dispute between the parties concerning such economic value, the economic value provided for in Paragraph 1 shall be deemed to exceed ¥20,000,000. ***See also* Rules 53-61 at A-59-61.**			

INSTITUTIONAL					AD HOC
CIETAC ARBITRATION RULES (2000)	HKIAC ARBITRATION RULES (1985)	JCAA ARBITRATION RULES (1997)	KCAB ARBITRATION RULES (2000)	SIAC ARBITRATION RULES (1997)	UNCITRAL ARBITRATION RULES (1976)
		Rule 33 - Submission of Written Statements 1. Each party may submit to the arbitral tribunal, at hearings or otherwise, written statements setting forth such party's case on the law and the facts (hereinafter the "written statements"). The arbitral tribunal may urge the submission of written statements. **Rule 34 - Clarification of the Case** The arbitral tribunal may, to assist it in understanding the case, require a party to explain such party's case or conduct an on-site inspection or investigation in the presence of the parties.	**Article 35 - Proceedings of Hearing** (3) The Tribunal may, at the beginning of the hearing, ask for statements clarifying issues involved in the dispute.	**Rule 22 - Hearings** 22.4 The Tribunal may in advance of hearings, submit to the parties, a list of questions which it wishes them to treat with special attention.	

INSTITUTIONAL					AD HOC
CIETAC ARBITRATION RULES (2000)	**HKIAC ARBITRATION RULES (1985)**	**JCAA ARBITRATION RULES (1997)**	**KCAB ARBITRATION RULES (2000)**	**SIAC ARBITRATION RULES (1997)**	**UNCITRAL ARBITRATION RULES (1976)**
Article 14 A Claimant submitting an Application for Arbitration must: (1) Submit an Application for Arbitration in writing, which shall, *inter alia*, contain: (a) the names and addresses of the Claimant and the Respondent, including the zip code, telephone, telex, fax, and cable numbers or any other means of electronic telecommunications, if any; (b) the arbitration agreement relied upon by the Claimant; (c) the facts of the case and the main points of dispute; and (d) the Claimant's claim and the facts and reasons on which his claim is based. The Application for Arbitration shall be signed by, and/or affixed with the seal of, the Claimant and/or	**Article 18 - Statement of Claim** 1. Unless the statement of claim was contained in the notice of arbitration, within a period of time to be determined by the arbitral tribunal, the claimant shall communicate his statement of claim in writing to the respondent and to each of the arbitrators. A copy of the contract, and of the arbitration agreement if not contained in the contract, shall be annexed thereto. 2. The statement of claim shall include the following particulars: (a) The names and addresses of the parties; (b) A statement of the facts supporting the claim; (c) The points at issue; (d) The relief or remedy sought. The claimant may annex to his statement	**Rule 12 - Request for Arbitration** 1. To request the initiation of arbitral proceedings, the claimant shall submit to the Association a written request for arbitration setting forth the following: (1) a demand that the dispute be referred to arbitration under these Rules; (2) a reference to the arbitration agreement that is invoked; (3) the full personal or corporate names of the parties and their addresses; (4) if the claimant is represented by an agent, the name and address of such agent; (5) the relief or remedy claimed; (6) a summary of the dispute; and (7) the basis for the claim and the manner or method of proof. 2. The claimant shall	**Article 10 - Claim** (1) A person desiring to file a claim with the KCAB under these Rules shall submit the following documents to the Secretariat accompanied by the arbitration costs as provided in Chapter IX: a) A document certifying agreement on arbitration; b) A power of attorney, in case the claim is made by an agent. (2) The following matters shall be stated in the statement of claim: a) The full names of the parties and their addresses (in case of corporations, the full names and addresses of the representatives shall also be stated); b) In case the Claimant is represented by an agent, the full name and address of the agent; c) The purport of the	**Rule 18 - Submission of Written Statements and Documents** 18.2 Within thirty (30) days of receipt of notification from the Registrar that the Tribunal has been constituted, the Claimant shall, if it has not done so, send to the Respondent a Statement of Case setting out in full detail the facts and any contention of law on which it relies, and the relief claimed. 18.5 The periods of time fixed by the Tribunal for the submission of written statements (including the Statement of Case and Statement of Defence) shall not exceed forty-five (45) days. However the Tribunal may extend the time-limits on such terms as it may deem appropriate. 18.6 All statements referred to in this Rule shall be accompanied by copies (or, if they	**Article 18 - Statement of Claim** 1. Unless the statement of claim was contained in the notice of arbitration, within a period of time to be determined by the arbitral tribunal, the claimant shall communicate his statement of claim in writing to the respondent and to each of the arbitrators. A copy of the contract, and of the arbitration agreement if not contained in the contract, shall be annexed thereto. 2. The statement of claim shall include the following particulars: (a) The names and addresses of the parties; (b) A statement of the facts supporting the claim; (c) The points at issue; (d) The relief or remedy sought. The claimant may annex to his statement

INSTITUTIONAL					AD HOC
CIETAC ARBITRATION RULES (2000)	HKIAC ARBITRATION RULES (1985)	JCAA ARBITRATION RULES (1997)	KCAB ARBITRATION RULES (2000)	SIAC ARBITRATION RULES (1997)	UNCITRAL ARBITRATION RULES (1976)
the authorized agent of the Claimant. (2) Attach to the Application for Arbitration the relevant documentary evidence which supports the facts on which the Claimant's claim is based. (3) Pay an arbitration fee in advance to the Arbitration Commission according to the Arbitration Fee Schedule of the Arbitration Commission.	of claim all documents he deems relevant or may add a reference to the documents or other evidence he will submit. ***See also* Article 3.3(e) at A-29, Article 3.4(c) at A-29 and Article 23 at A-35.**	submit to the Association, together with the written request for arbitration, a copy of the arbitration clause or the separate arbitration agreement containing the arbitration agreement provided for in (2) of the preceding Paragraph. 3. If the claimant is represented by an agent in the arbitral proceedings, such agent shall submit a power of attorney to the Association together with the written request for arbitration. 4. The claimant shall, when it requests the initiation of arbitral proceedings, pay the request fee and the administrative fee provided for in the Arbitration Fee Regulations of the Association. If the claimant fails to pay such request fee and/or administrative fee, the Association may treat the request for arbitration as if it had not been made	claim; d) The grounds for the claim and the method of proof. **Article 11 - Acceptance and Notification of Statement of Claim** (1) The Secretariat shall, upon submission of a statement of claim, examine whether such claim is in conformity with the provisions of Article 10 and accept it upon confirmation of its conformity. (2) The Secretariat shall, upon acceptance of the statement of claim, give such notice to both parties. In this case, a copy of the statement of claim shall be served on the Respondent accompanied by such notice.	are especially voluminous, lists) of all essential documents on which the party concerned relies and which have not previously been submitted by any party, and (where appropriate) by any relevant samples. 18.7 Copies of all statements referred to in this Rule shall be served on the Tribunal and the Registrar. 18.9 If the Claimant fails within the time specified under these Rules or as may be fixed by the Tribunal, to submit its Statement of Case, the Tribunal may issue an order for the termination of the arbitral proceedings or make such other directions as may be appropriate in the circumstances. If the Respondent fails to submit a Statement of Defence, or if at any point any party fails to avail itself of the opportunity to present its case in the manner directed by the Tribunal, the Tribunal may nevertheless	of claim all documents he deems relevant or may add a reference to the documents or other evidence he will submit. ***See also* Article 3.3(e) at A-102, Article 3.4(c) at A-103 and Article 23 at A-109.**

INSTITUTIONAL					AD HOC
CIETAC ARBITRATION RULES (2000)	HKIAC ARBITRATION RULES (1985)	JCAA ARBITRATION RULES (1997)	KCAB ARBITRATION RULES (2000)	SIAC ARBITRATION RULES (1997)	UNCITRAL ARBITRATION RULES (1976)
		and return the written request for arbitration to the claimant with notification to such effect. 5. Arbitral proceedings shall be deemed to be initiated on the date on which the Association receives the written request for arbitration. ***See also* Rule 18 at A-48-49.**		proceed with the arbitration and make the award. ***See also* Rule 3 at A-87.**	

ARBITRAL PROCEEDINGS

STATEMENT OF DEFENSE/COUNTERCLAIMS/REPLY

INSTITUTIONAL					AD HOC
CIETAC ARBITRATION RULES (2000)	HKIAC ARBITRATION RULES (1985)	JCAA ARBITRATION RULES (1997)	KCAB ARBITRATION RULES (2000)	SIAC ARBITRATION RULES (1997)	UNCITRAL ARBITRATION RULES (1976)
Article 17 The Respondent shall, within 45 days from the date of receipt of the Notice of Arbitration, submit his written defense and relevant documentary evidence to the secretariat of the Arbitration Commission. **Article 18** The Respondent shall, at the latest within 60 days from the date of receipt of the Notice of Arbitration, file with the secretariat of the Arbitration Commission his counterclaim in writing, if any. The arbitration tribunal may extend that time limit if it deems that there are justified reasons. When filing a counterclaim, the Respondent must state in his written statement of counterclaim his specific claim and facts and reasons upon which his claim is based, and attach to his written statement of counterclaim any relevant documentary	**Article 19 - Statement of Defense** 1. Within a period of time to be determined by the arbitral tribunal, the respondent shall communicate his statement of defence in writing to the claimant and to each of the arbitrators. 2. The statement of defence shall reply to the particulars (b), (c) and (d) of the statement of claim (article 18, para. 2). The respondent may annex to his statement the documents on which he relies for his defence or may add a reference to the documents or other evidence he will submit. 3. In his statement of defence, or at a later stage in the arbitral proceedings if the arbitral tribunal decides that the delay was justified under the circumstances, the respondent may make a counter-claim arising out of the same contract or rely on a claim arising out of the	**Rule 15 - Answer** 1. The respondent shall, within four (4) weeks from the Basic Date, submit to the Association a written answer setting forth the following: (1) the full personal or corporate names of the parties and their addresses; (2) if the respondent is represented by an agent, the name and address of such agent; (3) confirmation or denial of the claims; (4) a summary of the dispute; and (5) the basis for the answer and the manner or method of proof. 2. If the respondent is represented by an agent in the arbitral proceedings, such agent shall submit a power of attorney to the Association together with the written answer. 3. Subsequent to	**Article 12 - Defence** (1) The Respondent may, within 15 days in case of Domestic Arbitration and within 30 days in case of International Arbitration from the date of receipt of the notice in accordance with Paragraph (2) of Article 11 (hereinafter referred to as "Basic Date"), file a defence with the same Secretariat by submitting the following documents: a) A statement of defence; b) The original or reproduced copy of documentary evidence, if any, proving the grounds stated in the said defence; c) A power of attorney, in case the said defence is made by an agent. (2) The following matters shall be stated in the statement of defence provided in a) of Paragraph (1):	**Rule 18 - Submission of Written Statements and Documents** 18.3 Within thirty (30) days of receipt of the Statement of Case by the Respondent, or, where the Statement of Case was served with the Notice of Arbitration, the notification referred to in Rule 18.2, the Respondent shall send to the Claimant, a Statement of Defence stating in full detail which of the facts and contentions of law in the Statement of Case it admits or denies, on what grounds, and on what other facts and contentions of law it relies. Any counterclaims shall be submitted with the Statement of Defence in the same manner as claims are set out in the Statement of Case. 18.5 The periods of time fixed by the Tribunal for the submission of written statements (including the Statement of Case	**Article 19 - Statement of Defense** 1. Within a period of time to be determined by the arbitral tribunal, the respondent shall communicate his statement of defence in writing to the claimant and to each of the arbitrators. 2. The statement of defence shall reply to the particulars (b), (c) and (d) of the statement of claim (article 18, para. 2). The respondent may annex to his statement the documents on which he relies for his defence or may add a reference to the documents or other evidence he will submit. 3. In his statement of defence, or at a later stage in the arbitral proceedings if the arbitral tribunal decides that the delay was justified under the circumstances, the respondent may make a counter-claim arising out of the same contract or rely on a

INSTITUTIONAL					AD HOC
CIETAC ARBITRATION RULES (2000)	HKIAC ARBITRATION RULES (1985)	JCAA ARBITRATION RULES (1997)	KCAB ARBITRATION RULES (2000)	SIAC ARBITRATION RULES (1997)	UNCITRAL ARBITRATION RULES (1976)
evidence. When filing a counterclaim, the Respondent must pay an arbitration fee in advance according to the Arbitration Fee Schedule of the Arbitration Commission.	same contract for the purpose of a set-off. 4. The provisions of article 18, paragraph 2, shall apply to a counter-claim and a claim relied on for the purpose of a set-off. ***See also* Article 23 at A-35.**	submission of the written answer, the Association shall send, without delay, a copy thereof to the other party or parties and, if an arbitrator has or arbitrators have been appointed, to such arbitrator or arbitrators. 4. If the written answer contains a counterclaim, the provisions of the following Rule shall apply to such counterclaim. **Rule 16 - Counterclaim** 1. The respondent may, only within six (6) weeks from the Basic Date, submit a counterclaim that is related to the claimant's claim(s) and covered by the same arbitration agreement. The arbitral tribunal shall examine any such counterclaim together with the claimant's claim(s). 2. The provisions of Rules 12, 13 and 15 shall apply *mutatis mutandis* to any counterclaim provided	a) The full names of the parties and their addresses (in case of corporations, the full names and their addresses including the full names of representatives and their addresses shall also be stated); b) In case the Respondent is represented by an agent, the full name and address of the agent; c) The purport of the defence; d) The grounds for the defence and the method of proof. (3) The Secretariat shall, upon receipt of the statement of defence, examine whether such defence is in conformity with the provision of Paragraph (2) of this Article, and upon confirmation of its conformity, accept it. (4) The Secretariat shall, upon acceptance of the statement of defence, give notice to the same effect to both	and Statement of Defence) shall not exceed forty-five (45) days. However the Tribunal may extend the time-limits on such terms as it may deem appropriate. 18.6 All statements referred to in this Rule shall be accompanied by copies (or, if they are especially voluminous, lists) of all essential documents on which the party concerned relies and which have not previously been submitted by any party, and (where appropriate) by any relevant samples. 18.7 Copies of all statements referred to in this Rule shall be served on the Tribunal and the Registrar. 18.8 As soon as practicable following completion of the submission of the statements specified in this Rule, the Tribunal shall proceed in such manner as has been agreed by the	claim arising out of the same contract for the purpose of a set-off. 4. The provisions of article 18, paragraph 2, shall apply to a counter-claim and a claim relied on for the purpose of a set-off. ***See also* Article 23 at A-109.**

INSTITUTIONAL					AD HOC
CIETAC ARBITRATION RULES (2000)	HKIAC ARBITRATION RULES (1985)	JCAA ARBITRATION RULES (1997)	KCAB ARBITRATION RULES (2000)	SIAC ARBITRATION RULES (1997)	UNCITRAL ARBITRATION RULES (1976)
		for in the preceding Paragraph. ***See also* Rule 18 at A-48-49.**	parties. In this case, a copy of the said defense shall be served on the Claimant. (5) If no statement of defence is filed within the period provided in Paragraph (1) hereinabove, the Respondent is considered to have dismissed the claim. **Article 14 - Counterclaim** (1) The Respondent may submit a counterclaim at any time during the arbitral proceeding. However, if a counterclaim is filed late in the proceeding and has an undue effect on the other party or delays the completion of the proceeding, then the Tribunal may, pursuant to the other party's request or at its own discretion, deny filing of such counterclaim. (2) The proceedings of the Respondent's counterclaim shall be annexed to the Claimant's request for arbitration.	parties, or pursuant to its authority under these Rules. 18.9 If the Claimant fails within the time specified under these Rules or as may be fixed by the Tribunal, to submit its Statement of Case, the Tribunal may issue an order for the termination of the arbitral proceedings or make such other directions as may be appropriate in the circumstances. If the Respondent fails to submit a Statement of Defence, or if at any point any party fails to avail itself of the opportunity to present its case in the manner directed by the Tribunal, the Tribunal may nevertheless proceed with the arbitration and make the award. ***See also* Rule 4 at A-87-88.**	

INSTITUTIONAL					AD HOC
CIETAC ARBITRATION RULES (2000)	HKIAC ARBITRATION RULES (1985)	JCAA ARBITRATION RULES (1997)	KCAB ARBITRATION RULES (2000)	SIAC ARBITRATION RULES (1997)	UNCITRAL ARBITRATION RULES (1976)
			(3) The provisions of Article 10 through Article 13 shall apply *mutatis mutandis* to the acceptance of a counterclaim, its notice and the answer thereto. **Article 15 - Request by Tribunal for Filing of Counterclaim** When the Tribunal decides that the Respondent's defence includes the grounds as well as the purport of a counterclaim, the Tribunal may request to the Respondent that a clarification be made as to whether such counterclaim would be filed as provided in Article 14. ***See also* Article 13 at A-69.**		

ARBITRAL PROCEEDINGS
AMENDMENTS TO CLAIMS/DEFENSES

INSTITUTIONAL					AD HOC
CIETAC ARBITRATION RULES (2000)	HKIAC ARBITRATION RULES (1985)	JCAA ARBITRATION RULES (1997)	KCAB ARBITRATION RULES (2000)	SIAC ARBITRATION RULES (1997)	UNCITRAL ARBITRATION RULES (1976)
Article 19 The Claimant may request to amend his claim and the Respondent may request to amend his counterclaim. However, the arbitration tribunal may refuse such an amendment if it considers that the request has been raised too late and may affect the progress of the arbitration proceedings.	**Article 20 - Amendments to the Claim or Defence** During the course of the arbitral proceedings either party may amend or supplement his claim or defence unless the arbitral tribunal considers it inappropriate to allow such amendment having regard to the delay in making it or prejudice to the other party or any other circumstances. However, a claim may not be amended in such a manner that the amended claim falls outside the scope of the arbitration clause or separate arbitration agreement.	**Rule 17 - Amendments to Claims or Counterclaims** 1. Either the claimant or the counterclaimant may, to the extent that the claim and counterclaim are covered by the same arbitration agreement, amend or supplement its claim (which shall hereinafter include a counterclaim for purposes of this Rule) by submitting a written request for amendment to the Association; provided that, after the establishment of the arbitral tribunal, such claimant or counterclaimant shall submit a written application for approval of such amendment to the arbitral tribunal and obtain its approval thereof. 2. The arbitral tribunal shall hear the other party's opinion before giving the approval provided for in the preceding Paragraph. 3. The arbitral tribunal	**Article 16 - Amendment and Supplement of Claim and Defence** (1) A party or parties desiring, after filing of a statement of claim or defence, to amend or supplement the said statement, shall file such a request with the Secretariat in writing. (2) During the course of the arbitral proceedings, any amendments or supplement to claims shall be subject to the approval of the Tribunal. However, if the said amendments or supplement are filed late in the proceeding and have an undue effect on the other party or delay the completion of the proceeding, then the Tribunal may, pursuant to the other party's request or at its own discretion, deny filing of such amendments or supplement. (3) The provisions of Article 10 through Article 13 shall apply	**Rule 25 - Additional Powers of the Tribunal** Unless the parties at any time agree otherwise, and subject to any mandatory limitations of any applicable law, the Tribunal shall have the power, on the application of any party or of its own motion, but in either case only after giving the parties a proper opportunity to state their views, to: (c) allow any party, upon such terms (as to costs and otherwise) as it shall determine, to amend any pleading or submissions.	**Article 20 - Amendments to the Claim or Defence** During the course of the arbitral proceedings either party may amend or supplement his claim or defence unless the arbitral tribunal considers it inappropriate to allow such amendment having regard to the delay in making it or prejudice to the other party or any other circumstances. However, a claim may not be amended in such a manner that the amended claim falls outside the scope of the arbitration clause or separate arbitration agreement.

INSTITUTIONAL					AD HOC
CIETAC ARBITRATION RULES (2000)	HKIAC ARBITRATION RULES (1985)	JCAA ARBITRATION RULES (1997)	KCAB ARBITRATION RULES (2000)	SIAC ARBITRATION RULES (1997)	UNCITRAL ARBITRATION RULES (1976)
		shall not give any approval provided for in Paragraph 1 if it considers it inappropriate to approve such amendment in view of the substantial delay in conducting the arbitral proceedings or prejudice to the other party that such amendment will cause or any other circumstances. 4. The provisions of Rules 15 or 16 shall apply *mutatis mutandis* to an answer to or counterclaim with respect to an amended claim; provided that such answer or counterclaim shall be submitted within three (3) weeks from the date on which the secretariat or the clerk in charge sends written notice of such amendment to such other party.	*mutatis mutandis* to the amendments provided in Paragraph (1).		

INSTITUTIONAL					AD HOC
CIETAC ARBITRATION RULES (2000)	**HKIAC ARBITRATION RULES (1985)**	**JCAA ARBITRATION RULES (1997)**	**KCAB ARBITRATION RULES (2000)**	**SIAC ARBITRATION RULES (1997)**	**UNCITRAL ARBITRATION RULES (1976)**
	Article 22 - Further Written Statements The arbitral tribunal shall decide which further written statements, in addition to the statement of claim and the statement of defence, shall be required from the parties or may be presented by them and shall fix the periods of time for communicating such statements.	**Rule 33 - Submission of Written Statements** 1. Each party may submit to the arbitral tribunal, at hearings or otherwise, written statements setting forth such party's case on the law and the facts (hereinafter the "written statements"). The arbitral tribunal may urge the submission of written statements. 2. Any party submitting written statements shall submit to the Association a number of copies thereof equal to the number of arbitrators and parties. The clerk in charge shall keep one copy for the record and, without delay, deliver personally or send one copy each to the arbitrators and parties (except the party submitting such written statements). 3. The arbitral tribunal shall confirm at hearings the receipt of the written statements submitted otherwise than at a hearing.	**Article 39 - Filing of Statements and Other Documents** (1) The statements and other documents not filed with the Tribunal at the hearing, but arranged for filing at the hearings or subsequently by mutual agreement of the parties or at the request of the Tribunal shall be filed with the Secretariat, which, in turn, shall deliver them to the Tribunal. In such case, both parties shall be afforded opportunity to examine such documents.	**Rule 18 - Submission of Written Statements and Documents** 18.4 The Tribunal shall decide which further written statements, in addition to the Statement of Case and the Statement of Defence, shall be required from the parties or may be presented by them and shall fix the periods of time for communicating such statements. **Rule 25 - Additional Powers of the Tribunal** Unless the parties at any time agree otherwise, and subject to any mandatory limitations of any applicable law, the Tribunal shall have the power, on the application of any party or of its own motion, but in either case only after giving the parties a proper opportunity to state their views, to: (i) to make orders or give directions to any	**Article 22 - Further Written Statements** The arbitral tribunal shall decide which further written statements, in addition to the statement of claim and the statement of defence, shall be required from the parties or may be presented by them and shall fix the periods of time for communicating such statements.

INSTITUTIONAL					AD HOC
CIETAC ARBITRATION RULES (2000)	HKIAC ARBITRATION RULES (1985)	JCAA ARBITRATION RULES (1997)	KCAB ARBITRATION RULES (2000)	SIAC ARBITRATION RULES (1997)	UNCITRAL ARBITRATION RULES (1976)
		Rule 34 - Clarification of the Case The arbitral tribunal may, to assist it in understanding the case, require a party to explain such party's case or conduct an on-site inspection or investigation in the presence of the parties.		party for interrogatories. (k) to make orders or give directions to any party for giving of evidence by affidavit.	

INSTITUTIONAL					AD HOC
CIETAC ARBITRATION RULES (2000)	HKIAC ARBITRATION RULES (1985)	JCAA ARBITRATION RULES (1997)	KCAB ARBITRATION RULES (2000)	SIAC ARBITRATION RULES (1997)	UNCITRAL ARBITRATION RULES (1976)
Article 18 The Respondent shall, at the latest within 60 days from the date of receipt of the Notice of Arbitration, file with the secretariat of the Arbitration Commission his counterclaim in writing, if any. The arbitration tribunal may extend that time limit if it deems that there are justified reasons. . . . **Article 52** The arbitration tribunal shall render an arbitral award within 9 months as from the date on which the arbitration tribunal is formed. The Secretary-General of the Arbitration Commission may extend this time limit at the request of the arbitration tribunal if the Secretary-General of the Arbitration Commission considers that it is really necessary and the reasons for extension are truly justified.	**Article 23 - Periods of Time** The periods of time fixed by the arbitral tribunal for the communication of written statements (including the statement of claim and statement of defence) should not exceed forty-five days. However, the arbitral tribunal may extend the time-limits if it concludes that an extension is justified. ***See also* Article 2 at A-28.**	**Rule 63 - Extension of Period of Time** 2. The arbitral tribunal may, if deemed necessary, extend any period of time provided for in these Rules (including a period of time determined by the arbitral tribunal) except for the period of time provided for in Rule 59. In the event of such an extension, the arbitral tribunal shall, without delay, notify the parties thereof.	**Article 47 - Extensions of Period** The parties may modify any period prescribed under these Rules by a mutual agreement in writing. The Tribunal for good cause may extend any period established by these Rules except the period for making an award. The Tribunal shall notify the parties through the Secretariat of any such extension and reasons therefor.	**Rule 18 - Submission of Written Statements and Documents** 18.1 The Tribunal may determine the periods of time within which the parties shall submit their written statements. If no specific periods of time are determined by the Tribunal the parties shall proceed as set out in this Rule 18. 18.5 The periods of time fixed by the Tribunal for the submission of written statements (including the Statement of Case and Statement of Defence) shall not exceed forty-five (45) days. However the Tribunal may extend the time-limits on such terms as it may deem appropriate. 18.8 As soon as practicable following completion of the submission of the statements specified in this Rule, the Tribunal shall proceed in such manner as has been agreed by the parties, or pursuant to its	**Article 23 - Periods of Time** The periods of time fixed by the arbitral tribunal for the communication of written statements (including the statement of claim and statement of defence) should not exceed forty-five days. However, the arbitral tribunal may extend the time-limits if it concludes that an extension is justified. ***See also* Article 2 at A-102.**

INSTITUTIONAL					AD HOC
CIETAC ARBITRATION RULES (2000)	HKIAC ARBITRATION RULES (1985)	JCAA ARBITRATION RULES (1997)	KCAB ARBITRATION RULES (2000)	SIAC ARBITRATION RULES (1997)	UNCITRAL ARBITRATION RULES (1976)
				authority under these Rules. **Rule 25 - Additional Powers of the Tribunal** Unless the parties at any time agree otherwise, and subject to any mandatory limitations of any applicable law, the Tribunal shall have the power, on the application of any party or of its own motion, but in either case only after giving the parties a proper opportunity to state their views to: (d) extend or abbreviate any time limits provided by these Rules or by its directions.	

DISCLOSURE/DISCOVERY

INSTITUTIONAL					AD HOC
CIETAC ARBITRATION RULES (2000)	HKIAC ARBITRATION RULES (1985)	JCAA ARBITRATION RULES (1997)	KCAB ARBITRATION RULES (2000)	SIAC ARBITRATION RULES (1997)	UNCITRAL ARBITRATION RULES (1976)
Article 38 The parties shall produce evidence in support of the facts on which their claim, defense or counterclaim is based. The arbitration tribunal may, on its own initiative, undertake investigations and collect evidence as it considers necessary. When investigating and collecting evidence by itself, the arbitration tribunal shall promptly inform the parties to be present if it considers necessary. Should one party or both parties fail to appear, the investigation and collection of evidence shall not be affected.	**Article 24 - Evidence and Hearings** 2. The arbitral tribunal may, if it considers it appropriate, require a party to deliver to the tribunal and to the other party, within such a period of time as the arbitral tribunal shall decide, a summary of the documents and other evidence which that party intends to present in support of the facts in issue set out in his statement of claim or statement of defence. 3. At any time during the arbitral proceedings the arbitral tribunal may require the parties to produce documents, exhibits or other evidence within such a period of time as the tribunal shall determine.	**Rule 34 - Clarification of the Case** The arbitral tribunal may, to assist it in understanding the case, require a party to explain such party's case or conduct an on-site inspection or investigation in the presence of the parties. **Rule 35 - Examination of Evidence** 1. Each party shall have the burden of proving the facts relied on to support such party's claim or defense. 5. The arbitral tribunal may, when it deems it necessary or when there has been a petition from a party, refer inquiries to, and request responses from, public or private bodies. The arbitral tribunal shall disclose responses thus obtained to the parties.	**Article 40 - Inspection or Investigation** Should the Tribunal deem it necessary to make an inspection or investigation, it shall, prior to making such inspection or investigation, direct the Secretariat to notify the parties of the purpose, time, date and place for such inspection or investigation. Any party who so desires, may present himself at such inspection or investigation. **Article 42 - Evidence** (2) The Tribunal may, where it is deemed necessary, request the production of evidence or the voluntary appearance of a witness or an expert witness at the hearings. However, the Tribunal may, at its discretion, proceed with the hearing even if evidence has not been submitted and/or neither a witness nor an expert witness has appeared within the designated time.	**Rule 18 - Submission of Written Statements and Documents** 18.6 All statements referred to in this Rule shall be accompanied by copies (or, if they are especially voluminous, lists) of all essential documents on which the party concerned relies and which have not previously been submitted by any party and (where appropriate) by any relevant samples. **Rule 22 - Hearings** 22.7 All statements, documents or other information supplied to the Tribunal by one party shall be communicated to the other party. Also, any expert report or evidentiary document on which the Tribunal may rely in making its decision shall be communicated to the parties.	**Article 24 - Evidence and Hearings** 2. The arbitral tribunal may, if it considers it appropriate, require a party to deliver to the tribunal and to the other party, within such a period of time as the arbitral tribunal shall decide, a summary of the documents and other evidence which that party intends to present in support of the facts in issue set out in his statement of claim or statement of defence. 3. At any time during the arbitral proceedings the arbitral tribunal may require the parties to produce documents, exhibits or other evidence within such a period of time as the tribunal shall determine.

INSTITUTIONAL					AD HOC
CIETAC ARBITRATION RULES (2000)	HKIAC ARBITRATION RULES (1985)	JCAA ARBITRATION RULES (1997)	KCAB ARBITRATION RULES (2000)	SIAC ARBITRATION RULES (1997)	UNCITRAL ARBITRATION RULES (1976)
				Rule 24 - Experts Appointed by the Tribunal 24.1 Unless otherwise agreed by the parties, the Tribunal: (b) may require a party to give any such expert(s) any relevant information or to produce, or to provide access to any relevant documents, goods or property for inspection by the expert(s). **Rule 25 - Additional Powers of the Tribunal** Unless the parties at any time agree otherwise, and subject to any mandatory limitations of any applicable law, the Tribunal shall have the power, on the application of any party or of its own motion, but in either case only after giving the parties a proper opportunity to state their views, to: (e) conduct such enquiries as may appear to the Tribunal to be necessary or	

INSTITUTIONAL					AD HOC
CIETAC ARBITRATION RULES (2000)	HKIAC ARBITRATION RULES (1985)	JCAA ARBITRATION RULES (1997)	KCAB ARBITRATION RULES (2000)	SIAC ARBITRATION RULES (1997)	UNCITRAL ARBITRATION RULES (1976)
				expedient; (f) order the parties to make any property or thing available for inspection, in their presence, by the Tribunal or any expert; (h) order any party to produce to the Tribunal, and to the other parties for inspection, and to supply copies of, any documents or classes of documents in their possession or power which the Tribunal determines to be relevant; (i) to make orders or give directions to any party for interrogatories; (k) to make orders or give directions to any party for giving of evidence by affidavit.	

ARBITRAL PROCEEDINGS

HEARINGS

INSTITUTIONAL					AD HOC
CIETAC ARBITRATION RULES (2000)	HKIAC ARBITRATION RULES (1985)	JCAA ARBITRATION RULES (1997)	KCAB ARBITRATION RULES (2000)	SIAC ARBITRATION RULES (1997)	UNCITRAL ARBITRATION RULES (1976)
Article 32 The arbitration tribunal will hold oral hearings. At the request of the parties or with their consent, the arbitration tribunal may, if it also considers oral hearings unnecessary, hear and decide a case on the basis of documents only. **Article 33** The date of the first oral hearing shall be decided by the arbitration tribunal in consultation with the secretariat of the Arbitration Commission. The secretariat shall notify the two parties of the decision 30 days before the date of the hearing. Any party having justified reasons may request a postponement of the hearing, but a written request must be submitted to the secretariat of the Arbitration Commission 12 days before the date of the hearing. The arbitration tribunal will then decide whether to	**Article 15 - General Provisions** 2. If either party so requests at any stage of the proceedings, the arbitral tribunal shall hold hearings for the presentation of evidence by witnesses, including expert witnesses, or for oral argument. In the absence of such a request, the arbitral tribunal shall decide whether to hold such hearings or whether the proceedings shall be conducted on the basis of documents and other materials. **Article 25 - Evidence and Hearings** 1. In the event of an oral hearing, the arbitral tribunal shall give the parties adequate advance notice of the date, time and place thereof. 2. If witnesses are to be heard, at least fifteen days before the hearing each party shall communicate to the arbitral tribunal and to the other party the names and	**Rule 32 - Hearings** 1. The date and place of hearings shall be decided by the arbitral tribunal upon consultation with the parties. If a hearing lasts more than one (1) day, it shall be held on consecutive days, to the extent possible. 2. After the date and place of hearing have been decided, the clerk in charge shall, without delay, notify the parties thereof. One notice shall suffice even if hearings are held on consecutive days. 3. Oral argumentations on the law and the facts and applications to present evidence and examination thereof shall occur at hearings. 4. The date of a hearing shall be changed at the request of both parties. In the event that one of the parties requests that the date of a hearing be changed, the arbitral tribunal may change	**Article 27 - Time, Date and Place** (1) The Tribunal shall determine the time, date, place and manner of each arbitration hearing. (2) The Secretariat shall notify each party of decision provided in Paragraph (1) 10 days prior to the opening date of the hearing for Domestic Arbitration, and 20 days prior to the opening date of the hearing for International Arbitration unless the terms thereof have been modified by mutual agreement. (3) In determining the manner of hearings under the provisions of Paragraph (1) hereinabove, the Tribunal shall give sufficient consideration in order to prevent a delay of the proceedings through such ways as an intensive hearing, etc.	**Rule 22 - Hearings** 22.1 Unless the parties have agreed on documents-only arbitration, the Tribunal shall, if either party so requests, hold a hearing for the presentation of evidence by witnesses, including expert witnesses, or for oral submissions. 22.2 The Tribunal shall fix the date, time and place of any meeting and hearing in the arbitration, and the sole or presiding arbitrator shall give the parties reasonable notice thereof. 22.3 If any party to the proceedings fails to appear at a hearing, without showing sufficient cause for such failure, the Tribunal may proceed with the arbitration and may make the award on the evidence before it. 22.4 The Tribunal may in advance of hearings, submit to the parties, a list of questions which it	**Article 15 - General Provisions** 2. If either party so requests at any stage of the proceedings, the arbitral tribunal shall hold hearings for the presentation of evidence by witnesses, including expert witnesses, or for oral argument. In the absence of such a request, the arbitral tribunal shall decide whether to hold such hearings or whether the proceedings shall be conducted on the basis of documents and other materials. **Article 25 - Evidence and Hearings** 1. In the event of an oral hearing, the arbitral tribunal shall give the parties adequate advance notice of the date, time and place thereof. 2. If witnesses are to be heard, at least fifteen days before the hearing each party shall communicate to the arbitral tribunal and to the other party the names and

INSTITUTIONAL					AD HOC
CIETAC ARBITRATION RULES (2000)	**HKIAC ARBITRATION RULES (1985)**	**JCAA ARBITRATION RULES (1997)**	**KCAB ARBITRATION RULES (2000)**	**SIAC ARBITRATION RULES (1997)**	**UNCITRAL ARBITRATION RULES (1976)**
postpone the hearing or not. **Article 34** The notice of the date of hearing subsequent to the first hearing is not subject to the 30-day time limit. ***See also* Articles 35-37 at A-11-12 and Articles 42-43 at A-12-13.**	addresses of the witnesses he intends to present, the subject upon and the languages in which such witnesses will give their testimony. 3. The arbitral tribunal shall make arrangements for the translation of oral statements made at a hearing and for a record of the hearing if either is deemed necessary by the tribunal under the circumstances of the case, or if the parties have agreed thereto and have communicated such agreement to the tribunal at least fifteen days before the hearing. 4. Hearings shall be held *in camera* unless the parties agree otherwise. The arbitral tribunal may require the retirement of any witness or witnesses during the testimony of other witnesses. The arbitral tribunal is free to determine the manner in which witnesses are examined.	such date only if it determines that there are unavoidable circumstances. 5. The request provided for in the preceding Paragraph shall be made in writing, unless made at a hearing. **Rule 37 - Principle of Appearance by the Parties** 1. Hearings shall in principle be held in the presence of both parties. 2. If one or both parties fails or fail to appear without good cause, a hearing may be held in its or their absence; provided that, if both of the parties fail to appear, the examination proceedings may not be terminated on the date when such hearing is held. 3. If one of the parties fails to appear, the examination proceedings may be conducted based on the allegations and proof of the party who	**Article 31 - Attendance at Hearings** (1) Parties are entitled to attend the hearing. (2) Persons not privy to arbitration, but who have an interest in the outcome of the arbitration award, may submit *prima facie* evidence of such interest to the Tribunal, and, subject to approval from the Tribunal, may attend the hearing. (3) The Tribunal may order any witness to retire during the testimony of another witness. **Article 32 - Adjournments or Continuations** The Tribunal may, on justifiable grounds, take adjournments or change the date of hearing upon the request of both parties or on its own motion. However, the adjournment should be made within 15 days in case of Domestic Arbitration and within	wishes them to treat with special attention. 22.5 All meetings and hearings shall be in private unless the parties agree otherwise. 22.6 The Tribunal may declare the hearings closed if it is satisfied that the parties have no further proof to offer or witnesses to be heard or submissions to make. The Tribunal may on its own motion or upon application of a party but before any award is made, reopen the hearings. 22.7 All statements, documents or other information supplied to the Tribunal by one party shall be communicated to the other party. Also, any expert report or evidentiary document on which the Tribunal may rely in making its decision shall be communicated to the parties.	addresses of the witnesses he intends to present, the subject upon and the languages in which such witnesses will give their testimony. 3. The arbitral tribunal shall make arrangements for the translation of oral statements made at a hearing and for a record of the hearing if either is deemed necessary by the tribunal under the circumstances of the case, or if the parties have agreed thereto and have communicated such agreement to the tribunal at least fifteen days before the hearing. 4. Hearings shall be held *in camera* unless the parties agree otherwise. The arbitral tribunal may require the retirement of any witness or witnesses during the testimony of other witnesses. The arbitral tribunal is free to determine the manner in which witnesses are examined.

INSTITUTIONAL					AD HOC
CIETAC ARBITRATION RULES (2000)	HKIAC ARBITRATION RULES (1985)	JCAA ARBITRATION RULES (1997)	KCAB ARBITRATION RULES (2000)	SIAC ARBITRATION RULES (1997)	UNCITRAL ARBITRATION RULES (1976)
	***See also* HKIAC As Arbitration Administrator: Liaison at A-26.**	has appeared. ***See also* Rule 31 at A-52, Rule 43(1)-(2) at A-56, and Rule 47 at A-57.**	30 days in case of International Arbitration, not subject to renewal of second adjournment. **Article 34 - Hearing** (1) Statements and statements of defence containing the statements of claim and the form of presenting evidence may be submitted so that the hearing may be conducted by the Tribunal in a manner that will most expeditiously and accurately permit full presentation of the evidence and arguments of the parties. (2) The Tribunal, of its own motion or upon the request of the parties, may submit the summarized text of the statements and statements of defence submitted by the parties or summarize the text and present it to the parties for confirmation. In such case, the Tribunal may hear and award only such summarized issues.		

Hearings

Institutional					Ad Hoc
CIETAC ARBITRATION RULES (2000)	HKIAC ARBITRATION RULES (1985)	JCAA ARBITRATION RULES (1997)	KCAB ARBITRATION RULES (2000)	SIAC ARBITRATION RULES (1997)	UNCITRAL ARBITRATION RULES (1976)
			Article 35 - Proceedings of Hearing (1) A hearing shall commence with the announcement of a case and both parties' names. (2) The Clerk shall keep and provide minutes of the proceedings, containing the following records: a) Date and place of the hearing; b) The names of the arbitrator(s), the parties and their agents, and if witnesses are used, their names and addresses; c) The statements of the parties or their agents, or a summary of each hearing. However, unless otherwise instructed by the Tribunal with regard to the results of the examination of evidence, a recording may be used as a substitute. (3) The Tribunal may,		

INSTITUTIONAL					AD HOC
CIETAC ARBITRATION RULES (2000)	HKIAC ARBITRATION RULES (1985)	JCAA ARBITRATION RULES (1997)	KCAB ARBITRATION RULES (2000)	SIAC ARBITRATION RULES (1997)	UNCITRAL ARBITRATION RULES (1976)
			at the beginning of the hearing, ask for statements clarifying issues involved in the dispute. (4) The party requesting arbitration shall present his statement on the purport and grounds of the claims, and introduce documentary evidence and his witnesses. The Respondent shall present his defence, and introduce documentary evidence and his witnesses. (5) Exhibits, when produced by either party, may be accepted as evidence by the Tribunal, and the exhibits so accepted shall be filed in their numerical order by the Clerk and shall be made a part of the record. (6) The Tribunal may vary the procedure when it may be deemed necessary but the Tribunal shall afford full and equal opportunity to both parties for the presentation of any		

INSTITUTIONAL					AD HOC
CIETAC ARBITRATION RULES (2000)	HKIAC ARBITRATION RULES (1985)	JCAA ARBITRATION RULES (1997)	KCAB ARBITRATION RULES (2000)	SIAC ARBITRATION RULES (1997)	UNCITRAL ARBITRATION RULES (1976)
			materials or relevant evidence. (7) If the parties repeatedly submit a series of statements to show cause of action or as legal defence as to cause undue confusion, the Tribunal may order the presentation of a summary of statements prior to the conclusion of the hearing. ***See also* Articles 28-30 at A-74 and Article 45 at A-78-79.**		

ARBITRAL PROCEEDINGS

EVIDENCE

INSTITUTIONAL					AD HOC
CIETAC ARBITRATION RULES (2000)	**HKIAC ARBITRATION RULES (1985)**	**JCAA ARBITRATION RULES (1997)**	**KCAB ARBITRATION RULES (2000)**	**SIAC ARBITRATION RULES (1997)**	**UNCITRAL ARBITRATION RULES (1976)**
Article 38 The parties shall produce evidence in support of the facts on which their claim, defense or counterclaim is based. The arbitration tribunal may, on its own initiative, undertake investigations and collect evidence as it considers necessary. When investigating and collecting evidence by itself, the arbitration tribunal shall promptly inform the parties to be present if it considers necessary. Should one party or both parties fail to appear, the investigation and collection of evidence shall not be affected. **Article 41** The evidence submitted by the parties will be examined and evaluated by the arbitration tribunal. The arbitration tribunal shall decide whether to adopt the expert's report and the	**Article 24 - Evidence and Hearings** 1. Each party shall have the burden of proving the facts relied on to support his claim or defence. **Article 25 - Evidence and Hearings** 5. Evidence of witnesses may also be presented in the form of written statements signed by them. 6. The arbitral tribunal shall determine the admissibility, relevance, materiality and weight of the evidence offered.	**Rule 35 - Examination of Evidence** 1. Each party shall have the burden of proving the facts relied on to support such party's claim or defense. 2. The arbitral tribunal may, when it deems it necessary, examine evidence that a party has not applied to present. 3. Such examination of evidence may be made other than at a hearing. If the arbitral tribunal decides to examine evidence other than at a hearing, the parties shall be given the opportunity to be present. 4. The arbitral tribunal is not authorized to administer an oath to any witness or expert. 5. The arbitral tribunal may, when it deems it necessary or when there has been a petition from a party, refer inquiries to, and	**Article 42 - Evidence** (1) The parties may offer any evidence they so desire to support their contention or request that any witness or expert witness voluntarily appear at the hearings. However, the Tribunal may refuse to investigate such evidence by finding there exists no relevancy between the evidence so produced and the contention of the parties concerned. (2) The Tribunal may, where it is deemed necessary, request the production of evidence or the voluntary appearance of a witness or an expert witness at the hearings. However, the Tribunal may, at its discretion, proceed with the hearing even if evidence has not been submitted and/or neither a witness nor an expert witness has appeared within the designated time. (3) In the event that the Tribunal is unable	**Rule 22 - Hearings** 22.1 Unless the parties have agreed on documents-only arbitration, the Tribunal shall, if either party so requests, hold a hearing for the presentation of evidence by witnesses, including expert witnesses, or for oral submissions. **Rule 26 - Jurisdiction of The Tribunal** 26.3 In addition to the jurisdiction to exercise the powers defined elsewhere in these Rules, the Tribunal shall have jurisdiction to determine any question of law arising in the arbitration; proceed with the arbitration notwithstanding the failure or refusal of any party to comply with these Rules or with the Tribunal's orders or directions, or to attend any meeting or hearing, but only after giving that party written notice that it intends to do so; and to receive and take into account	**Article 24 - Evidence and Hearings** 1. Each party shall have the burden of proving the facts relied on to support his claim or defence. **Article 25 - Evidence and Hearings** 5. Evidence of witnesses may also be presented in the form of written statements signed by them. 6. The arbitral tribunal shall determine the admissibility, relevance, materiality and weight of the evidence offered.

INSTITUTIONAL					AD HOC
CIETAC ARBITRATION RULES (2000)	HKIAC ARBITRATION RULES (1985)	JCAA ARBITRATION RULES (1997)	KCAB ARBITRATION RULES (2000)	SIAC ARBITRATION RULES (1997)	UNCITRAL ARBITRATION RULES (1976)
		from, public or private bodies. The arbitral tribunal shall disclose responses thus obtained to the parties. **Rule 36 - Application to Present Evidence** 1. A party may apply to present evidence by submitting any of the following documents to the arbitral tribunal: (1) application for documentary evidence (a document explaining the documentary evidence attached thereto); (2) application to examine a witness (a written application, specifying the witness and the matters with respect to which such witness is to be examined, to examine a witness); or (3) application for an expert opinion or verification (a written application for an expert opinion or verification setting forth the matters for which an expert opinion is required or the items to be verified and the	evidence necessary for an arbitration award, the Tribunal may file an application with the competent court upon its own initiative or upon the request of any party. (4) All evidence shall be submitted and examined in the presence of all the parties, and sole arbitrator or the majority of the arbitrators, except where any of the parties is absent without sufficient reason or has waived his right to be present. (5) The Tribunal shall decide at his own discretion the relevancy and materiality of the evidence offered. **Article 40 - Inspection or Investigation** Should the Tribunal deem it necessary to make an inspection or investigation, it shall, prior to making such inspection or investigation, direct the Secretariat to notify the	evidence as it shall determine to be relevant, whether or not strictly admissible in law. ***See also* Rule 25 at A-95.**	

INSTITUTIONAL					AD HOC
CIETAC ARBITRATION RULES (2000)	HKIAC ARBITRATION RULES (1985)	JCAA ARBITRATION RULES (1997)	KCAB ARBITRATION RULES (2000)	SIAC ARBITRATION RULES (1997)	UNCITRAL ARBITRATION RULES (1976)
		method thereof). 2. An application to present evidence may be made other than at a hearing. 3. Any party submitting any of the documents provided for in Paragraph 1 shall submit to the Association a number of copies thereof equal to the number of arbitrators and parties. The clerk in charge shall keep one of the copies for the record and promptly deliver personally or send one copy each to the arbitrators and the parties (except the party submitting such document). 4. A party, except the party who has applied to present evidence, may submit to the arbitral tribunal a document setting forth its views with respect to the application to present evidence. If a party does submit such a document, the provisions of the preceding two (2) Paragraphs shall apply *mutatis mutandis*	parties of the purpose, time, date and place for such inspection or investigation. Any party who so desires, may present himself at such inspection or investigation. ***See also* Article 45 at A-78-79.**		

INSTITUTIONAL					AD HOC
CIETAC ARBITRATION RULES (2000)	HKIAC ARBITRATION RULES (1985)	JCAA ARBITRATION RULES (1997)	KCAB ARBITRATION RULES (2000)	SIAC ARBITRATION RULES (1997)	UNCITRAL ARBITRATION RULES (1976)
		5. The arbitral tribunal may, any time after the lapse of a reasonable period of time necessary for the document provided for in Paragraph 4 to be submitted, determine whether to adopt or reject the application to present evidence. After the arbitral tribunal makes such determination, the clerk in charge shall, without delay, notify the parties of the result thereof. 6. The arbitral tribunal shall, at a hearing, confirm its receipt of documents provided for in Paragraphs 1 and 4 that are submitted other than at a hearing and determine whether to adopt or reject any applications to present evidence (or, if already determined pursuant to the provisions of the preceding Paragraph, confirm such determination).			

ARBITRAL PROCEEDINGS
WITNESSES

INSTITUTIONAL					AD HOC
CIETAC ARBITRATION RULES (2000)	**HKIAC ARBITRATION RULES (1985)**	**JCAA ARBITRATION RULES (1997)**	**KCAB ARBITRATION RULES (2000)**	**SIAC ARBITRATION RULES (1997)**	**UNCITRAL ARBITRATION RULES (1976)**
Article 32 The arbitration tribunal will hold oral hearings. At the request of the parties or with their consent, the arbitration tribunal may, if it also considers oral hearings unnecessary, hear and decide a case on the basis of documents only. ***See also* Article 37 at A-12 and Article 43 at A-13.**	**Article 25 - Evidence and Hearings** 2. If witnesses are to be heard, at least fifteen days before the hearing each party shall communicate to the arbitral tribunal and to the other party the names and addresses of the witnesses he intends to present, the subject upon and the languages in which such witnesses will give their testimony. 4. Hearings shall be held *in camera* unless the parties agree otherwise. The arbitral tribunal may require the retirement of any witness or witnesses during the testimony of other witnesses. The arbitral tribunal is free to determine the manner in which witnesses are examined. 5. Evidence of witnesses may also be presented in the form of written statements signed by them.	**Rule 35 - Examination of Evidence** 4. The arbitral tribunal is not authorized to administer an oath to any witness or expert. **Rule 36 - Application to Present Evidence** 1. A party may apply to present evidence by submitting any of the following documents to the arbitral tribunal: (2) application to examine a witness (a written application, specifying the witness and the matters with respect to which such witness is to be examined, to examine a witness). ***See also* Rule 39 at A-55.**	**Article 35 - Proceedings of Hearing** (4) The party requesting arbitration shall present his statement on the purport and grounds of the claims, and introduce documentary evidence and his witnesses. The Respondent shall present his defence, and introduce documentary evidence and his witnesses. **Article 42 - Evidence** (1) The parties may offer any evidence they so desire to support their contention or request that any witness or expert witness voluntarily appear at the hearings. However, the Tribunal may refuse to investigate such evidence by finding there exists no relevancy between the evidence so produced and the contention of the parties concerned.	**Rule 22 - Hearings** 22.1 Unless the parties have agreed on documents-only arbitration, the Tribunal shall, if either party so requests, hold a hearing for the presentation of evidence by witnesses, including expert witnesses, or for oral submissions. **Rule 23 - Witnesses** 23.1 Before any hearing, the Tribunal may require any party to give notice of the identity of witnesses it wishes to call, as well as the subject matter of their testimony and its relevance to the issues. 23.2 The Tribunal has discretion to allow, refuse, or limit the appearance of witnesses, whether witnesses of fact or expert witnesses. 23.3 Any witness who gives oral evidence may be questioned by each of the parties or their representatives, under the control of	**Article 25 - Evidence and Hearings** 2. If witnesses are to be heard, at least fifteen days before the hearing each party shall communicate to the arbitral tribunal and to the other party the names and addresses of the witnesses he intends to present, the subject upon and the languages in which such witnesses will give their testimony. 4. Hearings shall be held *in camera* unless the parties agree otherwise. The arbitral tribunal may require the retirement of any witness or witnesses during the testimony of other witnesses. The arbitral tribunal is free to determine the manner in which witnesses are examined. 5. Evidence of witnesses may also be presented in the form of written statements signed by them.

INSTITUTIONAL					AD HOC
CIETAC ARBITRATION RULES (2000)	HKIAC ARBITRATION RULES (1985)	JCAA ARBITRATION RULES (1997)	KCAB ARBITRATION RULES (2000)	SIAC ARBITRATION RULES (1997)	UNCITRAL ARBITRATION RULES (1976)
			Article 31 - Attendance at Hearings (3) The Tribunal may order any witness to retire during the testimony of another witness.	the Tribunal. The Tribunal may put questions at any stage of the examination of the witnesses. 23.4 Subject to such order or direction which the Tribunal may make, the testimony of witnesses may be presented in written form, either as signed statements or by duly sworn affidavits. Subject to Rule 23.2, any party may request that such a witness should attend for oral examination at a hearing. If he fails to attend, the Tribunal may place such weight on the written testimony as it thinks fit, or exclude it altogether. 23.5 Subject to the mandatory provisions of any applicable law, it shall be proper for any party or its representatives to interview any witness or potential witness prior to his appearance at any hearing.	

ARBITRAL PROCEEDINGS

EXPERTS

INSTITUTIONAL					AD HOC
CIETAC ARBITRATION RULES (2000)	HKIAC ARBITRATION RULES (1985)	JCAA ARBITRATION RULES (1997)	KCAB ARBITRATION RULES (2000)	SIAC ARBITRATION RULES (1997)	UNCITRAL ARBITRATION RULES (1976)
Article 39 The arbitration tribunal may consult an expert or appoint an appraiser for clarification of the specific issues relating to a case. Such an expert or appraiser may be either a Chinese or foreign organization or citizen. The arbitration tribunal has the power to order the parties to submit or produce to the expert or appraiser any relevant materials, documents, or properties and goods for check-up, inspection and/or appraisal, and the parties are so obliged as well. **Article 40** The expert's report and the appraiser's report shall be copied to the parties so that the parties may have the opportunity to give their opinions thereon. At the request of any party to the case and with the approval of the arbitration tribunal,	**Article 27 - Experts** 1. The arbitral tribunal may appoint one or more experts to report to it, in writing, on specific issues to be determined by the tribunal. A copy of the expert's terms of reference, established by the arbitral tribunal, shall be communicated to the parties. 2. The parties shall give the expert any relevant information or produce for his inspection any relevant documents or goods that he may require of them. Any dispute between a party and such expert as to the relevance of the required information or production shall be referred to the arbitral tribunal for decision. 3. Upon receipt of the expert's report, the arbitral tribunal shall communicate a copy of the report to the parties who shall be given the opportunity to express, in writing,	**Rule 35 - Examination of Evidence** 4. The arbitral tribunal is not authorized to administer an oath to any witness or expert. **Rule 36 - Application to Present Evidence** 1. A party may apply to present evidence by submitting any of the following documents to the arbitral tribunal: (3) application for an expert opinion or verification (a written application for an expert opinion or verification setting forth the matters for which an expert opinion is required or the items to be verified and the method thereof).	**Article 42 - Evidence** (1) The parties may offer any evidence they so desire to support their contention or request that any witness or expert witness voluntarily appear at the hearings. However, the Tribunal may refuse to investigate such evidence by finding there exists no relevancy between the evidence so produced and the contention of the parties concerned. (2) The Tribunal may, where it is deemed necessary, request the production of evidence or the voluntary appearance of a witness or an expert witness at the hearings. However, the Tribunal may, at its discretion, proceed with the hearing even if evidence has not been submitted and/or neither a witness nor an expert witness has appeared within the designated time.		**Article 27 - Experts** 1. The arbitral tribunal may appoint one or more experts to report to it, in writing, on specific issues to be determined by the tribunal. A copy of the expert's terms of reference, established by the arbitral tribunal, shall be communicated to the parties. 2. The parties shall give the expert any relevant information or produce for his inspection any relevant documents or goods that he may require of them. Any dispute between a party and such expert as to the relevance of the required information or production shall be referred to the arbitral tribunal for decision. 3. Upon receipt of the expert's report, the arbitral tribunal shall communicate a copy of the report to the parties who shall be given the opportunity to express, in writing,

INSTITUTIONAL					AD HOC
CIETAC ARBITRATION RULES (2000)	HKIAC ARBITRATION RULES (1985)	JCAA ARBITRATION RULES (1997)	KCAB ARBITRATION RULES (2000)	SIAC ARBITRATION RULES (1997)	UNCITRAL ARBITRATION RULES (1976)
the expert and appraiser may be present at the hearing, and, if considered necessary and appropriate by the arbitration tribunal, be required to give explanations of their reports. **Article 41** The evidence submitted by the parties will be examined and evaluated by the arbitration tribunal. The arbitration tribunal shall decide whether to adopt the expert's report and the appraiser's report. ***See also* Article 37 at A-12.**	their opinion on the report. A party shall be entitled to examine any document on which the expert has relied in his report. 4. At the request of either party the expert, after delivery of the report, may be heard at a hearing where the parties shall have the opportunity to be present and to interrogate the expert. At this hearing either party may present expert witnesses in order to testify on the points at issue. The provisions of article 25 shall be applicable to such proceedings.				their opinion on the report. A party shall be entitled to examine any document on which the expert has relied in his report. 4. At the request of either party the expert, after delivery of the report, may be heard at a hearing where the parties shall have the opportunity to be present and to interrogate the expert. At this hearing either party may present expert witnesses in order to testify on the points at issue. The provisions of article 25 shall be applicable to such proceedings.

INSTITUTIONAL					AD HOC
CIETAC ARBITRATION RULES (2000)	HKIAC ARBITRATION RULES (1985)	JCAA ARBITRATION RULES (1997)	KCAB ARBITRATION RULES (2000)	SIAC ARBITRATION RULES (1997)	UNCITRAL ARBITRATION RULES (1976)
Article 23 When a party applies for property preservative measures, the Arbitration Commission shall submit the party's application to the intermediate people's court for a ruling in the place where the domicile of the party against whom the property preservative measures are sought is located or in the place where the property of the said party is located. When a party applies for taking interim measures of protection of evidence, the Arbitration Commission shall submit the party's application to the intermediate people's court in the place where the evidence is located for a ruling.	**Article 26 - Interim Measures of Protection** 1. At the request of either party, the arbitral tribunal may take any interim measures it deems necessary in respect of the subject-matter of the dispute, including measures for the conservation of the goods forming the subject-matter in dispute, such as ordering their deposit with a third person or the sale of perishable goods. 2. Such interim measures may be established in the form of an interim award. The arbitral tribunal shall be entitled to require security for the costs of such measures. 3. A request for interim measures addressed by any party to a judicial authority shall not be deemed incompatible with the agreement to arbitrate, or as a waiver of that agreement.	**Rule 51 - Interlocutory Award** The arbitral tribunal may, when it deems it appropriate, make an interlocutory award to decide a dispute arising during the course of the arbitral proceedings. The provisions of Rule 49, Paragraph 1 and Rule 50, Paragraph 1 shall apply *mutatis mutandis* to such interlocutory award; provided that the statement of a reason for the interlocutory award may be dispensed with.	**Article 41 - Interim Measure** (1) The Tribunal, with the application of any party, may issue to any party such orders as may be deemed necessary to safeguard the property which is the subject matter of the dispute without prejudice to the right of the parties or to the final determination of the dispute. (2) The Tribunal may, at its discretion, order any party applying for the interim measure to provide a proper security.	**Rule 25 - Additional Powers of the Tribunal** Unless the parties at any time agree otherwise, and subject to any mandatory limitations of any applicable law, the Tribunal shall have the power, on the application of any party or of its own motion, but in either case only after giving the parties a proper opportunity to state their views, to: (g) order the preservation, storage, sale or other disposal of any property or thing which is the subject-matter of the dispute; (j) to make orders or give directions to any party for an interim injunction or any other interim measure; (l) to make orders or give directions to any party for ensuring that any award which may be made in the arbitral proceedings is not rendered ineffectual by the dissipation of	**Article 26 - Interim Measures of Protection** 1. At the request of either party, the arbitral tribunal may take any interim measures it deems necessary in respect of the subject-matter of the dispute, including measures for the conservation of the goods forming the subject-matter in dispute, such as ordering their deposit with a third person or the sale of perishable goods. 2. Such interim measures may be established in the form of an interim award. The arbitral tribunal shall be entitled to require security for the costs of such measures. 3. A request for interim measures addressed by any party to a judicial authority shall not be deemed incompatible with the agreement to arbitrate, or as a waiver of that agreement.

INSTITUTIONAL					AD HOC
CIETAC ARBITRATION RULES (2000)	HKIAC ARBITRATION RULES (1985)	JCAA ARBITRATION RULES (1997)	KCAB ARBITRATION RULES (2000)	SIAC ARBITRATION RULES (1997)	UNCITRAL ARBITRATION RULES (1976)
	***See also* Article 32.1 at A-38.**			assets by a party. **Rule 27 - Deposits and Security** 27.4 Without prejudice to the right of any party to apply to a competent court for pre-award conservatory measures, the Tribunal shall also have the power to order any party to provide security for all or part of any amount in dispute in the arbitration.	***See also* Article 32.1 at A-112.**

ARBITRAL PROCEEDINGS

DEFAULT

INSTITUTIONAL					AD HOC
CIETAC ARBITRATION RULES (2000)	HKIAC ARBITRATION RULES (1985)	JCAA ARBITRATION RULES (1997)	KCAB ARBITRATION RULES (2000)	SIAC ARBITRATION RULES (1997)	UNCITRAL ARBITRATION RULES (1976)
Article 21 The progress of arbitration proceedings shall not be affected notwithstanding the failure of the Respondent to file his defense in writing or the failure of the Claimant to submit his written defense against the Respondent's counterclaim. **Article 42** Should one of the parties fail to appear at the hearing, the arbitration tribunal may proceed with the hearing and make an award by default. ***See also* Article 57 at A-15.**	**Article 28 - Default** 1. If, within the period of time fixed by the arbitral tribunal, the claimant has failed to communicate his claim without showing sufficient cause for such failure, the arbitral tribunal shall issue an order for the termination of the arbitral proceedings. If, within the period of time fixed by the arbitral tribunal, the respondent has failed to communicate his statement of defence without showing sufficient cause for such failure, the arbitral tribunal shall order that the proceedings continue. 2. If one of the parties, duly notified under these Rules, fails to appear at a hearing, without showing sufficient cause for such failure, the arbitral tribunal may proceed with the arbitration. 3. If one of the parties, duly invited to produce documentary evidence, fails to do so	**Rule 37 - Principle of Appearance by the Parties** 1. Hearings shall in principle be held in the presence of both parties. 2. If one or both parties fails or fail to appear without good cause, a hearing may be held in its or their absence; provided that, if both of the parties fail to appear, the examination proceedings may not be terminated on the date when such hearing is held. 3. If one of the parties fails to appear, the examination proceedings may be conducted based on the allegations and proof of the party who has appeared.	**Article 12 - Defence** (5) If no statement of defence is filed within the period provided in Paragraph (1) hereinabove, the Respondent is considered to have dismissed the claim. **Article 36 - Parties' Lack of Care** If the party requesting arbitration fails to state a specific claim or present a reason or documentary evidence, which unduly hinders the arbitration proceeding, the Tribunal may close the hearings. The Tribunal may also close the hearings if the parties show lack of care in stating claims or presenting evidence, and it is deemed improper to proceed with the hearing. **Article 37 - Arbitration in the Absence of Parties** (1) The arbitration may proceed in the absence of either party who, after due notice	**Rule 18 - Submission of Written Statements and Documents** 18.9 If the Claimant fails within the time specified under these Rules or as may be fixed by the Tribunal, to submit its Statement of Case, the Tribunal may issue an order for the termination of the arbitral proceedings or make such other directions as may be appropriate in the circumstances. If the Respondent fails to submit a Statement of Defence, or if at any point any party fails to avail itself of the opportunity to present its case in the manner directed by the Tribunal, the Tribunal may nevertheless proceed with the arbitration and make the award. **Rule 22 - Hearings** 22.3 If any party to the proceedings fails to appear at a hearing, without showing sufficient cause for such failure, the	**Article 28 - Default** 1. If, within the period of time fixed by the arbitral tribunal, the claimant has failed to communicate his claim without showing sufficient cause for such failure, the arbitral tribunal shall issue an order for the termination of the arbitral proceedings. If, within the period of time fixed by the arbitral tribunal, the respondent has failed to communicate his statement of defence without showing sufficient cause for such failure, the arbitral tribunal shall order that the proceedings continue. 2. If one of the parties, duly notified under these Rules, fails to appear at a hearing, without showing sufficient cause for such failure, the arbitral tribunal may proceed with the arbitration. 3. If one of the parties, duly invited to produce documentary evidence, fails to do so

INSTITUTIONAL					AD HOC
CIETAC ARBITRATION RULES (2000)	HKIAC ARBITRATION RULES (1985)	JCAA ARBITRATION RULES (1997)	KCAB ARBITRATION RULES (2000)	SIAC ARBITRATION RULES (1997)	UNCITRAL ARBITRATION RULES (1976)
	within the established period of time, without showing sufficient cause for such failure, the arbitral tribunal may make the award on the evidence before it.		fails to be present, and even if present, does not participate in the hearing. (2) In case of Paragraph (1), the documents or other evidence produced by the absent party or otherwise not participating in the hearing shall be deemed to have been orally stated or submitted thereat and the hearing necessary for making an award may proceed with a party present. (3) If the parties have been properly notified of the hearing but fail to attend the hearings two or more times, or even if the parties attend but fail to participate in the hearing, the Tribunal may declare a suspension of the arbitration proceedings.	Tribunal may proceed with the arbitration and may make the award on the evidence before it. **Rule 26 - Jurisdiction of The Tribunal** 26.3 In addition to the jurisdiction to exercise the powers defined elsewhere in these Rules, the Tribunal shall have jurisdiction to determine any question of law arising in the arbitration; proceed with the arbitration notwithstanding the failure or refusal of any party to comply with these Rules or with the Tribunal's orders or directions, or to attend any meeting or hearing, but only after giving that party written notice that it intends to do so; and to receive and take into account such written or oral evidence as it shall determine to be relevant, whether or not strictly admissible in law. ***See also* Rule 30.4 at A-98-99.**	within the established period of time, without showing sufficient cause for such failure, the arbitral tribunal may make the award on the evidence before it.

ARBITRAL PROCEEDINGS

Waiver of Rules

Institutional					Ad Hoc
CIETAC ARBITRATION RULES (2000)	**HKIAC ARBITRATION RULES (1985)**	**JCAA ARBITRATION RULES (1997)**	**KCAB ARBITRATION RULES (2000)**	**SIAC ARBITRATION RULES (1997)**	**UNCITRAL ARBITRATION RULES (1976)**
Article 51 The party who knows or should have known that any provision or requirement of these Rules has not been complied with and yet proceeds with the arbitration proceedings without explicitly raising in writing his objection to non-compliance in a timely manner shall be taken to have waived his right to object.	**Article 30 - Waiver of Rules** A party who knows that any provision of, or requirement under, these Rules has not been complied with and yet proceeds with the arbitration without promptly stating his objection to such non-compliance, shall be deemed to have waived his right to object.	**Rule 46 - Right to Object** A party who knows or ought to know that the arbitral proceedings have not been conducted properly and who fails to object without delay, shall be deemed to have waived its right to object; provided that no party shall be deemed to have waived any right that it cannot waive.	**Article 46 - Waiver of the Right to Protest** Any party who proceeds with the arbitration, with knowledge or being able to have known that any provision or requirement of these Rules has not been complied with, shall be deemed to have lost his right to object unless he states objection thereto without delay.	**Rule 34 - General Provisions** 34.1 A party who knows that any provision of, or requirement under, these Rules has not been complied with and yet proceeds with the arbitration without promptly stating its objection to such non-compliance, shall be deemed to have waived its right to object. ***See also* Rule 34.4 at A-100.**	**Article 30 - Waiver of Rules** A party who knows that any provision of, or requirement under, these Rules has not been complied with and yet proceeds with the arbitration without promptly stating his objection to such non-compliance, shall be deemed to have waived his right to object.

ARBITRAL PROCEEDINGS

Closure of Hearings/Proceedings

Institutional					Ad Hoc
CIETAC ARBITRATION RULES (2000)	**HKIAC ARBITRATION RULES (1985)**	**JCAA ARBITRATION RULES (1997)**	**KCAB ARBITRATION RULES (2000)**	**SIAC ARBITRATION RULES (1997)**	**UNCITRAL ARBITRATION RULES (1976)**
	Article 29 - Closure of Hearings 1. The arbitral tribunal may inquire of the parties if they have any further proof to offer or witnesses to be heard or submissions to make and, if there are none, it may declare the hearings closed. 2. The arbitral tribunal may, if it considers it necessary owing to exceptional circumstances, decide, on its own motion or upon application of a party, to reopen the hearings at any time before the award is made.	**Rule 45 - Conclusion and Reopening of Examination Proceedings** 1. The arbitral tribunal may decide to conclude the examination upon determining that the proceedings have matured enough for the arbitral tribunal to render an arbitral award or that the proceedings should be terminated because it is impossible to continue. If such decision is made other than at a hearing, an appropriate period of time for advance notice shall be provided. 2. The arbitral tribunal shall declare the proceedings closed upon determining that the proceedings should be terminated and concluding the examination. The provisions applied to arbitral awards shall apply *mutatis mutandis* to such declaration. 3. The arbitral tribunal may, if it deems it	**Article 43 - Closing of Hearings** (1) The Tribunal shall, when it believes that all contentions and evidence of the parties have been put forth, declare the hearings closed. (2) If it is required that a summary of statements be submitted, the hearings shall be deemed to be closed as of the final date set by the Tribunal for the submission of the aforementioned documents. **Article 44 - Reopening of Hearings** (1) The hearing may be reopened by the Tribunal on its own discretion, or upon application of a party for good cause, at any time before an award is rendered. (2) If the reopening of the hearing provided in Paragraph (1) would prevent the making of the award within the specific time agreed	**Rule 22 - Hearings** 22.6 The Tribunal may declare the hearings closed if it is satisfied that the parties have no further proof to offer or witnesses to be heard or submissions to make. The Tribunal may on its own motion or upon application of a party but before any award is made, reopen the hearings.	**Article 29 - Closure of Hearings** 1. The arbitral tribunal may inquire of the parties if they have any further proof to offer or witnesses to be heard or submissions to make and, if there are none, it may declare the hearings closed. 2. The arbitral tribunal may, if it considers it necessary owing to exceptional circumstances, decide, on its own motion or upon application of a party, to reopen the hearings at any time before the award is made.

INSTITUTIONAL					AD HOC
CIETAC ARBITRATION RULES (2000)	HKIAC ARBITRATION RULES (1985)	JCAA ARBITRATION RULES (1997)	KCAB ARBITRATION RULES (2000)	SIAC ARBITRATION RULES (1997)	UNCITRAL ARBITRATION RULES (1976)
		necessary, reopen the examination. The arbitral tribunal shall, if it decides to reopen the examination, promptly notify the parties in writing of such decision and the reasons therefor. 4. An examination shall, in principle, not be reopened after the lapse of three (3) weeks from the date of the decision to conclude the examination.	upon by the parties in the arbitration agreement, the hearings may not be reopened unless the parties agree upon the extension of such time limit. (3) When hearings are reopened, the closing date of the hearings shall be the date on which the proceedings of the reopened hearings were concluded.		

TIME LIMITS FOR AWARD

INSTITUTIONAL					AD HOC
CIETAC ARBITRATION RULES (2000)	HKIAC ARBITRATION RULES (1985)	JCAA ARBITRATION RULES (1997)	KCAB ARBITRATION RULES (2000)	SIAC ARBITRATION RULES (1997)	UNCITRAL ARBITRATION RULES (1976)
Article 52 The arbitration tribunal shall render an arbitral award within 9 months as from the date on which the arbitration tribunal is formed. The Secretary-General of the Arbitration Commission may extend this time limit at the request of the arbitration tribunal if the Secretary-General of the Arbitration Commission considers that it is really necessary and the reasons for extension are truly justified.		**Rule 48 - Time of Arbitral Award** 1. Once the arbitral tribunal has determined that the proceedings have matured enough for it to render an arbitral award and concluded the examination, the arbitral tribunal shall make an arbitral award within five (5) weeks from the date of such conclusion; provided that the arbitral tribunal may, if it deems it necessary in view of the complexities of the case or for any other reason, extend such period of time to an appropriate period of not more than eight (8) weeks. 2. The arbitral tribunal shall, upon conclusion of the examination pursuant to the preceding Paragraph, notify the parties of the period of time during which it shall make an arbitral award.	**Article 47 - Extensions of Period** The parties may modify any period prescribed under these Rules by a mutual agreement in writing. The Tribunal for good cause may extend any period established by these Rules except the period for making an award. The Tribunal shall notify the parties through the Secretariat of any such extension and reasons therefor. **Article 48 - Arbitral Award** (1) The award shall be rendered promptly unless otherwise agreed by the parties or specified by law, not later than 30 days from the date of closing the hearings.	**Rule 28 - The Award** 28.1 Unless all parties agree otherwise, the Tribunal shall make its award in writing within forty-five (45) days from the date on which the hearings are closed and shall state the reasons upon which its award is based. The award shall state its date and shall be signed by the arbitrator or arbitrators.	

ARBITRAL DECISIONS/AWARDS

QUORUM/DISSENTS

Institutional					Ad Hoc
CIETAC ARBITRATION RULES (2000)	**HKIAC ARBITRATION RULES (1985)**	**JCAA ARBITRATION RULES (1997)**	**KCAB ARBITRATION RULES (2000)**	**SIAC ARBITRATION RULES (1997)**	**UNCITRAL ARBITRATION RULES (1976)**
Article 54 Where a case is heard by an arbitration tribunal composed of three arbitrators, the arbitral award shall be decided by the majority of the arbitrators and the minority opinion may be recorded and placed on file. When the arbitration tribunal cannot attain a majority opinion, the arbitral award shall be decided in accordance with the presiding arbitrator's opinion. **Article 56** Unless the arbitral award is made in accordance with the opinion of the presiding arbitrator or the sole arbitrator, the arbitral award shall be signed by a majority of arbitrators. An arbitrator who has a dissenting opinion may sign or not sign his name on the arbitral award. The arbitrators shall submit the draft arbitral award to the Arbitration Commission before signing the award. The	**Article 31 - Decisions** 1. When there are three arbitrators, any award or other decision of the arbitral tribunal shall be made by a majority of the arbitrators. **Article 32 - Form and Effect of the Award** 4. An award shall be signed by the arbitrators and it shall contain the date on which and the place where the award was made. Where there are three arbitrators and one of them fails to sign, the award shall state the reason for the absence of the signature. ***See also* Article 31.2 at A-37.**	**Rule 6 - Decision of Arbitral Tribunal** 1. If the number of arbitrators is more than one, decisions of the arbitral tribunal, including the arbitral award, shall be made by a majority of votes of the arbitrators. 2. If the voting of the arbitral tribunal results in a tie, the presiding arbitrator, if one has been appointed, shall cast the deciding vote. **Rule 49 - Arbitral Award** 4. If there are more than one arbitrator and an arbitrator fails to sign and affix its seal to the arbitral award, the arbitral tribunal shall set forth the reasons for such failure in the arbitral award.	**Article 33 - Decisions of Tribunal** Whenever there is more than one arbitrator, simple majority rule shall apply for all decisions, including that of the arbitral awards, unless parties agree otherwise. However, if no majority rule is reached with regard to a procedural matter, then the presiding arbitrator shall decide. **Article 48 - Arbitral Award** (2) Where the Tribunal is composed of more than one arbitrator and less than a majority of arbitrators refuse to partake in the arbitration decision or do not participate in the arbitration decision without just cause, the award shall be made by the remaining majority of arbitrators. **Article 49 - Form of Award** (2) If an award is to be	**Rule 28 - The Award** 28.2 If any arbitrator refuses or fails to comply with the mandatory provisions of any applicable law relating to the making of the award, having been given a reasonable opportunity to do so, the remaining arbitrators shall proceed in his absence. 28.3 Where there is more than one arbitrator and they fail to agree on any issue, they shall decide by a majority. Failing a majority decision on any issue, the presiding arbitrator of the Tribunal shall make the award alone as if he were sole arbitrator. If an arbitrator refuses or fails to sign the award, the signatures of the majority shall be sufficient, provided that the reasons for the omitted signature is stated. ***See also* Rule 17.3 at A-91.**	**Article 31 - Decisions** 1. When there are three arbitrators, any award or other decision of the arbitral tribunal shall be made by a majority of the arbitrators. **Article 32 - Form and Effect of the Award** 4. An award shall be signed by the arbitrators and it shall contain the date on which and the place where the award was made. Where there are three arbitrators and one of them fails to sign, the award shall state the reason for the absence of the signature. ***See also* Article 31.2 at A-111.**

INSTITUTIONAL					AD HOC
CIETAC ARBITRATION RULES (2000)	**HKIAC ARBITRATION RULES (1985)**	**JCAA ARBITRATION RULES (1997)**	**KCAB ARBITRATION RULES (2000)**	**SIAC ARBITRATION RULES (1997)**	**UNCITRAL ARBITRATION RULES (1976)**
Arbitration Commission may remind the arbitrator of any issue related to the form of the arbitral award on condition that the arbitrator's independence of decision is not affected. The Arbitration Commission's stamp shall be affixed to the arbitral award. The date on which the arbitral award is made is the date on which the arbitral award comes into legal effect.			made by more than one arbitrator and less than a majority of the arbitrators refuse or fail to sign the award, the remaining arbitrators must specify the reasons on it and sign thereon. ***See also* Article 51 at A-80.**		

ARBITRAL DECISIONS/AWARDS

PLACE, FORM, NOTIFICATION AND EFFECT OF AWARD

INSTITUTIONAL			AD HOC		
CIETAC ARBITRATION RULES (2000)	**HKIAC ARBITRATION RULES (1985)**	**JCAA ARBITRATION RULES (1997)**	**KCAB ARBITRATION RULES (2000)**	**SIAC ARBITRATION RULES (1997)**	**UNCITRAL ARBITRATION RULES (1976)**
Article 55 The arbitration tribunal shall state in the arbitral award the claims, the facts of the dispute, the reasons on which the arbitral award is based, the result of the arbitral award, the allocation of the arbitration costs, the date on which and the place at which the arbitral award is made. The facts of the dispute and the reasons on which the arbitral award is based may not be stated in the arbitral award if the parties have agreed not to state them in the arbitral award, or the arbitral award is made in accordance with the contents of the settlement agreement reached between the parties. **Article 56** Unless the arbitral award is made in accordance with the opinion of the presiding arbitrator or the sole arbitrator, the arbitral award shall be signed by a majority of	**Article 32 - Form and Effect of the Award** 1. In addition to making a final award, the arbitral tribunal shall be entitled to make interim, interlocutory, or partial awards. 2. The award shall be made in writing and shall be final and binding on the parties. The parties undertake to carry out the award without delay. 3. The arbitral tribunal shall state the reasons upon which the award is based, unless the parties have agreed that no reasons are to be given. 4. An award shall be signed by the arbitrators and it shall contain the date on which and the place where the award was made. Where there are three arbitrators and one of them fails to sign, the award shall state the reason for the absence of the signature. 5. The award may be made public only with	**Rule 49 - Arbitral Award** 1. The arbitral award shall state the following and bear the signature and seal of each arbitrator; provided that the statement of Item (4) below shall be omitted if the parties have agreed that no statement is necessary and in the case provided for in the following Paragraph and the reason for such omission shall be set forth in the arbitral award: (1) the full personal or corporate names of the parties and their addresses; (2) if a party is represented by an agent, the name and address of such agent; (3) the text of the award; (4) the reasons for the award; and (5) the date of the award.	**Article 49 - Form of Award** (1) The arbitral award shall be made in writing, stating the following particulars and shall be signed by the arbitrator: a) The full personal or corporate names of the parties and their addresses. In case a party is represented by an agent, the full name and address of the agent; b) Principal and Reason upon which the award is based; c) Date of award; d) Place of arbitration. (2) If an award is to be made by more than one arbitrator and less than a majority of the arbitrators refuse or fail to sign the award, the remaining arbitrators must specify the reasons on it and sign thereon. **Article 52 - Scope of Award** (1) The Tribunal may	**Rule 28 - The Award** 28.1 Unless all parties agree otherwise, the Tribunal shall make its award in writing within forty-five (45) days from the date on which the hearings are closed and shall state the reasons upon which its award is based. The award shall state its date and shall be signed by the arbitrator or arbitrators. 28.2 If any arbitrator refuses or fails to comply with the mandatory provisions of any applicable law relating to the making of the award, having been given a reasonable opportunity to do so, the remaining arbitrators shall proceed in his absence. 28.3 Where there is more than one arbitrator and they fail to agree on any issue, they shall decide by a majority. Failing a majority decision on any issue, the presiding arbitrator of the Tribunal shall	**Article 32 - Form and Effect of the Award** 1. In addition to making a final award, the arbitral tribunal shall be entitled to make interim, interlocutory, or partial awards. 2. The award shall be made in writing and shall be final and binding on the parties. The parties undertake to carry out the award without delay. 3. The arbitral tribunal shall state the reasons upon which the award is based, unless the parties have agreed that no reasons are to be given. 4. An award shall be signed by the arbitrators and it shall contain the date on which and the place where the award was made. Where there are three arbitrators and one of them fails to sign, the award shall state the reason for the absence of the signature. 5. The award may be made public only with

INSTITUTIONAL			AD HOC		
CIETAC ARBITRATION RULES (2000)	**HKIAC ARBITRATION RULES (1985)**	**JCAA ARBITRATION RULES (1997)**	**KCAB ARBITRATION RULES (2000)**	**SIAC ARBITRATION RULES (1997)**	**UNCITRAL ARBITRATION RULES (1976)**
arbitrators. An arbitrator who has a dissenting opinion may sign or not sign his name on the arbitral award. The arbitrators shall submit the draft arbitral award to the Arbitration Commission before signing the award. The Arbitration Commission may remind the arbitrator of any issue related to the form of the arbitral award on condition that the arbitrator's independence of decision is not affected. The Arbitration Commission's stamp shall be affixed to the arbitral award. The date on which the arbitral award is made is the date on which the arbitral award comes into legal effect. **Article 57** An interlocutory award or partial award may be made on any issue of the case at any time	the consent of both parties. 6. Copies of the award signed by the arbitrators shall be communicated to the parties by the arbitral tribunal. 7. If the arbitration law of the country where the award is made requires that the award be filed or registered by the arbitral tribunal, the tribunal shall comply with this requirement within the period of time required by law. **See also Article 16.4 at A-33 and HKIAC As Arbitration Administrator: Registration of Awards at A-26.**	2. If the arbitral tribunal deems it appropriate, it may, at the request of the parties reaching a settlement during the course of the arbitral proceedings, set forth the contents of any such settlement in its arbitral award. 3. The arbitral tribunal shall set forth in the text of its arbitral award the total amount and the allocation of the administrative fee, the hearing fee, the necessary expenses incurred during the proceedings and the arbitrators' remuneration and shall, if there is a party who has deposited an amount of money less than the amount allocated in the text of the arbitral award, set forth an order to the effect that the balance shall be paid to the other party. 4. If there are more than one arbitrator and an arbitrator fails to sign and affix its seal to the arbitral award, the arbitral tribunal	not only order the specific performance of a contract but may also grant any remedy and relief which is deemed just and equitable within the scope of the arbitration agreement of the parties. (2) The Tribunal shall assess the arbitration costs provide in Chapter IX to the party or parties responsible. **Article 55 - Delivery of Arbitral Award** (1) The Secretariat shall deliver a duly authenticated arbitral award to each party or his agent in ways provided in Paragraph (1) through (3) of Article 4 of the Act. The original arbitral award shall be delivered to the competent court, enclosed with a document certifying the delivery. (2) Service under the provisions of Paragraph (1) may be conducted after all the arbitration costs provided in Chapter IX	make the award alone as if he were sole arbitrator. If an arbitrator refuses or fails to sign the award, the signatures of the majority shall be sufficient, provided that the reasons for the omitted signature is stated. 28.4 The sole arbitrator or presiding arbitrator shall be responsible for delivering the award to the Registrar, who shall transmit certified copies to the parties provided that the costs of the arbitration have been paid to the Centre in accordance with Rule 30. 28.5 The Tribunal may award simple or compound interest on any sum which is the subject of the reference at such rates as the Tribunal determines to be appropriate, in respect of any period which the Tribunal determines to be appropriate ending not later than the date upon which the award is complied with.	the consent of both parties. 6. Copies of the award signed by the arbitrators shall be communicated to the parties by the arbitral tribunal. 7. If the arbitration law of the country where the award is made requires that the award be filed or registered by the arbitral tribunal, the tribunal shall comply with this requirement within the period of time required by law. **See also Article 16.4 at A-107.**

INSTITUTIONAL				AD HOC	
CIETAC ARBITRATION RULES (2000)	**HKIAC ARBITRATION RULES (1985)**	**JCAA ARBITRATION RULES (1997)**	**KCAB ARBITRATION RULES (2000)**	**SIAC ARBITRATION RULES (1997)**	**UNCITRAL ARBITRATION RULES (1976)**
in the course of arbitration before the final award is made if considered necessary by the arbitration tribunal, or if the parties make such a proposal and it is agreed to by the arbitration tribunal. Either party's failure to perform the interlocutory award will not affect the continuation of the arbitration proceedings, nor will it prevent the arbitration tribunal from making a final award. **Article 60** The arbitral award is final and binding upon both disputing parties. Neither party may bring a suit before a law court or make a request to any other organization for revising the arbitral award. **Article 63** The parties must automatically execute the arbitral award within the time limit specified in the arbitral award. If no time limit		shall set forth the reasons for such failure in the arbitral award. **Rule 50 - Service and Deposit of Arbitral Award** 1. The clerk in charge shall serve an authenticated copy of the arbitral award on each party by hand delivery, by delivery-certified registered mail or any other method proving receipt. 2. Service under the preceding Paragraph shall occur after the fees, the necessary expenses incurred during the proceedings and the arbitrators' remuneration have been fully paid to the Association. 3. After serving authenticated copies of the arbitral award, the clerk in charge shall, without delay, deposit the original text of the arbitral award with a court of appropriate jurisdiction together with	have been paid in full by the responsible party or parties to the Secretariat unless other circumstances arise. ***See also* Article 48(3) at A-80.**	28.6 The Tribunal may make separate final awards on different issues at different times, which shall be subject to correction under the procedure specified in Rule 29. Unless otherwise stated by the Tribunal, such awards shall be individually enforceable as soon as they are made. 28.7 In the event of a settlement, the Tribunal may render a consent award recording the settlement if any party so requests. If the parties do not require a consent award, then on confirmation in writing by the parties to the Registrar that a settlement has been reached, the Tribunal shall be discharged and the reference to arbitration concluded, subject to payment by the parties of any outstanding costs of the arbitration in accordance with Rule 30. 28.8 By agreeing to have an arbitration under these Rules, the	

INSTITUTIONAL			AD HOC		
CIETAC ARBITRATION RULES (2000)	HKIAC ARBITRATION RULES (1985)	JCAA ARBITRATION RULES (1997)	KCAB ARBITRATION RULES (2000)	SIAC ARBITRATION RULES (1997)	UNCITRAL ARBITRATION RULES (1976)
is specified in the arbitral award, the parties shall carry out the arbitral award immediately. In case one party fails to execute the arbitral award, the other party may apply to the Chinese court for enforcement of the arbitral award pursuant to Chinese law or apply to the competent foreign court for enforcement of the arbitral award according to the 1958 Convention on Recognition and Enforcement of Foreign Arbitral Awards or other international treaties that China has concluded or acceded to.		certificates of service. **Rule 51 - Interlocutory Award** The arbitral tribunal may, when it deems it appropriate, make an interlocutory award to decide a dispute arising during the course of the arbitral proceedings. The provisions of Rule 49, Paragraph 1 and Rule 50, Paragraph 1 shall apply *mutatis mutandis* to such interlocutory award; provided that the statement of a reason for the interlocutory award may be dispensed with.		parties undertake to carry out the award without delay. Awards shall be final and binding on the parties from the date they are made.	

ARBITRAL DECISIONS/AWARDS
CURRENCY OF AWARD/INTEREST

INSTITUTIONAL					AD HOC
CIETAC ARBITRATION RULES (2000)	HKIAC ARBITRATION RULES (1985)	JCAA ARBITRATION RULES (1997)	KCAB ARBITRATION RULES (2000)	SIAC ARBITRATION RULES (1997)	UNCITRAL ARBITRATION RULES (1976)
		Rule 52 - Application of Expedited Procedures 2. The amount of interest and other fruits, compensation for damages, penalty for breach of contract and expenses incidental to a principal claim shall not be included in either the amount or the economic value of the claim provided for in the preceding Paragraph.		**Rule 28 - The Award** 28.5 The Tribunal may award simple or compound interest on any sum which is the subject of the reference at such rates as the Tribunal determines to be appropriate, in respect of any period which the Tribunal determines to be appropriate ending not later than the date upon which the award is complied with.	

Determination and Allocation of Arbitration Costs

Institutional					Ad Hoc
CIETAC ARBITRATION RULES (2000)	**HKIAC ARBITRATION RULES (1985)**	**JCAA ARBITRATION RULES (1997)**	**KCAB ARBITRATION RULES (2000)**	**SIAC ARBITRATION RULES (1997)**	**UNCITRAL ARBITRATION RULES (1976)**
Article 58 The arbitration tribunal has the power to determine in the arbitral award the arbitration fee and other expenses to be paid by the parties to the Arbitration Commission. **Article 59** The arbitration tribunal has the power to decide in the arbitral award that the losing party shall pay the winning party as compensation a proportion of the expenses reasonably incurred by the winning party in dealing with the case. The amount of such compensation shall not in any case exceed 10% of the total amount awarded to the winning party. **Article 88** Apart from charging arbitration fees from the parties according to the arbitration Fee Schedule of the Arbitration Commission, the	**Article 38 - Costs** The arbitral tribunal shall fix the costs of arbitration in its award. The term "costs" includes only: (a) The fees of the arbitral tribunal to be stated separately as to each arbitrator and to be fixed by the tribunal itself in accordance with article 39; (b) The travel and other expenses incurred by the arbitrators; (c) The costs of expert advice and of other assistance required by the arbitral tribunal; (d) The travel and other expenses of witnesses to the extent such expenses are approved by the arbitral tribunal; (e) The costs for legal representation and assistance of the successful party if such costs were claimed during the arbitral proceedings, and only to the extent that the arbitral	**Rule 28 - Allocation of Expenses of Non-resident Arbitrator** 1. If a party has appointed an arbitrator who is not resident in Japan, such party shall bear the expenses required due to such arbitrator's non-residence; provided that the arbitral tribunal may allocate such expenses in a manner different therefrom. 2. If the Association has, or the arbitrators have, appointed an arbitrator who is not resident in Japan, the arbitral tribunal shall allocate such expenses in its arbitral award. **Rule 38 - Allocation of the Cost of Examining Evidence and Other Expenses** The necessary costs incurred to examine evidence, make inquiries and conduct inspections or investigations under the provisions of Rule 34 shall, if such expense was the	**Article 52 - Scope of Award** (2) The Tribunal shall assess the arbitration costs provided in Chapter IX to the party or parties responsible. **Article 61 - Costs of Arbitration** (1) The costs of arbitration comprise the fees, the expenses and the allowances as prescribed in Article 62 through Article 64 of these Rules. (2) The costs of arbitration prescribed in Paragraph (1) shall be borne by the parties in accordance with the apportionment fixed in the award. However, such arbitration costs shall be borne equally by the parties unless the award assesses such costs of arbitration or any part thereof against any specified party in the award. (3) Even where the proceedings shall be conducted only on the basis of the documents under	**Rule 30 - Costs** 30.1 The costs of the arbitration shall be taxed by the Registrar or fixed by the Tribunal in its award. The term "costs of the arbitration" includes: (a) the fees of the Tribunal; (b) the travel and other expenses incurred by the arbitrators; (c) the costs of expert advice and of other assistance required by the Tribunal; (d) any fees and expenses of the appointing authority, if applicable; and (e) expenses reasonably incurred by the Centre in connection with the arbitration as well as its administrative charges, but shall not include the legal or other costs incurred by the parties themselves. 30.2 The Tribunal shall specify in the award, the total amount of the	**Article 38 - Costs** The arbitral tribunal shall fix the costs of arbitration in its award. The term "costs" includes only: (a) The fees of the arbitral tribunal to be stated separately as to each arbitrator and to be fixed by the tribunal itself in accordance with article 39; (b) The travel and other expenses incurred by the arbitrators; (c) The costs of expert advice and of other assistance required by the arbitral tribunal; (d) The travel and other expenses of witnesses to the extent such expenses are approved by the arbitral tribunal; (e) The costs for legal representation and assistance of the successful party if such costs were claimed during the arbitral proceedings, and only to the extent that the arbitral

INSTITUTIONAL					AD HOC
CIETAC ARBITRATION RULES (2000)	HKIAC ARBITRATION RULES (1985)	JCAA ARBITRATION RULES (1997)	KCAB ARBITRATION RULES (2000)	SIAC ARBITRATION RULES (1997)	UNCITRAL ARBITRATION RULES (1976)
Arbitration Commission may collect from the parties other extra, reasonable and actual expenses including arbitrators' special remuneration and their travel and boarding expenses for dealing with the case, as well as the fees and expenses for experts, appraisers and interpreters appointed by the arbitration tribunal, etc. If a case is withdrawn after the parties have reached between themselves an amicable settlement or is concluded with an arbitral award made according to paragraph 4 of Article 44, the Arbitration Commission may charge a certain amount of fees from the parties in consideration of the quantity of work and the amount of the actual expenses incurred by the Arbitration Commission.	tribunal determines that the amount of such costs is reasonable; (f) Any fees and expenses of the appointing authority as well as the expenses of the Secretary-General of the Permanent Court of Arbitration at The Hague. **Article 40 - Costs** 1. Except as provided in paragraph 2, the costs of arbitration shall in principle be borne by the unsuccessful party. However, the arbitral tribunal may apportion each of such costs between the parties if it determines that apportionment is reasonable, taking into account the circumstances of the case. 2. With respect to the costs of legal representation and assistance referred to in article 38, paragraph (e), the arbitral tribunal, taking into account the	result of an order by the arbitral tribunal, be equally borne by the parties and, if such expense was the result of a petition by a party, be borne by such party; provided that, notwithstanding the foregoing, the arbitral tribunal may reallocate expenses in view of the circumstances. **Rule 43 - Record of Hearings and Making a Stenographic Transcript** 3. The cost of making a stenographic transcript shall, if ordered by the arbitral tribunal, be borne equally by each party or, if ordered at a party's request, be borne by the requesting party; provided that the arbitral tribunal may, in view of the circumstances, allocate such cost among the parties. **Rule 49 - Arbitral Award** 3. The arbitral tribunal shall set forth in the	Article 45, the provisions of this Article through Article 65 shall apply to the costs of arbitration. (4) Any interest incurred pursuant to the advance payment of the arbitration costs need not be refunded. ***See also* Article 18(6) at A-70 and Articles 62-65 at A-83.**	costs of the arbitration. Unless the parties shall agree otherwise, the Tribunal shall determine the proportions in which the parties shall pay all or part of them to the Centre. If the Tribunal has determined that all or any part of the costs of the arbitration shall be paid by any party other than a party which has already paid them to the Centre, the latter shall have the right to recover the appropriate amount from the former. 30.3 The Tribunal shall have the authority to order in its award that all or a part of the legal or other costs of a party (apart from the costs of the arbitration) be paid by another party. Such costs shall, unless the award otherwise directs, be taxable by the Registrar. 30.4 If the arbitration is abandoned, suspended or concluded, by agreement or otherwise, before the final award is made,	tribunal determines that the amount of such costs is reasonable; (f) Any fees and expenses of the appointing authority as well as the expenses of the Secretary-General of the Permanent Court of Arbitration at The Hague. **Article 40 - Costs** 1. Except as provided in paragraph 2, the costs of arbitration shall in principle be borne by the unsuccessful party. However, the arbitral tribunal may apportion each of such costs between the parties if it determines that apportionment is reasonable, taking into account the circumstances of the case. 2. With respect to the costs of legal representation and assistance referred to in article 38, paragraph (e), the arbitral tribunal, taking into account the

INSTITUTIONAL					AD HOC
CIETAC ARBITRATION RULES (2000)	HKIAC ARBITRATION RULES (1985)	JCAA ARBITRATION RULES (1997)	KCAB ARBITRATION RULES (2000)	SIAC ARBITRATION RULES (1997)	UNCITRAL ARBITRATION RULES (1976)
	circumstances of the case, shall be free to determine which party shall bear such costs or may apportion such costs between the parties if it determines that apportionment is reasonable. 3. When the arbitral tribunal issues an order for the termination of the arbitral proceedings or makes an award on agreed terms, it shall fix the costs of arbitration referred to in article 38 and article 39, paragraph 1, in the text of that order or award. 4. No additional fees may be charged by an arbitral tribunal for interpretation or correction or completion of its award under articles 35 to 37. ***See also* Article 41 at A-41.**	text of its arbitral award the total amount and the allocation of the administrative fee, the hearing fee, the necessary expenses incurred during the proceedings and the arbitrators' remuneration and shall, if there is a party who has deposited an amount of money less than the amount allocated in the text of the arbitral award, set forth an order to the effect that the balance shall be paid to the other party. **Rule 64 - Obligation to Pay Fees, etc.** 1. The parties shall be jointly and severally liable for payment to the Association of the fees provided for in the Arbitration Fee Regulations, necessary expenses incurred during the proceedings and the arbitrators' remuneration. 2. Any dispute arising between the Association and the parties with respect to the payments provided for in the preceding		the parties shall be jointly and severally liable to pay the costs of the arbitration as determined by the Tribunal. In the event that the costs so determined are less than the deposits made, there shall be a refund in such proportions as the parties may agree, or failing agreement, in the same proportions as the deposits were made. 30.5 A certificate signed by the Registrar on the amount of costs or fees taxed shall form part of the award of the Tribunal. **Rule 31 - Amount of Tribunal's Fees** 31.1 The fees of the Tribunal shall be reasonable in amount, taking into account the amount in dispute, the complexity of the subject-matter, the time spent by the arbitrators and any other relevant circumstances of the case.	circumstances of the case, shall be free to determine which party shall bear such costs or may apportion such costs between the parties if it determines that apportionment is reasonable. 3. When the arbitral tribunal issues an order for the termination of the arbitral proceedings or makes an award on agreed terms, it shall fix the costs of arbitration referred to in article 38 and article 39, paragraph 1, in the text of that order or award. 4. No additional fees may be charged by an arbitral tribunal for interpretation or correction or completion of its award under articles 35 to 37. ***See also* Article 41 at A-115.**

<table>
<tr><th colspan="5">INSTITUTIONAL</th><th>AD HOC</th></tr>
<tr><th>CIETAC ARBITRATION RULES (2000)</th><th>HKIAC ARBITRATION RULES (1985)</th><th>JCAA ARBITRATION RULES (1997)</th><th>KCAB ARBITRATION RULES (2000)</th><th>SIAC ARBITRATION RULES (1997)</th><th>UNCITRAL ARBITRATION RULES (1976)</th></tr>
<tr><td></td><td></td><td>Paragraph shall be determined by the arbitral tribunal established to determine the dispute between the parties.

Rule 65 - Allocation of Fees and Expenses

In addition to the expenses provided for in Rule 28, Paragraphs 1 and 2, Rule 38 and Rule 43, Paragraph 3 (including the application mutatis mutandis of the provisions of such Paragraph under the provisions of Rule 44, Paragraphs 2 and 3), the parties shall bear, in the manner provided below, the fees provided for in the Arbitration Fee Regulations and the necessary expenses incurred during the proceedings:

(1) the request fee shall be borne by the party requesting the initiation of arbitral proceedings;

(2) the administrative fee, hearing fee and necessary expenses</td><td></td><td>31.2 If an appointing authority has been agreed upon by the parties or designated by the Chairman, and if that authority has issued a schedule of fees for arbitrators in international cases which it administers, the Tribunal in fixing its fees shall take that schedule of fees into account to the extent that it considers appropriate in the circumstances of the case.

31.3 If such appointing authority has not issued a schedule of fees for arbitrators in international cases, and if the parties fail to agree, an appropriate rate shall be determined by the Registrar and communicated in writing to the parties.

31.4 In all cases when a party so requests, the Tribunal shall fix its fees only after consultation with the Registrar who may advise the Tribunal concerning the fees.</td><td></td></tr>
</table>

INSTITUTIONAL					AD HOC
CIETAC ARBITRATION RULES (2000)	HKIAC ARBITRATION RULES (1985)	JCAA ARBITRATION RULES (1997)	KCAB ARBITRATION RULES (2000)	SIAC ARBITRATION RULES (1997)	UNCITRAL ARBITRATION RULES (1976)
		incurred during the proceedings shall be borne subject to the allocation determined by the arbitral tribunal and set forth in the arbitral award; and (3) the hearing schedule alteration fee shall be borne, if the alteration is requested by one of the parties, by such party, and, in any other case, equally by both parties. **Rule 66 - Allocation of Remuneration for Arbitrators** The parties shall bear equally the cost of the remuneration fixed by the Association for the arbitrators; provided that the arbitral tribunal may, in view of the circumstances, allocate such cost in any other manner. **Rule 67 - Payment to the Association** 1. The parties shall pay to the Association, in the manner and within the period of time determined by the arbitral tribunal, a sum		***See also* Rule 27 at A-96.**	

INSTITUTIONAL					AD HOC
CIETAC ARBITRATION RULES (2000)	HKIAC ARBITRATION RULES (1985)	JCAA ARBITRATION RULES (1997)	KCAB ARBITRATION RULES (2000)	SIAC ARBITRATION RULES (1997)	UNCITRAL ARBITRATION RULES (1976)
		of money fixed by it to cover the hearing fee, the hearing schedule alteration fee, the arbitrators' remuneration and necessary expenses incurred during the proceedings. 2. If a party fails to make payment as provided for in the preceding Paragraph, the arbitral tribunal may suspend or terminate the arbitral proceedings unless the other party makes such payment on behalf of the first party. 3. If, subsequent to termination of the arbitral proceedings, the total sum of money paid under the provisions of Paragraph 1 exceeds the total sum of the administrative fee and other fees and expenses determined by the arbitral tribunal under the provisions of Rule 49, Paragraph 3 and the hearing schedule alteration fee, the Association shall refund the difference to either or both of the parties.			

INSTITUTIONAL					AD HOC
CIETAC ARBITRATION RULES (2000)	HKIAC ARBITRATION RULES (1985)	JCAA ARBITRATION RULES (1997)	KCAB ARBITRATION RULES (2000)	SIAC ARBITRATION RULES (1997)	UNCITRAL ARBITRATION RULES (1976)
		See also Rule 12.4 at A-46 and Rule 44 at A-56-57.			

ARBITRAL DECISIONS/AWARDS

CORRECTION, INTERPRETATION OR SUPPLEMENTATION OF AWARD

INSTITUTIONAL					AD HOC
CIETAC ARBITRATION RULES (2000)	**HKIAC ARBITRATION RULES (1985)**	**JCAA ARBITRATION RULES (1997)**	**KCAB ARBITRATION RULES (2000)**	**SIAC ARBITRATION RULES (1997)**	**UNCITRAL ARBITRATION RULES (1976)**
Article 61 Either party may request in writing that a correction be made to any writing, typing, calculating errors or any errors of a similar nature contained in the arbitral award within 30 days from the date of receipt of the arbitral award; if there is really an error in the arbitral award, the arbitration tribunal shall make a correction in writing within 30 days from the date of receipt of the written request for correction. The arbitration tribunal may likewise correct any errors in writing on its own initiative within 30 days from the date on which the arbitral award is issued. The correction in writing forms a part of the arbitral award. **Article 62** If anything claimed or counterclaimed is found to have been omitted in the arbitral award, either of the parties may make a request in writing to	**Article 35 - Interpretation of the Award** 1. Within thirty days after the receipt of the award, either party, with notice to the other party, may request that the arbitral tribunal give an interpretation of the award. 2. The interpretation shall be given in writing within forty-five days after the receipt of the request. The interpretation shall form part of the award and the provisions of article 32, paragraphs 2 to 7, shall apply. **Article 36 - Correction of the Award** 1. Within thirty days after the receipt of the award, either party, with notice to the other party, may request the arbitral tribunal to correct in the award any errors in computation, any clerical or typographical errors, or any errors of similar nature. The arbitral		**Article 54 - Correction or Interpretation of Award and Additional Award** (1) The Tribunal may correct, by its decision, any error in computation, any clerical or typographical error, or any other obvious error of a similar nature in the arbitral award. In case such error can not be corrected by the Tribunal concerned, the Secretariat may correct that error. (2) If the parties request the interpretation of a specific point or any part of the award within the 30 days of receipt of the duly authenticated arbitral award, the Tribunal shall, if so agreed by the parties, decide on it within 30 days of receipt of the request. (3) The Tribunal shall make an additional award as to claims presented in the arbitral proceedings but omitted from the	**Rule 29 - Correction of Awards and Additional Awards** 29.1 Within thirty (30) days of receipt of the award, unless another period of time has been agreed upon by the parties, a party may by notice to the Registrar request the Tribunal to correct in the award any error in computation, any clerical or typographical error or any error of a similar nature. If the Tribunal considers the request to be justified, it shall make the correction(s) within thirty (30) days of receipt of the request. Any correction, which shall take the form of a separate memorandum, shall become part of the award. 29.2 The Tribunal may correct any error of the type referred to in Rule 29.1 on its own initiative within thirty (30) days of the date of the award. 29.3 Unless otherwise agreed by the parties,	**Article 35 - Interpretation of the Award** 1. Within thirty days after the receipt of the award, either party, with notice to the other party, may request that the arbitral tribunal give an interpretation of the award. 2. The interpretation shall be given in writing within forty-five days after the receipt of the request. The interpretation shall form part of the award and the provisions of article 32, paragraphs 2 to 7, shall apply. **Article 36 - Correction of the Award** 1. Within thirty days after the receipt of the award, either party, with notice to the other party, may request the arbitral tribunal to correct in the award any errors in computation, any clerical or typographical errors, or any errors of similar nature. The arbitral

INSTITUTIONAL					AD HOC
CIETAC ARBITRATION RULES (2000)	HKIAC ARBITRATION RULES (1985)	JCAA ARBITRATION RULES (1997)	KCAB ARBITRATION RULES (2000)	SIAC ARBITRATION RULES (1997)	UNCITRAL ARBITRATION RULES (1976)
the arbitration tribunal for an additional award within 30 days from the date on which the arbitral award is received. If there is really something omitted, the arbitration tribunal shall make an additional award within 30 days from the date of receipt of the written request. The arbitration tribunal may likewise make an additional award on its own initiative within 30 days from the date on which the arbitral award is issued. The additional award forms a part of the arbitral award previously issued.	tribunal may within thirty days after the communication of the award make such corrections on its own initiative. 2. Such corrections shall be in writing, and the provisions of article 32, paragraphs 2 to 7, shall apply. **Article 37 - Additional Award** 1. Within thirty days after the receipt of the award, either party, with notice to the other party, may request the arbitral tribunal to make an additional award as to claims presented in the arbitral proceedings but omitted from the award. 2. If the arbitral tribunal considers the request for an additional award to be justified and considers that the omission can be rectified without any further hearings or evidence, it shall complete its award within sixty days after the receipt of the request.		award within 60 days of receipt of the request by the parties. (4) All of the corrections, interpretations and the additional awards as provided in this Article shall form part of the award.	a party may, within thirty (30) days of receipt of the award, and with notice to the other party or parties, by notice to the Registrar request the Tribunal to make an additional award as to claims presented in the arbitral proceedings but not dealt with in the award. If the Tribunal considers the request to be justified, it shall make the additional award within forty-five (45) days of receipt of the request. 29.4 The provisions of Rule 28 shall apply *mutatis mutandis* to a correction of the award and to any additional award.	tribunal may within thirty days after the communication of the award make such corrections on its own initiative. 2. Such corrections shall be in writing, and the provisions of article 32, paragraphs 2 to 7, shall apply. **Article 37 - Additional Award** 1. Within thirty days after the receipt of the award, either party, with notice to the other party, may request the arbitral tribunal to make an additional award as to claims presented in the arbitral proceedings but omitted from the award. 2. If the arbitral tribunal considers the request for an additional award to be justified and considers that the omission can be rectified without any further hearings or evidence, it shall complete its award within sixty days after the receipt of the request.

ARBITRAL DECISIONS/AWARDS

Correction, Interpretation or Supplementation of Award

Institutional					Ad Hoc
CIETAC Arbitration Rules (2000)	HKIAC Arbitration Rules (1985)	JCAA Arbitration Rules (1997)	KCAB Arbitration Rules (2000)	SIAC Arbitration Rules (1997)	UNCITRAL Arbitration Rules (1976)
	3. When an additional award is made, the provisions of article 32, paragraphs 2 to 7, shall apply.				3. When an additional award is made, the provisions of article 32, paragraphs 2 to 7, shall apply.

INSTITUTIONAL					AD HOC
CIETAC ARBITRATION RULES (2000)	HKIAC ARBITRATION RULES (1985)	JCAA ARBITRATION RULES (1997)	KCAB ARBITRATION RULES (2000)	SIAC ARBITRATION RULES (1997)	UNCITRAL ARBITRATION RULES (1976)
Article 44 If the parties reach an amicable settlement agreement by themselves, they may either request the arbitration tribunal to conclude the case by making an award in accordance with the contents of their amicable settlement agreement, or request a dismissal of the case. The Secretary-General of the Arbitration Commission shall decide on the dismissal of an arbitration case if the decision on dismissal is made before the formation of the arbitration tribunal, and the arbitration tribunal shall decide thereon if the decision on dismissal is made after the formation of the arbitration tribunal. If the party or the parties refer the dismissed case again to the Arbitration Commission for arbitration, the Chairman of the Arbitration	**Article 34 - Settlement or Other Grounds for Termination** 1. If, before the award is made, the parties agree on a settlement of the dispute, the arbitral tribunal shall either issue an order for the termination of the arbitral proceedings or, if requested by both parties and accepted by the tribunal, record the settlement in the form of an arbitral award on agreed terms. The arbitral tribunal is not obliged to give reasons for such an award. 2. If, before the award is made, the continuation of the arbitral proceedings becomes unnecessary or impossible for any reason not mentioned in paragraph 1, the arbitral tribunal shall inform the parties of its intention to issue an order for the termination of the proceedings. The arbitral tribunal shall have the power to issue such an order	**Rule 39 - Assignment of Arbitrator's Authority** The arbitral tribunal may, when it deems it necessary and upon obtaining the consent of the parties, cause one or more of the arbitrators constituting the arbitral tribunal to examine witnesses, make verifications, conduct inspections or investigations under the provisions of Rule 34 or mediate a settlement. **Rule 49 - Arbitral Award** 2. If the arbitral tribunal deems it appropriate, it may, at the request of the parties reaching a settlement during the course of the arbitral proceedings, set forth the contents of any such settlement in its arbitral award.	**Article 53 - Arbitral Award based on Settlement** If the parties reach a settlement during the course of the arbitral proceedings, the Tribunal may, upon their request, record the agreed settlement in the form of an Award. ***See also* Article 18 at A-70.**	**Rule 18 - Submission of Written Statements and Documents** 18.9 If the Claimant fails within the time specified under these Rules or as may be fixed by the Tribunal, to submit its Statement of Case, the Tribunal may issue an order for the termination of the arbitral proceedings or make such other directions as may be appropriate in the circumstances. If the Respondent fails to submit a Statement of Defence, or if at any point any party fails to avail itself of the opportunity to present its case in the manner directed by the Tribunal, the Tribunal may nevertheless proceed with the arbitration and make the award. **Rule 28 - The Award** 28.7 In the event of a settlement, the Tribunal may render a consent award recording the settlement if any party so requests. If the	**Article 34 - Settlement or Other Grounds for Termination** 1. If, before the award is made, the parties agree on a settlement of the dispute, the arbitral tribunal shall either issue an order for the termination of the arbitral proceedings or, if requested by both parties and accepted by the tribunal, record the settlement in the form of an arbitral award on agreed terms. The arbitral tribunal is not obliged to give reasons for such an award. 2. If, before the award is made, the continuation of the arbitral proceedings becomes unnecessary or impossible for any reason not mentioned in paragraph 1, the arbitral tribunal shall inform the parties of its intention to issue an order for the termination of the proceedings. The arbitral tribunal shall have the power to issue such an order

INSTITUTIONAL					AD HOC
CIETAC ARBITRATION RULES (2000)	**HKIAC ARBITRATION RULES (1985)**	**JCAA ARBITRATION RULES (1997)**	**KCAB ARBITRATION RULES (2000)**	**SIAC ARBITRATION RULES (1997)**	**UNCITRAL ARBITRATION RULES (1976)**
Commission shall decide whether to accept the reference or not. If the parties reach a settlement agreement by themselves through conciliation without involvement of the Arbitration Commission, any of them may, based on an arbitration agreement concluded between them providing for arbitration by the Arbitration Commission and their settlement agreement, request the Arbitration Commission to appoint a sole arbitrator to render an arbitration award in accordance with the contents of the settlement agreement. ***See also* Articles 45-50 at A-13-14 and Article 88 at A-21.**	unless a party raises justifiable grounds for objection. 3. Copies of the order for termination of the arbitral proceedings or of the arbitral award on agreed terms, signed by the arbitrators, shall be communicated by the arbitral tribunal to the parties. Where an arbitral award on agreed terms is made, the provisions of article 32, paragraphs 2 and 4 to 7, shall apply. ***See also* Article 28.1 at A-37 and Article 41.4 at A-41.**			parties do not require a consent award, then on confirmation in writing by the parties to the Registrar that a settlement has been reached, the Tribunal shall be discharged and the reference to arbitration concluded, subject to payment by the parties of any outstanding costs of the arbitration in accordance with Rule 30.	unless a party raises justifiable grounds for objection. 3. Copies of the order for termination of the arbitral proceedings or of the arbitral award on agreed terms, signed by the arbitrators, shall be communicated by the arbitral tribunal to the parties. Where an arbitral award on agreed terms is made, the provisions of article 32, paragraphs 2 and 4 to 7, shall apply. ***See also* Article 28.1 at A-111 and Article 41.4 at A-115.**

INSTITUTIONAL					AD HOC
CIETAC ARBITRATION RULES (2000)	HKIAC ARBITRATION RULES (1985)	JCAA ARBITRATION RULES (1997)	KCAB ARBITRATION RULES (2000)	SIAC ARBITRATION RULES (1997)	UNCITRAL ARBITRATION RULES (1976)
Article 60 The arbitral award is final and binding upon both disputing parties. Neither party may bring a suit before a law court or make a request to any other organization for revising the arbitral award. **Article 63** The parties must automatically execute the arbitral award within the time limit specified in the arbitral award. If no time limit is specified in the arbitral award, the parties shall carry out the arbitral award immediately. In case one party fails to execute the arbitral award, the other party may apply to the Chinese court for enforcement of the arbitral award pursuant to Chinese law or apply to the competent foreign court for enforcement of the arbitral award according to the 1958 Convention on Recognition and	**Article 32 - Form and Effect of the Award** 2. The award shall be made in writing and shall be final and binding on the parties. The parties undertake to carry out the award without delay.			**Rule 28 - The Award** 28.6. The Tribunal may make separate final awards on different issues at different times, which shall be subject to correction under the procedure specified in Rule 29. Unless otherwise stated by the Tribunal, such awards shall be individually enforceable as soon as they are made. 28.8 By agreeing to have an arbitration under these Rules, the parties undertake to carry out the award without delay. Awards shall be final and binding on the parties from the date they are made. ***See also* Rule 25(m) at A-95.**	**Article 32 - Form and Effect of the Award** 2. The award shall be made in writing and shall be final and binding on the parties. The parties undertake to carry out the award without delay.

ARBITRAL DECISIONS/AWARDS

RECOURSE AGAINST AWARD

INSTITUTIONAL					AD HOC
CIETAC ARBITRATION RULES (2000)	HKIAC ARBITRATION RULES (1985)	JCAA ARBITRATION RULES (1997)	KCAB ARBITRATION RULES (2000)	SIAC ARBITRATION RULES (1997)	UNCITRAL ARBITRATION RULES (1976)
Enforcement of Foreign Arbitral Awards or other international treaties that China has concluded or acceded to.					

Index

APPENDIX

THE CHINA INTERNATIONAL ECONOMIC AND TRADE ARBITRATION COMMISSION ("CIETAC") ARBITRATION RULES

Effective as of October 1, 2000

CIETAC ARBITRATION RULES

CHAPTER I – GENERAL PROVISIONS

SECTION I – JURISDICTION

Article 1

These Rules are formulated in accordance with the Arbitration Law of the People's Republic of China and the provisions of other relevant laws, as well as the "Decision" of the former Administration Council of the Central People's Government and the "Notice" and "Official Reply" of the State Council.

Article 2

China International Economic and Trade Arbitration Commission (originally named the Foreign Trade Arbitration Commission of the China Council for the Promotion of International Trade, later renamed the Foreign Economic and Trade Arbitration Commission of the China Council for the Promotion of International Trade, and currently called the China International Economic and Trade Arbitration Commission, hereinafter referred to as the "Arbitration Commission") independently and impartially resolves, by means of arbitration, disputes arising from economic and trade transactions of a contractual or non-contractual nature.

The disputes stated in the preceding paragraph include:

(1) international or foreign-related disputes;

(2) disputes related to the Hong Kong SAR or the Macao SAR or the Taiwan region;

(3) disputes between foreign investment enterprises or between a foreign investment enterprise and a Chinese legal person, physical person and /or economic organization;

(4) disputes arising from project financing, invitations to tender and bidding submissions, project construction or other activities conducted by a Chinese legal person, physical person and /or other economic organization which utilize capital, technology or services from foreign countries, international organizations or from the Hong Kong SAR, the Macao SAR and the Taiwan region;

(5) disputes that may be taken cognizance of by the Arbitration Commission in accordance with special provisions of, or upon special authorization from, the laws or administrative regulations of the People's Republic of China.; and

(6) any other domestic disputes that the parties have agreed to arbitrate by the Arbitration Commission.

The Arbitration Commission does not accept the cases over the following disputes:

(1) marital, adoption, guardianship, support and succession disputes;

(2) administrative disputes that laws require to be handled by administrative authorities;

(3) labor disputes and disputes within the agricultural collective economic organizations over contracted management in agriculture.

Article 3

The Arbitration Commission will, upon the written application by one of the parties, accept a case in accordance with the arbitration agreement concluded between the parties, either before or after the occurrence of the dispute, in which it is provided that disputes are to be submitted to the Arbitration Commission for arbitration.

An arbitration agreement means an arbitration clause in a contract concluded between the parties or any other form of written agreement providing for settlement of dispute by arbitration.

Article 4

The Arbitration Commission has the power to decide on the existence and validity of an arbitration agreement and on jurisdiction over an arbitration case. If the parties concerned dispute the validity of an arbitration agreement, with one party requesting the Arbitration Commission to make a decision and the other party requesting the people's court to make a ruling, the people's court will make such a ruling.

Article 5

An arbitration clause contained in a contract shall be regarded as existing independently and separately from the other clauses of the contract, and an arbitration agreement attached to a contract shall be treated as a part of the contract existing independently and separately from the other parts of the contract. The validity of an arbitration clause or an arbitration agreement shall not be affected by any modification, rescission, termination, expiry, invalidity, or non-existence of the contract.

Article 6

Any objection to an arbitration agreement and/or the jurisdiction over an arbitration case shall be raised before the first hearing conducted by the arbitration tribunal. Where a case is examined on the basis of documents only, an objection to jurisdiction should be raised before submission of the first substantive defense.

Any objection to an arbitration agreement and/or the jurisdiction over an arbitration case shall not affect the hearing of the case according to the arbitration procedures.

Article 7

If the parties agree to submit their dispute to the Arbitration Commission for arbitration, it will be taken that they have agreed to the case being arbitrated under these Rules. However, if the parties have agreed otherwise, and subject to consent by the Arbitration Commission, the parties' agreement will prevail.

SECTION II – ORGANIZATION

Article 8

The Arbitration Commission has one honorary Chairman and several advisers.

Article 9

The Arbitration Commission consists of one Chairman, several Vice-Chairmen and a number of Commission members. The Chairman performs the functions and duties vested in him by these Rules and the Vice-Chairmen may also perform the Chairman's functions and duties with the Chairman's authorization.

The Arbitration Commission has a secretariat to handle its day-to-day work under the leadership of the Secretary-General of the Arbitration Commission.

Article 10

The Arbitration Commission establishes a Panel of Arbitrators. The arbitrators are selected and appointed by the Arbitration Commission from among Chinese and foreign persons with professional knowledge and practical experience in the fields of law, economics and trade, science and technology, etc.

Article 11

The Arbitration Commission is based in Beijing. The Arbitration Commission has a Shenzhen Sub-Commission in Shenzhen Special Economic Zone and a Shanghai Sub-Commission in Shanghai. These Sub-Commissions are an integral part of the Arbitration Commission.

The Sub-Commissions have their respective secretariats to handle their day-to-day work under the leadership of the Secretaries-General of the respective Sub-Commissions.

These Rules uniformly apply to the Arbitration Commission and its Sub-Commissions. When arbitration proceedings are conducted in the Sub-Commissions, the functions and duties under these Rules to be carried out by the Chairman, the secretariat and the Secretary-General of the Arbitration Commission shall be performed by the Vice-Chairmen as authorized by the Chairman, the secretariats and the Secretaries-General of the Sub-Commissions respectively, except for the circumstances provided for in Article 30 of these Rules.

Article 12

The Parties may agree to have their dispute arbitrated by the Arbitration Commission in Beijing or by the Shenzhen Sub-Commission in Shenzhen or by the Shanghai Sub-Commission in Shanghai.

In the absence of such an agreement, the Claimant will have option to submit the case to be arbitrated by the Arbitration Commission in Beijing or by the Shenzhen Sub-commission in Shenzhen or by the Shanghai Sub-Commission in Shanghai.

When deciding on where the case should be arbitrated, the first choice should be final. In case of any dispute, the Arbitration Commission will make a decision accordingly.

CHAPTER II – ARBITRATION PROCEEDINGS

SECTION I – APPLICATION FOR ARBITRATION, DEFENSE AND COUNTER-CLAIM

Article 13

The arbitration proceedings will commence from the date on which the Notice of Arbitration is issued by the Arbitration Commission or its Sub-Commissions.

Article 14

A Claimant submitting an Application for Arbitration must:

(1) Submit an Application for Arbitration in writing, which shall, *inter alia*, contain:

(a) the names and addresses of the Claimant and the Respondent, including the zip code, telephone, telex, fax, and cable numbers or any other means of electronic telecommunications, if any;

(b) the arbitration agreement relied upon by the Claimant;

(c) the facts of the case and the main points of dispute; and

(d) the Claimant's claim and the facts and reasons on which his claim is based.

The Application for Arbitration shall be signed by, and/or affixed with the seal of, the Claimant and/or the authorized agent of the Claimant.

(2) Attach to the Application for Arbitration the relevant documentary evidence which supports the facts on which the Claimant's claim is based.

(3) Pay an arbitration fee in advance to the Arbitration Commission according to the Arbitration Fee Schedule of the Arbitration Commission.

Article 15

Upon receipt of the Application for Arbitration and its attachments, if the secretariat of the Arbitration Commission, after examination, finds that the Claimant has not yet completed the formalities required for arbitration, it will request the Claimant to complete them. If it finds that the Claimant has completed such formalities, the secretariat should promptly send to the Respondent a Notice of Arbitration, together with one copy each of the Claimant's Application for Arbitration and its attachments as well as the Arbitration Rules, the Panel of Arbitrators and the Arbitration Fee Schedule of the Arbitration Commission. At the same time, the Notice of

Arbitration, the Arbitration Rules, the Panel of Arbitrators and Arbitration Fee Schedule should be sent to the Claimant as well.

The secretariat of the Arbitration Commission, after sending the Notice of Arbitration to the Claimant and Respondent, shall appoint one of its staff-members to take charge of procedural administration of the case.

Article 16

The Claimant and the Respondent shall, within 20 days as from the date of receipt of the Notice of Arbitration, each appoint an arbitrator from among the Panel of Arbitrators of the Arbitration Commission or authorize the Chairman of the Arbitration Commission to make such appointment.

Article 17

The Respondent shall, within 45 days from the date of receipt of the Notice of Arbitration, submit his written defense and relevant documentary evidence to the secretariat of the Arbitration Commission.

Article 18

The Respondent shall, at the latest within 60 days from the date of receipt of the Notice of Arbitration, file with the secretariat of the Arbitration Commission his counterclaim in writing, if any. The arbitration tribunal may extend that time limit if it deems that there are justified reasons.

When filing a counterclaim, the Respondent must state in his written statement of counterclaim his specific claim and facts and reasons upon which his claim is based, and attach to his written statement of counterclaim any relevant documentary evidence.

When filing a counterclaim, the Respondent must pay an arbitration fee in advance according to the Arbitration Fee Schedule of the Arbitration Commission.

Article 19

The Claimant may request to amend his claim and the Respondent may request to amend his counterclaim. However, the arbitration tribunal may refuse such an amendment if it considers that the request has been raised too late and may affect the progress of the arbitration proceedings.

Article 20

When submitting application for arbitration, written defense, statement of counterclaim, documentary evidence and other documents, the parties shall submit them in quintuplicate. If the number of the parties is more than two, additional copies shall be provided accordingly. If the arbitration tribunal is composed of only one arbitrator, the number of copies submitted may be reduced by two.

Article 21

The progress of arbitration proceedings shall not be affected notwithstanding the failure of the Respondent to file his defense in writing or the failure of the Claimant to submit his written defense against the Respondent's counterclaim.

Article 22

The parties may authorize arbitration agents to deal with the matters relating to arbitration; the authorized arbitration agent must produce a Power of Attorney to the Arbitration Commission.

Both Chinese and foreign citizens can be authorized to act as arbitration agents.

Article 23

When a party applies for property preservative measures, the Arbitration Commission shall submit the party's application to the intermediate people's court for a ruling in the place where the domicile of the party against whom the property preservative measures are sought is located or in the place where the property of the said party is located.

When a party applies for taking interim measures of protection of evidence, the Arbitration Commission shall submit the party's application to the intermediate people's court in the place where the evidence is located for a ruling.

SECTION II – FORMATION OF ARBITRAL TRIBUNAL

Article 24

Each of the parties shall appoint one arbitrator from among the Panel of Arbitrators of the Arbitration Commission or entrust the Chairman of the Arbitration Commission to make such appointment. A third arbitrator shall be jointly appointed by the parties or appointed by the Chairman of the Arbitration Commission upon the parties' joint authorization.

In case the two parties fail to jointly appoint a third arbitrator or fail to jointly entrust the Chairman of the Arbitration Commission to appoint a third arbitrator within 20 days from the date on which the Respondent receives the Notice of Arbitration, the third arbitrator will be appointed by the Chairman of the Arbitration Commission. The third arbitrator will act as the presiding arbitrator.

The presiding arbitrator and the two appointed arbitrators will jointly form an arbitration tribunal to jointly hear the case.

Article 25

The Claimant and the Respondent may jointly appoint or jointly authorize the Chairman of the Arbitration Commission to appoint a sole arbitrator to form an arbitration tribunal to hear the case alone.

If both parties agree to having a sole arbitrator to hear their case but are unable to agree on the choice of such a sole arbitrator within 20 days from the date on which the Respondent receives the Notice of Arbitration, the Chairman of the Arbitration Commission will make the appointment.

Article 26

If the Claimant or the Respondent fails to appoint or authorize the Chairman of the Arbitration Commission to appoint an arbitrator according to Article 16 of these Rules, the Chairman of the Arbitration Commission will appoint an arbitrator for the Claimant or the Respondent.

Article 27

Where there are two or more Claimants and/or Respondents involved in an arbitration case, the Claimants' side and/or the Respondents' side each shall, through consultation, appoint or entrust the Chairman of the Arbitration Commission to appoint one arbitrator from among the Panel of Arbitrators of the Arbitration Commission.

If the Claimants' side or the Respondents' side fails to make such appointment or entrustment within 20 days as from the date on which the Respondents' side receives the Notice of Arbitration, the appointment will be made by the Chairman of the Arbitration Commission.

Article 28

Any appointed arbitrator having a personal interest in the case shall himself disclose such circumstances to the Arbitration Commission and request a withdrawal from his office.

Article 29

Any party who has justified reasons to suspect the impartiality and independence of an appointed arbitrator may make a request in writing to the Arbitration Commission for that arbitrator's withdrawal. In the request, the facts and reasons on which the request is based shall be stated with the supporting evidence provided.

A challenge against an arbitrator must be put forward in writing no later than the first oral hearing. If the grounds for the challenge come out or are made known after the first oral hearing, the challenge may nevertheless be raised before the conclusion of the last hearing.

Article 30

The Chairman of the Arbitration Commission shall decide whether an arbitrator should be withdrawn.

Before any decision is made by the Chairman of the Arbitration Commission, the challenged arbitrator shall continue to perform the duties of an arbitrator.

Article 31

If an arbitrator is unable to perform the duties owing to his/her withdrawal, demise, removal from the Panel of Arbitrators or any other reasons, a substitute arbitrator shall be appointed in accordance with the procedure pursuant to which the original arbitrator was appointed.

After the appointment of the substitute arbitrator, the arbitration tribunal has discretion to decide whether to repeat the whole or a part of the previous procedures.

SECTION III – HEARING

Article 32

The arbitration tribunal will hold oral hearings. At the request of the parties or with their consent, the arbitration tribunal may, if it also considers oral hearings unnecessary, hear and decide a case on the basis of documents only.

Article 33

The date of the first oral hearing shall be decided by the arbitration tribunal in consultation with the secretariat of the Arbitration Commission. The secretariat shall notify the two parties of the decision 30 days before the date of the hearing. Any party having justified reasons may request a postponement of the hearing, but a written request must be submitted to the secretariat of the Arbitration Commission 12 days before the date of the hearing. The arbitration tribunal will then decide whether to postpone the hearing or not.

Article 34

The notice of the date of hearing subsequent to the first hearing is not subject to the 30-day time limit.

Article 35

Where the parties have agreed on the place of arbitration, the case shall be arbitrated in that place. Unless the parties agree otherwise, the cases accepted by the Arbitration Commission shall be heard in Beijing, or in other places with the approval of the Secretary-General of the Arbitration Commission. The cases accepted by a Sub-Commission of the Arbitration Commission shall be heard in the place where the Sub-Commission is located, or in other places with the approval of the Secretary-General of that Sub-Commission.

Article 36

The arbitration tribunal shall not hear cases in open session. However, if both parties request that an open session hearing be held, the arbitration tribunal shall decide whether to do so or not.

Article 37

For cases heard in closed session, the parties, their arbitration agents, witnesses, arbitrators, experts consulted by the arbitration tribunal and appraisers appointed by the arbitration tribunal and the relevant staff-members of the secretariat of the Arbitration Commission shall not disclose to outsiders the substantive or procedural matters of the case.

Article 38

The parties shall produce evidence in support of the facts on which their claim, defense or counterclaim is based. The arbitration tribunal may, on its own initiative, undertake investigations and collect evidence as it considers necessary.

When investigating and collecting evidence by itself, the arbitration tribunal shall promptly inform the parties to be present if it considers necessary. Should one party or both parties fail to appear, the investigation and collection of evidence shall not be affected.

Article 39

The arbitration tribunal may consult an expert or appoint an appraiser for clarification of the specific issues relating to a case. Such an expert or appraiser may be either a Chinese or foreign organization or citizen.

The arbitration tribunal has the power to order the parties to submit or produce to the expert or appraiser any relevant materials, documents, or properties and goods for check-up, inspection and/or appraisal, and the parties are so obliged as well.

Article 40

The expert's report and the appraiser's report shall be copied to the parties so that the parties may have the opportunity to give their opinions thereon. At the request of any party to the case and with the approval of the arbitration tribunal, the expert and appraiser may be present at the hearing, and, if considered necessary and appropriate by the arbitration tribunal, be required to give explanations of their reports.

Article 41

The evidence submitted by the parties will be examined and evaluated by the arbitration tribunal. The arbitration tribunal shall decide whether to adopt the expert's report and the appraiser's report.

Article 42

Should one of the parties fail to appear at the hearing, the arbitration tribunal may proceed with the hearing and make an award by default.

Article 43

During the hearing, the arbitration tribunal may make a record in writing and/or by tape-recording. The arbitration tribunal may, when it considers necessary, make a minute stating the main points of the hearing and ask the parties and/or their arbitration agents, witnesses and/or other persons involved to sign and/or affix their seal to it.

The record in writing or by tape-recording is only available for use and reference by the arbitration tribunal.

Article 44

If the parties reach an amicable settlement agreement by themselves, they may either request the arbitration tribunal to conclude the case by making an award in accordance with the contents of their amicable settlement agreement, or request a dismissal of the case.

The Secretary-General of the Arbitration Commission shall decide on the dismissal of an arbitration case if the decision on dismissal is made before the formation of the arbitration tribunal, and the arbitration tribunal shall decide thereon if the decision on dismissal is made after the formation of the arbitration tribunal.

If the party or the parties refer the dismissed case again to the Arbitration Commission for arbitration, the Chairman of the Arbitration Commission shall decide whether to accept the reference or not.

If the parties reach a settlement agreement by themselves through conciliation without involvement of the Arbitration Commission, any of them may, based on an arbitration agreement concluded between them providing for arbitration by the Arbitration Commission and their settlement agreement, request the Arbitration Commission to appoint a sole arbitrator to render an arbitration award in accordance with the contents of the settlement agreement.

Article 45

If both parties have a desire for conciliation or one party so desires and the other party agrees to it when consulted by the arbitration tribunal, the arbitration tribunal may conciliate the case under its cognizance in the process of arbitration.

Article 46

The arbitration tribunal may conciliate cases in the manner it considers appropriate.

Article 47

The arbitration tribunal shall terminate conciliation and continue the arbitration proceedings when one of the parties requests a termination of conciliation or when the arbitration tribunal believes that further efforts to conciliate will be futile.

Article 48

If the parties have reached an amicable settlement outside the arbitration tribunal in the course of conciliation conducted by the arbitration tribunal, such settlement shall be taken as one which has been reached through the arbitration tribunal's conciliation.

Article 49

The parties shall sign a settlement agreement in writing when an amicable settlement is reached through conciliation conducted by the arbitration tribunal, and the arbitration tribunal will close the case by making an arbitration award in accordance with the contents of the settlement agreement unless otherwise agreed by the parties.

Article 50

Should conciliation fail, any statement, opinion, view or proposal which has been made, raised, put forward, acknowledged, accepted or rejected by either party or by the arbitration tribunal in the process of conciliation shall not be invoked as grounds for any claim, defense and/or counterclaim in the subsequent arbitration proceedings, judicial proceedings or any other proceedings.

Article 51

The party who knows or should have known that any provision or requirement of these Rules has not been complied with and yet proceeds with the arbitration proceedings without explicitly raising in writing his objection to non-compliance in a timely manner shall be taken to have waived his right to object.

SECTION IV – AWARD

Article 52

The arbitration tribunal shall render an arbitral award within 9 months as from the date on which the arbitration tribunal is formed. The Secretary-General of the Arbitration Commission may extend this time limit at the request of the arbitration tribunal if the Secretary-General of the Arbitration Commission considers that it is really necessary and the reasons for extension are truly justified.

Article 53

The arbitration tribunal shall independently and impartially make its arbitral award on the basis of the facts, in accordance with the law and the terms of the contracts, with reference to international practices and in compliance with the principle of fairness and reasonableness.

Article 54

Where a case is heard by an arbitration tribunal composed of three arbitrators, the arbitral award shall be decided by the majority of the arbitrators and the minority opinion may be recorded and placed on file.

When the arbitration tribunal cannot attain a majority opinion, the arbitral award shall be decided in accordance with the presiding arbitrator's opinion.

Article 55

The arbitration tribunal shall state in the arbitral award the claims, the facts of the dispute, the reasons on which the arbitral award is based, the result of the arbitral award, the allocation of the arbitration costs, the date on which and the place at which the arbitral award is made. The facts of the dispute and the reasons on which the arbitral award is based may not be stated in the arbitral award if the parties have agreed not to state them in the arbitral award, or the arbitral award is made in accordance with the contents of the settlement agreement reached between the parties.

Article 56

Unless the arbitral award is made in accordance with the opinion of the presiding arbitrator or the sole arbitrator, the arbitral award shall be signed by a majority of arbitrators. An arbitrator who has a dissenting opinion may sign or not sign his name on the arbitral award.

The arbitrators shall submit the draft arbitral award to the Arbitration Commission before signing the award. The Arbitration Commission may remind the arbitrator of any issue related to the form of the arbitral award on condition that the arbitrator's independence of decision is not affected.

The Arbitration Commission's stamp shall be affixed to the arbitral award.

The date on which the arbitral award is made is the date on which the arbitral award comes into legal effect.

Article 57

An interlocutory award or partial award may be made on any issue of the case at any time in the course of arbitration before the final award is made if considered necessary by the arbitration tribunal, or if the parties make such a proposal and it is agreed to by the arbitration tribunal. Either party's failure to perform the interlocutory award will not affect the continuation of the arbitration proceedings, nor will it prevent the arbitration tribunal from making a final award.

Article 58

The arbitration tribunal has the power to determine in the arbitral award the arbitration fee and other expenses to be paid by the parties to the Arbitration Commission.

Article 59

The arbitration tribunal has the power to decide in the arbitral award that the losing party shall pay the winning party as compensation a proportion of the expenses reasonably incurred by the winning party in dealing with the case. The amount of such compensation shall not in any case exceed 10% of the total amount awarded to the winning party.

Article 60

The arbitral award is final and binding upon both disputing parties. Neither party may bring a suit before a law court or make a request to any other organization for revising the arbitral award.

Article 61

Either party may request in writing that a correction be made to any writing, typing, calculating errors or any errors of a similar nature contained in the arbitral award within 30 days from the date of receipt of the arbitral award; if there is really an error in the arbitral award, the arbitration tribunal shall make a correction in writing within 30 days from the date of receipt of the written request for correction. The arbitration tribunal may likewise correct any errors in writing on its own initiative within 30 days from the date on which the arbitral award is issued. The correction in writing forms a part of the arbitral award.

Article 62

If anything claimed or counterclaimed is found to have been omitted in the arbitral award, either of the parties may make a request in writing to the arbitration tribunal for an additional award within 30 days from the date on which the arbitral award is received. If there is really something omitted, the arbitration tribunal shall make an additional award within 30 days from the date of receipt of the written request. The arbitration tribunal may likewise make an additional award on its own initiative within 30 days from the date on which the arbitral award is issued. The additional award forms a part of the arbitral award previously issued.

Article 63

The parties must automatically execute the arbitral award within the time limit specified in the arbitral award. If no time limit is specified in the arbitral award, the parties shall carry out the arbitral award immediately.

In case one party fails to execute the arbitral award, the other party may apply to the Chinese court for enforcement of the arbitral award pursuant to Chinese law or apply to the competent foreign court for enforcement of the arbitral award according to the 1958 Convention on Recognition and Enforcement of Foreign Arbitral Awards or other international treaties that China has concluded or acceded to.

CHAPTER III – SUMMARY PROCEDURE

Article 64

Unless otherwise agreed by the parties, this Summary Procedure shall apply to any case in dispute where the amount of the claim totals not more than RMB 500,000 yuan, and to any case in dispute where the amount of the claim totals more than RMB 500,000 yuan provided that one party applies for arbitration under this Summary Procedure and the other party agrees in writing.

Article 65

When an application for arbitration is submitted to the Arbitration Commission, the secretariat of the Arbitration Commission shall, if such application is examined and found to be acceptable and qualified for application of the Summary Procedure, send a Notice of Arbitration immediately to the parties.

Unless both parties have jointly appointed one sole arbitrator from among the Panel of Arbitrators of the Arbitration Commission, they shall jointly appoint or jointly entrust the Chairman of the Arbitration Commission to appoint one sole arbitrator within 15 days from the date on which the Notice of Arbitration is received by the Respondent. Should the parties fail to make such appointment or entrustment, the Chairman of the Arbitration Commission shall immediately appoint one sole arbitrator to form an arbitration tribunal to hear the case.

Article 66

The Respondent shall, within 30 days from the date of receipt of the Notice of Arbitration, submit his defense and relevant documentary evidence to the secretariat of the Arbitration Commission; a counterclaim, if any, shall be filed with documentary evidence within the said time limit.

Article 67

The arbitration tribunal may hear the case in the way it considers appropriate. The arbitration tribunal may in its full discretion decide to hear the case only on the basis of the written materials and evidence submitted by the parties or to hold an oral hearing as well.

Article 68

The parties must hand in written materials and evidence required for arbitration in compliance with the requirements of the arbitration tribunal within the time limit given by the arbitration tribunal.

Article 69

For a case which needs an oral hearing, the secretariat of the Arbitration Commission shall, after the arbitration tribunal has fixed a date for hearing, inform the parties of the date of the hearing 15 days before the date of the hearing.

Article 70

If the arbitration tribunal decides to hear the case orally, only one oral hearing shall be held. However, the arbitration tribunal may hold two oral hearings if really necessary.

Article 71

Should one of the parties fail to act in compliance with this Summary Procedure during summary proceedings, such failure shall not affect the arbitration tribunal's conduct of the proceedings and the arbitration tribunal's power to render an arbitral award.

Article 72

The conduct of the summary proceedings shall not be affected by any amendment of the claim or by the filing of a counterclaim, except that the disputed amount of the revised arbitration claim or counterclaim is in conflict with the provision of Article 64.

Article 73

Where a case is heard orally, the arbitration tribunal shall make an arbitral award within 30 days from the date of the oral hearing if one hearing is to be held, or from the date of the second oral hearing if two oral hearings are to be held. Where a case is examined on the basis of documents only, the arbitration tribunal shall render an arbitral award within 90 days from the date on which the arbitration tribunal is formed. The Secretary-General of the Arbitration Commission may extend the said time limit if such extension is necessary and justified.

Article 74

For matters not covered in this Chapter, the relevant provisions in the other Chapters of these Rules shall apply.

CHAPTER IV – SPECIAL PROVISIONS FOR DOMESTIC ARBITRATION

Article 75

The provisions of this Chapter apply to the domestic arbitration cases accepted by the Arbitration Commission in respect of the disputes listed in Item (3), (4), (5) and (6) of paragraph 2, Article 2 of these Rules.

The provisions of Summary Procedure of Chapter III shall apply if the domestic arbitration cases fall within the scope of Article 64 of these Rules.

Article 76

After receipt of the Application for Arbitration, the Arbitration Commission, if considered that the application formalities stated in Article 14 of these Rules have been complied with, shall initiate the arbitration proceedings within 5 days and give notification to the parties. Or alternatively, the Arbitration Commission will initiate the arbitration proceedings immediately and notify the parties accordingly. If the Arbitration Commission considers that the application formalities have not been completed, it shall notify the applicant party in writing of its refusal and explain the reasons thereof.

Article 77

Upon receipt of the Application for Arbitration, if the Arbitration Commission considers that the Application does not fulfill the requirements set out in Article 14, it may ask the party to rectify it within a specified time limit. If no required rectification is made within that time limit, such Application for Arbitration will be rejected.

Article 78

When the Claimant or the Respondent is required to appoint or authorize the Chairman of the Arbitration Commission to appoint arbitrator(s) according to Article 16, 24, 25 and 27, the time limits provided for by each of the above-mentioned articles shall be 15 days.

Article 79

The Respondent shall, within 30 days from the date of receipt of the Notice of Arbitration, submit his written defense and relevant documentary evidence to the secretariat of the Arbitration Commission.

The Respondent shall, at the latest within 45 days from the date of receipt of the Notice of Arbitration, file with the Arbitration Commission his counterclaim in writing, if any. The arbitration tribunal may extend this time limit if it considers that there are justified reasons.

Article 80

For cases requiring oral hearing(s), the secretariat of the Arbitration Commission shall notify the parties involved of the hearing date at least 15 days in advance. The arbitration tribunal may, with consent from both parties, hold the hearing ahead of schedule. Any party may request a postponement of the hearing if it has justified reasons, but a written request must be submitted to the arbitration tribunal at least 7 days before the date of the hearing. The tribunal will then decide whether to postpone the hearing or not.

The notice of the date of hearing subsequent to the first hearing is not subject to the 15-day time limit stipulated by the preceding paragraph.

Article 81

If a case is heard orally, evidences shall be presented during the hearing(s) and be submitted within the time limit set by the arbitration tribunal.

Article 82

The arbitration tribunal shall make a record of the hearing(s) in writing. Any party or participant in the arbitration may apply for correction if any omission or mistake is found in the record of his own statement. If the arbitration tribunal refuses to correct, such application shall nevertheless be recorded.

The written record shall be signed or sealed by the arbitrator(s), the person who takes the notes, the parties, and other participants to the arbitration, if any.

Article 83

The arbitration tribunal shall render an arbitral award within 6 months as from the date on which the arbitration tribunal is formed. At the request of the arbitration tribunal, the Secretary-General of the Arbitration Commission may extend this time limit as he considers necessary and justifiable.

Article 84

For matters not covered in this Chapter, the relevant provisions in the other Chapters of these Rules shall apply.

CHAPTER V – SUPPLEMENTARY PROVISIONS

Article 85

The Chinese language is the official language of the Arbitration Commission. If the parties have agreed otherwise, their agreement shall prevail.

At the hearing, if the parties or their arbitration agents or witnesses require language interpretation, the secretariat of the Arbitration Commission may provide an interpreter for them. Or the parties may bring with them their own interpreter.

The arbitration tribunal and/or the secretariat of the Arbitration Commission may, as it considers necessary, request the parties to hand in the corresponding translation copies in Chinese language or other languages of the documents and evidential materials submitted by the parties.

Article 86

All the arbitration documents, notices and materials may be sent to the parties and/or their arbitration agents in person, or by registered letter or express airmail, telefax, telex, cable or by any other means considered proper by the secretariat of the Arbitration Commission.

Article 87

Any written correspondence to the parties and/or their arbitration agents shall be taken to have been properly served if it is delivered to the addressee or delivered at his place of business, habitual residence or mailing address, or if, after reasonable inquiries, none of the aforesaid addresses can be found, the written correspondence is sent to the addressee's last known place of business, habitual residence or mailing address by registered letter or by any other means which provides a record of the attempt to deliver it.

Article 88

Apart from charging arbitration fees from the parties according to the arbitration Fee Schedule of the Arbitration Commission, the Arbitration Commission may collect from the parties other extra, reasonable and actual expenses including arbitrators' special remuneration and their travel and boarding expenses for dealing with the case, as well as the fees and expenses for experts, appraisers and interpreters appointed by the arbitration tribunal, etc.

If a case is withdrawn after the parties have reached between themselves an amicable settlement or is concluded with an arbitral award made according to paragraph 4 of Article 44, the Arbitration Commission may charge a certain amount of fees from the parties in consideration of the quantity of work and the amount of the actual expenses incurred by the Arbitration Commission.

Article 89

Where an arbitration agreement or an arbitration clause contained in the contract provides for arbitration to be conducted by China International Economic and Trade Arbitration Commission or its Sub-Commissions or by the formerly named Foreign Trade Arbitration Commission or Foreign Economic and Trade Arbitration Commission of the China Council for the Promotion of International Trade, it shall be taken that the parties have unanimously agreed that the arbitration shall be conducted by China International Economic and Trade Arbitration Commission or by its Sub-Commissions.

Where an arbitration agreement or an arbitration clause contained in the contract provides for arbitration by China Council for the Promotion of International Trade/China Chamber of International Commerce or by the arbitration commission or court of arbitration of China Council for the Promotion of International Trade/China Chamber of International Commerce, it shall be taken that the parties have unanimously agreed that the arbitration shall be conducted by China International Economic and Trade Arbitration Commission.

Article 90

These Rules shall come into force as from October 1st, 2000. For cases accepted by the Arbitration Commission or by its Sub-Commissions before the date on which these Rules become effective, the Rules of Arbitration effective at the time of acceptance shall apply. However, these Rules will be applied if the parties so agree.

Article 91

The power to interpret these Rules is vested in the Arbitration Commission.

THE HONG KONG INTERNATIONAL ARBITRATION CENTRE ("HKIAC") PROCEDURES FOR ARBITRATION (INCLUDING THE UNCITRAL RULES)

Effective as of 1985

HKIAC PROCEDURES FOR ARBITRATION

(Including the UNCITRAL Rules)

UNCITRAL ARBITRATION RULES

The United Nations Commission on International Trade Law (UNCITRAL) adopted the present UNCITRAL Arbitration Rules in 1976.

The General Assembly of the United Nations by its Resolution 31/98 recommended the use of the UNCITRAL Arbitration Rules in the settlement of international disputes, particularly by reference to the Rules in international commercial contracts (see Page 4 for model clauses adopting the Rules).

THE UNCITRAL Arbitration Rules include provision for the parties to an arbitration to designate an appointing authority, who will appoint an arbitral tribunal if the parties do not, and will fulfil certain other functions. Prior designation of a suitable appointing authority enables cases to be processed more efficiently when they subsequently arise. The appointment of an experienced arbitration administrator and the availability of appropriate additional arbitration support services also help cases to proceed more smoothly.

THE HONG KONG INTERNATIONAL ARBITRATION CENTRE (HKIAC)

The HKIAC was established in 1985. It operates under a Council composed of business and professional people of many different nationalities and with a wide diversity of skills and experience. Its activities are based at the International Arbitration Centre in Hong Kong. They include the appointment of arbitrators, the provision of support services, and the administration of arbitrations under the HKIAC's own Arbitration Rules.

Administration of the HKIAC's arbitration activities is conducted by the Management Committee of the Council through the Centre's Secretary-General, who is the HKIAC's Chief Executive and Registrar. The task of ensuring the application of the HKIAC's arbitration rules is performed by a Court of Appointment consisting of persons with wide experience in the law and international commercial arbitration.

The HKIAC has extensive expertise and experience with which to provide services in international arbitrations. Such services are available for arbitration under the UNCITRAL Arbitration Rules, whether such arbitrations are in Hong Kong or elsewhere.

THE HKIAC AS APPOINTING AUTHORITY

The parties may designate the HKIAC as appointing authority at the same time as adopting the UNCITRAL Arbitration Rules or they may agree to do so after a dispute to which the Rules apply has arisen. (See Page 4 for the model clause designating the HKIAC as appointing authority where the UNCITRAL Arbitration Rules are being adopted.)

Appointment

The HKIAC selects the arbitral tribunal having regard to the particular requirements of each case and subject to any conditions agreed by the parties. Reference is made to the HKIAC's Panel of International Arbitrators, which is composed of arbitrators with substantial international experience and drawn from the major trading nations of the world. Appointments are made on behalf of the HKIAC by the Secretary-General on the advice of the Court of Appointment.

Challenge of Arbitrators

Arbitrators appointed by the HKIAC are required to confirm their independence and impartiality. Where a decision is required by the appointing authority under the Rules on any challenge of an arbitrator, such decision is made on behalf of the HKIAC by the Court of Appointment.

Replacement of Arbitrator

Replacement of an arbitrator is effected by the HKIAC in accordance with the Rules as necessary.

Assistance in Fixing Fees of Arbitrators

The fees for arbitrators appointed by the HKIAC are generally calculated by reference to work done by them in connection with the arbitration and are charged at rates appropriate to the particular circumstances of the case including its complexity and any special qualifications of the arbitrators. If the parties so wish the HKIAC will consult with the arbitral tribunal to establish the rates applicable to a particular case.

Advisory Comments Regarding Deposits

If requested under the Rules the HKIAC will consult with the arbitral tribunal to fix the amount of any deposits.

APPOINTMENT FEE SCHEDULE

In cases where the HKIAC is named in an arbitration clause or a separate arbitration agreement as the appointment authority an appointment fee, based on the following scale, is payable at the time the appointment or referral is made.

Amount of Claim	Fee
Up to $5 million	$ 3,000
Up to $50 million	$ 8,000
Up to $100 million	$12,000
Over $100 million	As appropriate

If an amount for the claim can be, or is, stated at the time of referral, a sum of $3,000 will be payable. This will be taken into account in determining the amount of the fee that will be payable when the amount in dispute is disclosed. This fee will cover all steps taken by the HKIAC in connection with the appointment of an arbitrator, or arbitrators.

THE HKIAC AS ARBITRATION ADMINISTRATOR

The parties or the arbitral tribunal may designate the HKIAC as arbitration administrator at the same time as adopting the UNCITRAL Arbitration Rules or they may agree to do so after a dispute to which the Rules apply has arisen. The arbitral tribunal may also at any time after its appointment designate the HKIAC as arbitration administrator. Where the HKIAC is designated arbitration administrator the following administrative services will be provided.

Communications

Communications and notices between the parties and the arbitral tribunal in the course of arbitration proceedings (except at meetings and hearings) will be addressed through the HKIAC, and deemed received by the addressee when received by the HKIAC. When passed on by the HKIAC to a party such communications and notices will be sent to the address of that party contained in the Notice of Arbitration or such other address as may have been notified in writing to the HKIAC by that party.

Liaison

The HKIAC will liaise with the arbitral tribunal and the parties to establish date, time and place of meetings and hearings, and otherwise, as required.

Procedural Advice

Upon request the HKIAC will advise generally on applicable procedure under the Rules and as directed by the arbitral tribunal.

Deposits

Upon request the HKIAC will hold deposits from the parties and account for the same.

Registration of Awards

Upon request the HKIAC will assist in the filing or registration of arbitral awards in countries where such filing or registration is required by law.

Administrative and other services performed by the HKIAC will be charged at an appropriate hourly rate.

ADDITIONAL ARBITRATION SUPPORT SERVICES OF THE HKIAC

A wide range of additional arbitration support services are available to the parties or the arbitral tribunal, as required, during the course of arbitration proceedings. These services are provided from the HKIAC's own resources where possible, or are otherwise obtainable through the HKIAC, and include:

- Hearing rooms and retiring rooms, at the Hong Kong International Arbitration Centre or elsewhere.

- Transcription, interpretation, typing and other secretarial and clerical assistance.
- Telephone, telex and other communications facilities; photocopying, printing and other office facilities.

The daily rate for the use of a hearing room at the Centre and other facilities (a conference room will usually be available for the use of parties in connection with an arbitration) is $1,800. One-third of the total payable for any booked period is payable at the time of making a reservation. The balance is payable on or before the date of the first hearing. There will be a charge of $600 in respect of days that are booked but unused subject to a minimum amount of the one-third sum payable on making a reservation being retained by the HKIAC. Other support services will be charged on an appropriate cost basis.

Note:
(a) Parties are jointly and severally liable for HKIAC fees.
(b) All invoices are payable upon presentation.
(c) Fees will be involved in Hong Kong dollars but may be paid in other convertible currencies at rates of exchange prevailing at the time of payment.
(d) The rates quoted above are those in force at the time of publication and may be varied from time to time.
(e) All figures quoted are in Hong Kong dollars, at the date of publication, May 1986, US$1.00 = HX$7.80.

MODEL CLAUSES

The Centre has adopted model clauses which those interested may wish to include in future contracts:

(a) "Any dispute, controversy, or claim arising out of or relating to this contract, or the breach, termination or invalidity thereof, shall be settled by arbitration in Hong Kong in accordance with the UNCITRAL Arbitration Rules in force at the date of this contract."

(b) "The appointing authority shall be administered by the Hong Kong International Arbitration Centre in accordance with its Procedures for Arbitration."

(d) "The parties agree to exclude any right of application or appeal to the Hong Kong Courts in connection with any question of law arising in the course of the arbitration or with respect to any award made."

(e) "The language(s) to be used in the arbitral proceedings shall be   ."

For domestic, i.e., Hong Kong, agreements the Centre recommends the inclusion of the following clause:

"Any dispute or difference arising out of or in connection with this contract shall be referred to and determined by arbitration at the Hong Kong International Arbitration Centre and in accordance with its Rules for Domestic Arbitration."

UNCITRAL ARBITRATION RULES

SECTION I – INTRODUCTORY RULES

Article 1 – Scope of Application

1. Where the parties to a contract have agreed in writing that disputes in relation to that contract shall be referred to arbitration under the UNCITRAL Arbitration Rules, then such disputes shall be settled in accordance with these Rules subject to such modification as the parties may agree in writing.

2. These Rules shall govern the arbitration except that where any of these Rules is in conflict with a provision of the law applicable to the arbitration from which the parties cannot derogate, that provision shall prevail.

Article 2 – Notice, Calculation of Periods of Time

1. For the purposes of these Rules, any notice, including a notification, communication or proposal, is deemed to have been received if it is physically delivered to the addressee or if it is delivered at his habitual residence, place of business or mailing address, or, if none of these can be found after making reasonable inquiry, then at the addressee's last-known residence or place of business. Notice shall be deemed to have been received on the day it is so delivered.

2. For the purposes of calculating a period of time under these Rules, such period shall begin to run on the day following the day when a notice, notification, communication or proposal is received. If the last day of such period is an official holiday or a non-business day at the residence or place of business of the addressee, the period is extended until the first business day which follows. Official holidays or non-business days occurring during the running of the period of time are included in calculating the period.

Article 3 – Notice of Arbitration

1. The party initiating recourse to arbitration (hereinafter called the "claimant") shall give to the other party (hereinafter called the "respondent") a notice of arbitration.

2. Arbitral proceedings shall be deemed to commence on the date on which the notice of arbitration is received by the respondent.

3. The notice of arbitration shall include the following:

(a) A demand that the dispute be referred to arbitration;

(b) The names and addresses of the parties;

(c) A reference to the arbitration clause or the separation arbitration agreement that is invoked;

(d) A reference to the contract out of or in relation to which the dispute arises;

(e) The general nature of the claim and an indication of the amount involved, if any;

(f) The relief or remedy sought;

(g) A proposal as to the number of arbitrators (i.e., one or three), if the parties have not previously agreed thereon.

4. The notice of arbitration may also include:

(a) The proposals for the appointments of a sole arbitrator and an appointing authority referred to in article 6, paragraph 1;

(b) The notification of the appointment of an arbitrator referred to in article 7;

(c) The statement of claim referred to in article 18.

Article 4 – Representation and Assistance

The parties may be represented or assisted by persons of their choice. The names and addresses of such persons must be communicated in writing to the other party; such communication must specify whether the appointment is being made for purposes of representation or assistance.

SECTION II – COMPOSITION OF THE ARBITRAL TRIBUNAL

Article 5 – Number of Arbitrators

If the parties have not previously agreed on the number of arbitrators (i.e., one or three), and if within fifteen days after the receipt by the respondent of the notice of arbitration the parties have not agreed that there shall be only one arbitrator, three arbitrators shall be appointed.

Article 6 – Appointment of Arbitrators (Articles 6 to 8)

1. If a sole arbitrator is to be appointed, either party may propose to the other:

(a) The names of one or more persons, one of whom would serve as the sole arbitrator; and

(b) If no appointing authority has been agreed upon by the parties, the name or names of one or more institutions or persons, one of whom would serve as appointing authority.

2. If within thirty days after receipt by a party of a proposal made in accordance with paragraph 1 the parties have not reached agreement on the choice of a sole arbitrator, the sole arbitrator shall be appointed by the appointing authority agreed upon by the parties. If no appointing authority has been agreed upon by the parties, or if the appointing authority agreed upon refuses to act or fails to appoint the arbitrator within sixty days of the receipt of a party's request therefor, either party may request the Secretary-General of the Permanent Court of Arbitration at The Hague to designate an appointing authority.

3. The appointing authority shall, at the request of one or the parties, appoint the sole arbitrator as promptly as possible. In making the appointment the appointing authority shall use the following list-procedure, unless both parties agree that the list-procedure should not be used or unless the appointing authority determines in its discretion that the use of the list-procedure is not appropriate for the case:

(a) At the request of one of the parties the appointing authority shall communicate to both parties an identical list containing at least three names;

(b) Within fifteen days after the receipt of this list, each party may return the list to the appointing authority after having deleted the name or names to which he objects and numbered the remaining names on the list in the order of his preference;

(c) After the expiration of the above period of time the appointing authority shall appoint the sole arbitrator from among the names approved on the lists returned to it and in accordance with the order of preference indicated by the parties;

(d) If for any reason the appointment cannot be made according to this procedure, the appointing authority may exercise its discretion in appointing the sole arbitrator.

4. In making the appointment, the appointing authority shall have regard to such considerations as are likely to secure the appointment of an independent and impartial arbitrator and shall take into account as well the advisability of appointing an arbitrator of a nationality other than the nationalities of the parties.

Article 7

1. If three arbitrators are to be appointed, each party shall appoint one arbitrator. The two arbitrators thus appointed shall choose the third arbitrator who will act as the presiding arbitrator of the tribunal.

2. If within thirty days after the receipt of a party's notification of the appointment of an arbitrator the other party has not notified the first party of the arbitrator he has appointed:

(a) The first party may request the appointing authority previously designated by the parties to appoint the second arbitrator; or

(b) If no such authority has been previously designated by the parties, or if the appointing authority previously designated refuses to act or fails to appoint the arbitrator within thirty days after receipt of a party's request therefor, the first party may request the Secretary-General of the Permanent Court of Arbitration at The Hague to designate the appointing authority. The first party may then request the appointing authority so designated to appoint the second arbitrator. In either case, the appointing authority may exercise its discretion in appointing the arbitrator.

3. If within thirty days after the appointment of the second arbitrator the two arbitrators have not agreed on the choice of the presiding arbitrator, the presiding arbitrator shall be

appointed by an appointing authority in the same way as a sole arbitrator would be appointed under article 6.

Article 8

1. When an appointing authority is requested to appoint an arbitrator pursuant to article 6 or article 7, the party which makes the request shall send to the appointing authority a copy of the notice of arbitration, a copy of the contract out of or in relation to which the dispute has arisen and a copy of the arbitration agreement if it is not contained in the contract. The appointing authority may require from either party such information as it deems necessary to fulfil its function.

2. Where the names of one or more persons are proposed for appointment as arbitrators, their full names, addresses and nationalities shall be indicated, together with a description of their qualifications.

Article 9 – Challenge of Arbitrators (Articles 9 to 12)

A prospective arbitrator shall disclose to those who approach him in connection with his possible appointment any circumstances likely to give rise to justifiable doubts as to his impartiality or independence. An arbitrator, once appointed or chosen, shall disclose such circumstances to the parties unless they have already been informed by him of these circumstances.

Article 10

1. Any arbitrator may be challenged if circumstances exist that give rise to justifiable doubts as to the arbitrator's impartiality or independence.

2. A party may challenge the arbitrator appointed by him only for reasons of which he becomes aware after the appointment has been made.

Article 11

1. A party who intends to challenge an arbitrator shall send notice of his challenge within fifteen days after the appointment of the challenged arbitrator has been notified to the challenging party or within fifteen days after the circumstances mentioned in articles 9 and 10 became known to that party.

2. The challenge shall be notified to the other party, to the arbitrator who is challenged and to the other members of the arbitral tribunal. The notification shall be in writing and shall state the reasons for the challenge.

3. When an arbitrator has been challenged by one party, the other party may agree to the challenge. The arbitrator may also, after the challenge, withdraw from his office. In neither case does this imply acceptance of the validity of the grounds for the challenge. In both cases the procedure provided in article 6 or 7 shall be used in full for the appointment of the substitute arbitrator, even if during the process of appointing the

challenged arbitrator a party had failed to exercise his right to appoint or to participate in the appointment.

Article 12

1. If the other party does not agree to the challenge and the challenged arbitrator does not withdraw, the decision on the challenge will be made:

(a) When the initial appointment was made by an appointing authority, by that authority;

(b) When the initial appointment was not made by an appointing authority, but an appointing authority has been previously designated, by that authority;

(c) In all other cases, by the appointing authority to be designated in accordance with the procedure for designating an appointing authority as provided for in article 6.

2. If the appointing authority sustains the challenge, a substitute arbitrator shall be appointed or chosen pursuant to the procedure applicable to the appointment or choice of an arbitrator as provided in articles 6 to 9 except that, when this procedure would call for the designation of an appointing authority, the appointment of the arbitrator shall be made by the appointing authority which decided on the challenge.

Article 13 – Replacement of an Arbitrator

1. In the event of the death or resignation of an arbitrator during the course of the arbitral proceedings, a substitute arbitrator shall be appointed or chosen pursuant to the procedure provided for in articles 6 to 9 that was applicable to the appointment or choice of the arbitrator being replaced.

2. In the event that an arbitrator fails to act or in the event of the *de jure* or *de facto* impossibility of his performing his functions, the procedure in respect of the challenge and replacement of an arbitrator as provided in the proceeding articles shall apply.

Article 14 – Repetition of Hearings in the Event of the Replacement of an Arbitrator

If under articles 11 to 13 the sole or presiding arbitrator is replaced, any hearings held previously shall be repeated; if any other arbitrator is replaced, such prior hearings may be repeated at the discretion of the arbitral tribunal.

SECTION III – ARBITRAL PROCEEDINGS

Article 15 – General Provisions

1. Subject to these Rules, the arbitral tribunal may conduct the arbitration in such manner as it considers appropriate, provided that the parties are treated with equality and that at any stage of the proceedings each party is given a full opportunity of presenting his case.

2. If either party so requests at any stage of the proceedings, the arbitral tribunal shall hold hearings for the presentation of evidence by witnesses, including expert witnesses, or for oral argument. In the absence of such a request, the arbitral tribunal shall decide whether to hold such hearings or whether the proceedings shall be conducted on the basis of documents and other materials.

3. All documents or information supplied to the arbitral tribunal by one party shall at the same time be communicated by that party to the other party.

Article 16 – Place of Arbitration

1. Unless the parties have agreed upon the place where the arbitration is to be held, such place shall be determined by the arbitral tribunal, having regard to the circumstances of the arbitration.

2. The arbitral tribunal may determine the locale of the arbitration within the country agreed upon by the parties. It may hear witnesses and hold meetings for consultation among its members at any place it deems appropriate, having regard to the circumstances of the arbitration.

3. The arbitral tribunal may meet at any place it deems appropriate for the inspection of goods, other property or documents. The parties shall be given sufficient notice to enable them to be present at such inspection.

4. The award shall be made at the place of arbitration.

Article 17 – Language

1. Subject to an agreement by the parties, the arbitral tribunal shall, promptly after its appointment, determine the language or languages to be used in the proceedings. This determination shall apply to the statement of claim, the statement of defence, and any further written statements and, if oral hearings take place, to the language or languages to be used in such hearings.

2. The arbitral tribunal may order that any documents annexed to the statement of claim or statement of defence, and any supplementary documents or exhibits submitted in the course of the proceedings, delivered in their original language, shall be accompanied by a translation into the language or languages agreed upon by the parties or determined by the arbitral tribunal.

Article 18 – Statement of Claim

1. Unless the statement of claim was contained in the notice of arbitration, within a period of time to be determined by the arbitral tribunal, the claimant shall communicate his statement of claim in writing to the respondent and to each of the arbitrators. A copy of the contract, and of the arbitration agreement if not contained in the contract, shall be annexed thereto.

2. The statement of claim shall include the following particulars:

(a) The names and addresses of the parties;

(b) A statement of the facts supporting the claim;

(c) The points at issue;

(d) The relief or remedy sought.

The claimant may annex to his statement of claim all documents he deems relevant or may add a reference to the documents or other evidence he will submit.

Article 19 – Statement of Defence

1. Within a period of time to be determined by the arbitral tribunal, the respondent shall communicate his statement of defence in writing to the claimant and to each of the arbitrators.

2. The statement of defence shall reply to the particulars (b), (c) and (d) of the statement of claim (article 18, para. 2). The respondent may annex to his statement the documents on which he relies for his defence or may add a reference to the documents or other evidence he will submit.

3. In his statement of defence, or at a later stage in the arbitral proceedings if the arbitral tribunal decides that the delay was justified under the circumstances, the respondent may make a counter-claim arising out of the same contract or rely on a claim arising out of the same contract for the purpose of a set-off.

4. The provisions of article 18, paragraph 2, shall apply to a counter-claim and a claim relied on for the purpose of a set-off.

Article 20 – Amendments to the Claim or Defense

During the course of the arbitral proceedings either party may amend or supplement his claim or defense unless the arbitral tribunal considers it inappropriate to allow such amendment having regard to the delay in making it or prejudice to the other party or any other circumstances. However, a claim may not be amended in such a manner that the amended claim falls outside the scope of the arbitration clause or separate arbitration agreement.

Article 21 – Pleas as to the Jurisdiction of the Arbitral Tribunal

1. The arbitral tribunal shall have the power to rule on objections that it has no jurisdiction, including any objections with respect to the existence or validity of the arbitration clause or of the separate arbitration agreement.

2. The arbitral tribunal shall have the power to determine the existence or the validity of the contract of which an arbitration clause forms a part. For the purposes of article 21, an

arbitration clause which forms part of a contract and which provides for arbitration under these Rules shall be treated as an agreement independent of the other terms of the contract. A decision by the arbitral tribunal that the contract is null and void shall not entail *ipso jure* the invalidity of the arbitration clause.

3. A plea that the arbitral tribunal does not have jurisdiction shall be raised not later than in the statement of defense or, with respect to a counterclaim, in the reply to the counterclaim.

4. In general, the arbitral tribunal should rule on a plea concerning its jurisdiction as a preliminary question. However, the arbitral tribunal may proceed with the arbitration and rule on such a plea in their first award.

Article 22 – Further Written Statements

The arbitral tribunal shall decide which further written statements, in addition to the statement of claim and the statement of defence, shall be required from the parties or may be presented by them and shall fix the periods of time for communicating such statements.

Article 23 – Periods of Time

The periods of time fixed by the arbitral tribunal for the communication of written statements (including the statement of claim and statement of defence) should not exceed forty-five days. However, the arbitral tribunal may extend the time-limits if it concludes that an extension is justified.

Article 24 – Evidence and Hearings (Articles 24 and 25)

1. Each party shall have the burden of proving the facts relied on to support his claim or defence.

2. The arbitral tribunal may, if it considers it appropriate, require a party to deliver to the tribunal and to the other party, within such a period of time as the arbitral tribunal shall decide, a summary of the documents and other evidence which that party intends to present in support of the facts in issue set out in his statement of claim or statement of defence.

3. At any time during the arbitral proceedings the arbitral tribunal may require the parties to produce documents, exhibits or other evidence within such a period of time as the tribunal shall determine.

Article 25

1. In the event of an oral hearing, the arbitral tribunal shall give the parties adequate advance notice of the date, time and place thereof.

2. If witnesses are to be heard, at least fifteen days before the hearing each party shall communicate to the arbitral tribunal and to the other party the names and addresses of the

witnesses he intends to present, the subject upon and the languages in which such witnesses will give their testimony.

3. The arbitral tribunal shall make arrangements for the translation of oral statements made at a hearing and for a record of the hearing if either is deemed necessary by the tribunal under the circumstances of the case, or if the parties have agreed thereto and have communicated such agreement to the tribunal at least fifteen days before the hearing.

4. Hearings shall be held *in camera* unless the parties agree otherwise. The arbitral tribunal may require the retirement of any witness or witnesses during the testimony of other witnesses. The arbitral tribunal is free to determine the manner in which witnesses are examined.

5. Evidence of witnesses may also be presented in the form of written statements signed by them.

6. The arbitral tribunal shall determine the admissibility, relevance, materiality and weight of the evidence offered.

Article 26 – Interim Measure of Protection

1. At the request of either party, that arbitral tribunal may take any interim measures it deems necessary in respect of the subject-matter of the dispute, including measures for the conservation of the goods forming the subject-matter in dispute, such as ordering their deposit with a third person or the sale of perishable goods.

2. Such interim measures may be established in the form of an interim award. The arbitral tribunal shall be entitled to require security for the costs of such measures.

3. A request for interim measures addressed by any party to a judicial authority shall not be deemed incompatible with the agreement to arbitrate, or as a waiver of that agreement.

Article 27 – Experts

1. The arbitral tribunal may appoint one or more experts to report to it, in writing, on specific issues to be determined by the tribunal. A copy of the expert's terms of reference, established by the arbitral tribunal, shall be communicated to the parties.

2. The parties shall give the expert any relevant information or produce for his inspection any relevant documents or goods that he may require of them. Any dispute between a party and such expert as to the relevance of the required information or production shall be referred to the arbitral tribunal for decision.

3. Upon receipt of the expert's report, the arbitral tribunal shall communicate a copy of the report to the parties who shall be given the opportunity to express, in writing, their opinion on the report. A party shall be entitled to examine any document on which the expert has relied in his report.

4. At the request of either party the expert, after delivery of the report, may be heard at a hearing where the parties shall have the opportunity to be present and to interrogate the expert. At this hearing either party may present expert witnesses in order to testify on the points at issue. The provisions of article 25 shall be applicable to such proceedings.

Article 28 – Default

1. If, within the period of time fixed by the arbitral tribunal, the claimant has failed to communicate his claim without showing sufficient cause for such failure, the arbitral tribunal shall issue an order for the termination of the arbitral proceedings. If, within the period of time fixed by the arbitral tribunal, the respondent has failed to communicate his statement of defence without showing sufficient cause for such failure, the arbitral tribunal shall order that the proceedings continue.

2. If one of the parties, duly notified under these Rules, fails to appear at a hearing, without showing sufficient cause for such failure, the arbitral tribunal may proceed with the arbitration.

3. If one of the parties, duly invited to produce documentary evidence, fails to do so within the established period of time, without showing sufficient cause for such failure, the arbitral tribunal may make the award on the evidence before it.

Article 29 – Closure of Hearings

1. The arbitral tribunal may inquire of the parties if they have any further proof to offer or witnesses to be heard or submissions to make and, if there are none, it may declare the hearings closed.

2. The arbitral tribunal may, if it considers it necessary owing to exceptional circumstances, decide, on its own motion or upon application of a party, to reopen the hearings at any time before the award is made.

Article 30 – Waiver of Rules

A party who knows that any provision of, or requirement under, these Rules has not been complied with and yet proceeds with the arbitration without promptly stating his objection to such non-compliance, shall be deemed to have waived his right to object.

SECTION IV – THE AWARD

Article 31 – Decisions

1. When there are three arbitrators, any award or other decision of the arbitral tribunal shall be made by a majority of the arbitrators.

2. In the case of questions of procedure, when there is no majority of when the arbitral tribunal so authorizes, the presiding arbitrator may decide on his own, subject to revisions, if any, by the arbitral tribunal.

Article 32 – Form of Effect of the Award

1. In addition to making a final award, the arbitral tribunal shall be entitled to make interim, interlocutory, or partial awards.

2. The award shall be made in writing and shall be final and binding on the parties. The parties undertake to carry out the award without delay.

3. The arbitral tribunal shall state the reasons upon which the award is based, unless the parties have agreed that no reasons are to be given.

4. An award shall be signed by the arbitrators and it shall contain the date on which and the place where the award was made. Where there are three arbitrators and one of them fails to sign, the award shall state the reason for the absence of the signature.

5. The award may be made public only with the consent of both parties.

6. Copies of the award signed by the arbitrators shall be communicated to the parties by the arbitral tribunal.

7. If the arbitration law of the country where the award is made requires that the award be filed or registered by the arbitral tribunal, the tribunal shall comply with this requirement within the period of time required by law.

Article 33 – Applicable Law, *Amiable Compositeur*

1. The arbitral tribunal shall apply the law designated by the parties as applicable to the substance of the dispute. Failing such designation by the parties, the arbitral tribunal shall apply the law determined by the conflict of laws rules which it considers applicable.

2. The arbitral tribunal shall decide as *amiable compositure* or *ex aequo et bono* only if the parties have expressly authorized the arbitral tribunal to do so and if the law applicable to the arbitral procedure permits such arbitration.

3. In all cases, the arbitral tribunal shall decide in accordance with the terms of the contract and shall take into account the usages of the trade applicable to the transaction.

Article 34 – Settlement or Other Grounds for Termination

1. If, before the award is made, the parties agree on a settlement of the dispute, the arbitral tribunal shall either issue an order for the termination of the arbitral proceedings or, if requested by both parties and accepted by the tribunal, record the settlement in the form of an arbitral award on agreed terms. The arbitral tribunal is not obliged to give reasons for such an award.

2. If, before the award is made, the continuation of the arbitral proceedings become unnecessary or impossible for any reason not mentioned in paragraph 1, the arbitral tribunal shall inform the parties of its intention to issue an order for the termination of the

proceedings. The arbitral tribunal shall have the power to issue such an order unless a party raises justifiable grounds for objection.

3. Copies of the order for termination of the arbitral proceedings or of the arbitral award on agreed terms, signed by the arbitrators, shall be communicated by the arbitral tribunal to the parties. Where an arbitral award on agreed terms is made, the provisions of article 32, paragraph 2 and 4 to 7, shall apply.

Article 35 – Interpretation of the Award

1. Within thirty days after the receipt of the award, either party, with notice to the other party, may request that the arbitral tribunal give an interpretation of the award.

2. The interpretation shall be given in writing within forty-five days after the receipt of the request. The interpretation shall form part of the award and the provisions of article 32, paragraphs 2 to 7, shall apply.

Article 36 – Correction of the Award

1. Within thirty days after the receipt of the award, either party, with notice to the other party, may request the arbitral tribunal to correct in the award any errors in computation, any clerical or typographical errors, or any errors of similar nature. The arbitral tribunal may within thirty days after the communication of the award make such corrections on its own initiative.

2. Such corrections shall be in writing, and the provisions of article 32, paragraphs 2 to 7, shall apply.

Article 37 – Additional Award

1. Within thirty days after the receipt of the award, either party, with notice to the other party, may request the arbitral tribunal to make an additional award as to claims presented in the arbitral proceedings but omitted from the award.

2. If the arbitral tribunal considers the request for an additional award to be justified and considered that the omission can be rectified without any further hearings or evidence, it shall complete its award within sixty days after the receipt of the request.

3. When an additional award is made, the provisions of article 32, paragraph 2 to 7, shall apply.

Article 38 – Costs (Articles 38 to 40)

The arbitral tribunal shall fix the costs of arbitration in its award. The term "costs" includes only:

(a) The fees of the arbitral tribunal to be stated separately as to each arbitrator and to be fixed by the tribunal itself in accordance with article 39;

(b) The travel and other expenses incurred by the arbitrators;

(c) The costs of expert advice and of other assistance required by the arbitral tribunal;

(d) The travel and other expenses of witnesses to the extent such expenses are approved by the arbitral tribunal;

(e) The costs for legal representation and assistance of the successful party if such costs were claimed during the arbitral proceedings, and only to the extent that the arbitral tribunal determines that the amount of such costs is reasonable;

(f) Any fees and expenses of the appointing authority as well as the expenses of the Secretary-General of the Permanent Court of Arbitration at The Hague.

Article 39

1. The fees of the arbitral tribunal shall be reasonable in amount, taking into account the amount in dispute, the complexity of the subject-matter, the time spent by the arbitrators and any other relevant circumstances of the case.

2. If an appointing authority has been agreed upon by the parties or designated by the Secretary-General of the Permanent Court of Arbitration at The Hague, and if that authority has issued a schedule of fees for arbitrators in international cases which it administers, the arbitral tribunal in fixing its fees shall take that schedule of fees into account to the extent that it considers appropriate in the circumstances of the case.

3. If such appointing authority has not issued a schedule of fees for arbitrators in international cases, any party may at any time request the appointing authority to furnish a statement setting forth the basis for establishing fees which is customarily followed in international cases in which the authority appoints arbitrators. If the appointing authority consents to provide such a statement, the arbitral tribunal in fixing its fees shall take such information into account to the extent that it considers appropriate in the circumstances of the case.

4. In cases referred to in paragraph 2 and 3, when a party so requests and the appointing authority consents to perform the function, the arbitral tribunal shall fix its fees only after consultation with the appointing authority which may make any comment it deems appropriate to the arbitral tribunal concerning the fees.

Article 40

1. Except as provided in paragraph 2, the costs of arbitration shall in principle be borne by the unsuccessful party. However, the arbitral tribunal may apportion each of such costs between the parties if it determines that apportionment is reasonable, taking into account the circumstances of the case.

2. With respect to the costs of legal representation and assistance referred to in article 38, paragraph *(e)*, the arbitral tribunal, taking into account the circumstances of the case,

shall be free to determine which party shall bear such costs or may apportion such costs between the parties if it determines that apportionment is reasonable.

3. When the arbitral tribunal issues an order for the termination of the arbitral proceedings or makes an award on agreed terms, it shall fix the costs of arbitration referred to in article 38 and article 39, paragraph 1, in the text of that order or award.

4. No additional fees may be charged by an arbitral tribunal for interpretation or correction or completion of its award under articles 35 to 37.

Article 41 – Deposit of Costs

1. The arbitral tribunal, on its establishment, may request each party to deposit an equal amount as an advance for the costs referred to in article 38, paragraphs *(a), (b)* and *(c).*

2. During the course of the arbitral proceedings the arbitral tribunal may request supplementary deposits from the parties.

3. If an appointing authority has been agreed upon by the parties or designated by the Secretary-General of the Permanent Court of Arbitration at The Hague, and when a party so requests and the appointing authority consents to perform the function, the arbitral tribunal shall fix the amounts of any deposits or supplementary deposits only after consultation with the appointing authority which may make any comments to the arbitral tribunal which it deems appropriate concerning the amount of such deposits and supplementary deposits.

4. If the required deposits are not paid in full within thirty days after the receipt of the request, the arbitral tribunal shall so inform the parties in order that one or another of them may make the required payment. If such payment is not made, the arbitral tribunal may order the suspension or termination of the arbitral proceedings.

5. After the award has been made, the arbitral tribunal shall render an accounting to the parties of the deposits received and return any unexpended balance to the parties.

THE JAPAN COMMERCIAL ARBITRATION ASSOCIATION ("JCAA") ARBITRATION RULES

Effective October 1, 1997

JCAA ARBITRATION RULES

CHAPTER I – GENERAL PROVISIONS

Rule 1 – Purpose

1. The purpose of these Rules shall be to provide such matters as are necessary for arbitration at The Japan Commercial Arbitration Association (hereinafter the "Association").

2. Arbitration under the UNCITRAL Arbitration Rules adopted by the United Nations Commission on International Trade Law on 28 April, 1976 and the Administrative and Procedural Rules for Arbitration under the UNCITRAL Arbitration Rules shall be governed otherwise.

Rule 2 – Application of these Rules

1. These Rules shall apply where the parties have agreed to submit their dispute to arbitration under the Rules of the Association or simply arbitration at the Association (hereinafter the "arbitration agreement").

2. These Rules shall apply if the parties agree, in writing, during the course of arbitral proceedings provided for in Rule 1, Paragraph 2, to conduct such arbitral proceedings pursuant to these Rules. In the case of such an agreement, the arbitral proceedings already conducted shall remain valid.

Rule 3 – Interpretation of these Rules

If any question arises concerning the interpretation of these Rules, the Association's interpretation shall prevail; provided that the interpretation of an arbitral tribunal shall, after such interpretation is made, prevail over that of the Association in the arbitration case before such tribunal.

Rule 4 – Arbitration Agreement

1. Arbitration agreements shall be made in writing.

2. When the parties have entered into an arbitration agreement, these Rules shall be deemed incorporated in such agreement; provided that the parties may agree otherwise to the extent that such agreement does not violate the spirit of these Rules.

Rule 5 – Arbitral Tribunal

1. Arbitration under these Rules shall be conducted by an arbitral tribunal composed of one or more arbitrators who have been appointed pursuant to the provisions of Rules 20 through 26 (including the application *mutatis mutandis* of Rule 26 under the provisions of Rule 41, Paragraph 2), Rule 29 and Rule 57.

2. If the arbitral tribunal is composed of more than one arbitrator, the arbitrators may, after all of them have been appointed, agree upon and appoint a presiding arbitrator from among themselves.

Rule 6 – Decision of Arbitral Tribunal

1. If the number of arbitrators is more than one, decisions of the arbitral tribunal, including the arbitral award, shall be made by a majority of votes of the arbitrators.

2. If the voting of the arbitral tribunal results in a tie, the presiding arbitrator, if one has been appointed, shall cast the deciding vote.

Rule 7 – Secretariat and Tribunal Clerk

1. Clerical work with respect to arbitration under these Rules shall be conducted by the Secretariat of the Association (hereinafter the "secretariat").

2. Clerical work of the arbitral tribunal shall be conducted by a staff member of the Association who has been appointed by the Association as the clerk in charge of such clerical work (hereinafter the "clerk in charge").

Rule 8 – Panel of Arbitrators

The Association shall prepare and maintain a panel of arbitrators to facilitate the appointment of arbitrators.

Rule 9 – Representation and Assistance

A party may be represented or assisted by any person of its choice in the proceedings under these Rules. Subsequent to such selection, the arbitral tribunal may, for good cause, reject a party's selection of such representative or assistant.

Rule 10 – Definition

1. "Basic Date" under these Rules shall be the date after the lapse of three (3) weeks from the date on which the Association sends a notice of acceptance of the request for arbitration provided for in Rule 13, Paragraph 1; provided that, if the respondent proves that it received such notice of acceptance after such date, the date on which the respondent received such notice shall be the Basic Date.

2. "Party or parties" under these Rules shall be either a claimant or respondent or both. Multiple claimants or respondents shall be deemed to be one party for purposes of the appointment of arbitrators.

3. "Document or documents" under these Rules shall include any document in which the contents of a communication have been recorded mechanically by way of telex, facsimile or other means.

4. “Agreement in writing” under these Rules shall mean the meeting of minds acknowledged in writing and the document need not be a single instrument.

Rule 11 – Means of Communication

Communication during arbitration under these Rules shall be by way of a document or other means of communication followed by a document.

CHAPTER II – REQUEST FOR ARBITRATION

Rule 12 – Request for Arbitration

1. To request the initiation of arbitral proceedings, the claimant shall submit to the Association a written request for arbitration setting forth the following:

(1) a demand that the dispute be referred to arbitration under these Rules;

(2) a reference to the arbitration agreement that is invoked;

(3) the full personal or corporate names of the parties and their addresses;

(4) if the claimant is represented by an agent, the name and address of such agent;

(5) the relief or remedy claimed;

(6) a summary of the dispute; and

(7) the basis for the claim and the manner or method of proof.

2. The claimant shall submit to the Association, together with the written request for arbitration, a copy of the arbitration clause or the separate arbitration agreement containing the arbitration agreement provided for in (2) of the preceding Paragraph.

3. If the claimant is represented by an agent in the arbitral proceedings, such agent shall submit a power of attorney to the Association together with the written request for arbitration.

4. The claimant shall, when it requests the initiation of arbitral proceedings, pay the request fee and the administrative fee provided for in the Arbitration Fee Regulations of the Association. If the claimant fails to pay such request fee and/or administrative fee, the Association may treat the request for arbitration as if it had not been made and return the written request for arbitration to the claimant with notification to such effect.

5. Arbitral proceedings shall be deemed to be initiated on the date on which the Association receives the written request for arbitration.

Rule 13 – Acceptance and Notification of Request for Arbitration

1. The Association, upon confirmation that the request for arbitration has been made in conformity with the provisions of Paragraphs 1 through 3 of the preceding Rule, shall notify, without delay, the claimant and the respondent of the acceptance of the request for arbitration. Copies of the written request for arbitration and the arbitration agreement shall be attached to the notice sent to the respondent.

2. The Association shall designate one of its offices as the secretariat in charge of administrative services and give notice thereof to each party when the Association notifies the parties of the acceptance of the request for arbitration provided for in the preceding Paragraph.

Rule 14 – Request for Separation of Arbitral Proceedings

1. If a request for arbitration against multiple respondents is submitted and any respondent submits a written request for separation of arbitral proceedings within three (3) weeks from the Basic Date and prior to the establishment of the arbitral tribunal, the claimant shall submit a new request for arbitration against each of such respondent and the other respondent(s).

2. All newly submitted requests for arbitration under the preceding Paragraph shall be deemed to have been submitted on the date on which the Association received the initial request for arbitration; provided that the Basic Date shall be determined based on the newly submitted requests for arbitration.

3. The provisions of Paragraph 1 shall not preclude the application of Rule 41.

Rule 15 – Answer

1. The respondent shall, within four (4) weeks from the Basic Date, submit to the Association a written answer setting forth the following:

(1) the full personal or corporate names of the parties and their addresses;

(2) if the respondent is represented by an agent, the name and address of such agent;

(3) confirmation or denial of the claims;

(4) a summary of the dispute; and

(5) the basis for the answer and the manner or method of proof.

2. If the respondent is represented by an agent in the arbitral proceedings, such agent shall submit a power of attorney to the Association together with the written answer.

3. Subsequent to submission of the written answer, the Association shall send, without delay, a copy thereof to the other party or parties and, if an arbitrator has or arbitrators have been appointed, to such arbitrator or arbitrators.

4. If the written answer contains a counterclaim, the provisions of the following Rule shall apply to such counterclaim.

Rule 16 – Counterclaim

1. The respondent may, only within six (6) weeks from the Basic Date, submit a counterclaim that is related to the claimant's claim(s) and covered by the same arbitration agreement. The arbitral tribunal shall examine any such counterclaim together with the claimant's claim(s).

2. The provisions of Rules 12, 13 and 15 shall apply *mutatis mutandis* to any counterclaim provided for in the preceding Paragraph.

Rule 17 – Amendments to Claims or Counterclaims

1. Either the claimant or the counterclaimant may, to the extent that the claim and counterclaim are covered by the same arbitration agreement, amend or supplement its claim (which shall hereinafter include a counterclaim for purposes of this Rule) by submitting a written request for amendment to the Association; provided that, after the establishment of the arbitral tribunal, such claimant or counterclaimant shall submit a written application for approval of such amendment to the arbitral tribunal and obtain its approval thereof.

2. The arbitral tribunal shall hear the other party's opinion before giving the approval provided for in the preceding Paragraph.

3. The arbitral tribunal shall not give any approval provided for in Paragraph 1 if it considers it inappropriate to approve such amendment in view of the substantial delay in conducting the arbitral proceedings or prejudice to the other party that such amendment will cause or any other circumstances.

4. The provisions of Rules 15 or 16 shall apply *mutatis mutandis* to an answer to or counterclaim with respect to an amended claim; provided that such answer or counterclaim shall be submitted within three (3) weeks from the date on which the secretariat or the clerk in charge sends written notice of such amendment to such other party.

Rule 18 – Number of Copies of Documents to be Submitted

1. The number of copies of documents to be submitted pursuant to the provisions of Rule 12, Paragraph 1 and Rule 15, Paragraph 1 (including the application *mutatis mutandis* of such provisions under Rule 16, Paragraph 2 and Paragraph 4 of the preceding Rule) and the provisions of Paragraph 1 of the preceding Rule shall be equal to the number of

arbitrators (three (3) if not yet determined) and the other party or parties plus one (1); provided that one copy of a power of attorney shall suffice.

Rule 19 – Withdrawal of Request for Arbitration

1. The claimant may, within thirty (30) days after the initiation of arbitral proceedings and before the appointment of any arbitrator, withdraw its request for arbitration upon written notice.

2. Except as provided in the preceding Paragraph, the claimant may withdraw its request for arbitration only with the written consent of the respondent.

3. Withdrawal of the request for arbitration shall become effective when the written notice of withdrawal and, in the case provided for in the preceding Paragraph, the respondent's written consent thereto reach the Association.

CHAPTER III – APPOINTMENT OF ARBITRATORS

Rule 20 – Qualification of Arbitrators

No person having a beneficial interest in the case under arbitration shall be an arbitrator.

Rule 21 – Agreement of Parties

1. The parties may, by written agreement, appoint one or more arbitrators or determine the number, the method or the period of time (or all of the above) of appointment of the arbitrators.

2. The parties shall notify the Association, within, at the latest, three (3) weeks from the Basic Date, of the contents of an agreement provided for in the preceding Paragraph.

Rule 22 – Appointment of Arbitrators where the Parties have Determined the Method of Appointment

1. If the parties have entered into an agreement provided for in the latter part of Paragraph 1 of the preceding Rule, an arbitrator shall be appointed pursuant to such agreement.

2. If one or both of the parties fails or fail to notify the Association of the appointment of an arbitrator, as provided for in the preceding Paragraph, within the period of time for appointment agreed upon by the parties or, if the parties have not agreed upon such period of time, within four (4) weeks from the earlier of the date on which the notice provided for in Paragraph 2 of the preceding Rule reaches the Association or the date provided for in the same Paragraph, the Association shall appoint such arbitrator. If the Association is to make such an appointment, it shall respect, to the extent possible, the contents of the agreement provided for in Paragraph 1 of the preceding Rule.

3. If the Association appoints an arbitrator under the provisions of the preceding Paragraph, the provisions of Rule 24, Paragraph 3 shall apply *mutatis mutandis*.

4. If the parties have not entered into an agreement provided for in the latter part of Paragraph 1 of the preceding Rule with respect to the number of arbitrators, such number shall be determined pursuant to the provisions of the following Rule.

Rule 23 – Number of Arbitrators

If the parties fail to notify the Association, within three (3) weeks from the Basic Date, of their agreement with respect to the number of arbitrators, such number shall be one (1); provided that if either party requests in writing, within four (4) weeks from the Basic Date, that such number be three (3) and the Association determines that such request is appropriate, such number shall be three (3).

Rule 24 – Appointment of Arbitrator (Single Arbitrator)

1. If the number of arbitrators is one (1) under the agreement provided for in Rule 21 or the provisions of the preceding Rule, the parties shall agree upon and appoint an arbitrator.

2. If the parties fail to notify the Association of the appointment of an arbitrator provided for in the preceding Paragraph within four (4) weeks from the date when the notice provided for in Rule 21, Paragraph 2 reaches the Association if the number of arbitrators fixed under an agreement provided for in Rule 21 is one (1) or the last day of the third week immediately following the Basic Date if the number of arbitrators fixed under the provisions of the preceding Rule is one (1), the Association shall appoint such arbitrator. If the Association is to make such an appointment, it shall respect, to the extent possible, the contents of an agreement, if one exists, provided for in Rule 21, Paragraph 1.

3. If the Association is to appoint an arbitrator pursuant to the provisions of the preceding Paragraph, the Association shall give due consideration to a written request, submitted by either party within one (1) week from the date on which it is determined that the Association shall make such appointment, that a person of a different nationality from those of the parties be appointed as such arbitrator.

Rule 25 – Appointment of Arbitrators (More than One)

1. If the parties agree under the provisions of Rule 21 that there shall be more than one arbitrator but not on the method of appointment or if the number of arbitrators is fixed at three (3) pursuant to the proviso of Rule 23, each party shall appoint the same number of arbitrators, the sum of which shall not exceed the number of arbitrators thus fixed, and if the number thus fixed is an odd number, the arbitrators appointed thereby shall appoint one (1) more arbitrator.

2. The parties shall appoint, within four (4) weeks from the date on which they have given notice under the provisions of Rule 21, Paragraph 2 or from the date on which the number of arbitrators is fixed at three (3) pursuant to the proviso of Rule 23, the same number of arbitrators which each party should appoint pursuant to the provisions of the preceding Paragraph.

3. If either party fails to appoint an arbitrator or arbitrators within the period of time provided for in the preceding Paragraph, the Association shall appoint such arbitrator or arbitrators.

4. If the number of arbitrators is odd and the arbitrators appointed by the parties or the arbitrators appointed pursuant to the provisions of the preceding Paragraph fail to appoint one (1) more arbitrator within three (3) weeks from the date on which the last of such arbitrators was appointed, the Association shall appoint such arbitrator.

5. If the Association is to make the appointment under the provisions of the preceding Paragraph, the provisions of Paragraph 3 of the preceding Rule shall apply *mutatis mutandis.*

Rule 26 – Appointment of Arbitrators where Third Party Participates in Proceedings

1. If, prior to the establishment of an arbitral tribunal, a third party participates or is allowed to participate in arbitral proceedings under the provisions of Rule 40, one or more arbitrators shall be appointed by agreement of the claimant, the respondent and such third party.

2. If the appointment of the number of arbitrators fixed by the agreement provided for in the preceding Paragraph has not been completed within three (3) weeks from the date on which such third party has participated in arbitral proceedings, the Association shall appoint the arbitrator(s) yet to be appointed.

3. If the number of arbitrators has not been agreed upon by the date fixed under the provisions of the preceding Paragraph, the Association shall appoint the number of arbitrator(s) determined by the Association.

Rule 27 – Notice of Appointment of Arbitrator

1. Upon appointment of an arbitrator by a party or the arbitrators, such party or arbitrators shall, without delay, submit to the Association a written notice of appointment of arbitrator setting forth such arbitrator's name, address and occupation, together with such arbitrator's written acceptance of appointment. The Association shall, without delay, send a copy of such notice to the other party and the arbitrator(s) already appointed.

2. Upon appointment of an arbitrator by the Association, it shall, without delay, notify the parties and the arbitrator(s) already appointed of such arbitrator's name, address and occupation.

Rule 28 – Allocation of Expenses of Non-resident Arbitrator

1. If a party has appointed an arbitrator who is not resident in Japan, such party shall bear the expenses required due to such arbitrator's non-residence; provided that the arbitral tribunal may allocate such expenses in a manner different therefrom.

2. If the Association has, or the arbitrators have, appointed an arbitrator who is not resident in Japan, the arbitral tribunal shall allocate such expenses in its arbitral award.

Rule 29 – Replacement of Arbitrator

1. If an arbitrator resigns or dies, the Association shall, without delay, notify the parties and the remaining arbitrator(s) thereof.

2. If the arbitrator who resigns or dies is one appointed by a party or parties or the remaining arbitrators, the party or parties or the remaining arbitrators shall appoint a substitute arbitrator within three (3) weeks from the date on which such party or parties or such arbitrators receive the notice provided for in the preceding Paragraph. If the arbitrator who resigns or dies is one appointed by the Association, the Association shall appoint a substitute arbitrator within three (3) weeks from the date on which it learns of such resignation or death.

3. If such party or parties or arbitrators fails or fail to appoint a substitute arbitrator within the period of time provided for in the preceding Paragraph, the Association shall appoint such substitute arbitrator.

Rule 30 – Removal of Arbitrator

1. The Association may remove any arbitrator who fails to perform its duties or unduly delays in the performance of its duties, or is legally or actually unable to perform its duties.

2. The provisions of Paragraph 2 of the preceding Rule shall apply *mutatis mutandis* to the appointment of a substitute arbitrator.

CHAPTER IV – ARBITRAL PROCEEDINGS

SECTION I – EXAMINATION PROCEEDINGS

Rule 31 – Supervision of Examination Proceedings

1. The examination proceedings, including hearings, shall be conducted under the supervision of the arbitral tribunal.

2. The arbitral tribunal shall treat the parties equally and give each party sufficient opportunity to state and prove its case and present a defense against the other party's case.

Rule 32 – Hearings

1. The date and place of hearings shall be decided by the arbitral tribunal upon consultation with the parties. If a hearing lasts more than one (1) day, it shall be held on consecutive days, to the extent possible.

2. After the date and place of hearing have been decided, the clerk in charge shall, without delay, notify the parties thereof. One notice shall suffice even if hearings are held on consecutive days.

3. Oral argumentations on the law and the facts and applications to present evidence and examination thereof shall occur at hearings.

4. The date of a hearing shall be changed at the request of both parties. In the event that one of the parties requests that the date of a hearing be changed, the arbitral tribunal may change such date only if it determines that there are unavoidable circumstances.

5. The request provided for in the preceding Paragraph shall be made in writing, unless made at a hearing.

Rule 33 – Submission of Written Statements

1. Each party may submit to the arbitral tribunal, at hearings or otherwise, written statements setting forth such party's case on the law and the facts (hereinafter the "written statements"). The arbitral tribunal may urge the submission of written statements.

2. Any party submitting written statements shall submit to the Association a number of copies thereof equal to the number of arbitrators and parties. The clerk in charge shall keep one copy for the record and, without delay, deliver personally or send one copy each to the arbitrators and parties (except the party submitting such written statements).

3. The arbitral tribunal shall confirm at hearings the receipt of the written statements submitted otherwise than at a hearing.

Rule 34 – Clarification of the Case

1. The arbitral tribunal may, to assist it in understanding the case, require a party to explain such party's case or conduct an on-site inspection or investigation in the presence of the parties.

Rule 35 – Examination of Evidence

1. Each party shall have the burden of proving the facts relied on to support such party's claim or defense.

2. The arbitral tribunal may, when it deems it necessary, examine evidence that a party has not applied to present.

3. Such examination of evidence may be made other than at a hearing. If the arbitral tribunal decides to examine evidence other than at a hearing, the parties shall be given the opportunity to be present.

4. The arbitral tribunal is not authorized to administer an oath to any witness or expert.

5. The arbitral tribunal may, when it deems it necessary or when there has been a petition from a party, refer inquiries to, and request responses from, public or private bodies. The arbitral tribunal shall disclose responses thus obtained to the parties.

Rule 36 – Application to Present Evidence

1. A party may apply to present evidence by submitting any of the following documents to the arbitral tribunal:

(1) application for documentary evidence (a document explaining the documentary evidence attached thereto);

(2) application to examine a witness (a written application, specifying the witness and the matters with respect to which such witness is to be examined, to examine a witness); or

(3) application for an expert opinion or verification (a written application for an expert opinion or verification setting forth the matters for which an expert opinion is required or the items to be verification and the method thereof).

2. An application to present evidence may be made other than at a hearing.

3. Any party submitting any of the documents provided for in Paragraph 1 shall submit to the Association a number of copies thereof equal to the number of arbitrators and parties. The clerk in charge shall keep one of the copies for the record and promptly deliver personally or send one copy each to the arbitrators and the parties (except the party submitting such document).

4. A party, except the party who has applied to present evidence, may submit to the arbitral tribunal a document setting forth its views with respect to the application to present evidence. If a party does submit such a document, the provisions of the preceding two (2) Paragraphs shall apply *mutatis mutandis.*

5. The arbitral tribunal may, any time after the lapse of a reasonable period of time necessary for the document provided for in Paragraph 4 to be submitted, determine whether to adopt or reject the application to present evidence. After the arbitral tribunal makes such determination, the clerk in charge shall, without delay, notify the parties of the result thereof.

6. The arbitral tribunal shall, at a hearing, confirm its receipt of documents provided for in Paragraphs 1 and 4 that are submitted other than at a hearing and determine whether to adopt or reject any applications to present evidence (or, if already determined pursuant to the provisions of the preceding Paragraph, confirm such determination).

Rule 37 – Principle of Appearance by the Parties

1. Hearings shall in principle be held in the presence of both parties.

2. If one or both parties fails or fail to appear without good cause, a hearing may be held in its or their absence; provided that, if both of the parties fail to appear, the examination proceedings may not be terminated on the date when such hearing is held.

3. If one of the parties fails to appear, the examination proceedings may be conducted based on the allegations and proof of the party who has appeared.

Rule 38 – Allocation of the Cost of Examining Evidence and Other Expenses

The necessary costs incurred to examine evidence, make inquiries and conduct inspections or investigations under the provisions of Rule 34 shall, if such expense was the result of an order by the arbitral tribunal, be equally borne by the parties and, if such expense was the result of a petition by a party, be borne by such party; provided that, notwithstanding the foregoing, the arbitral tribunal may reallocate expenses in view of the circumstances.

Rule 39 – Assignment of Arbitrator's Authority

The arbitral tribunal may, when it deems it necessary and upon obtaining the consent of the parties, cause one or more of the arbitrators constituting the arbitral tribunal to examine witnesses, make verifications, conduct inspections or investigations under the provisions of Rule 34 or mediate a settlement.

Rule 40 – Participation in Proceedings

1. Any person who is not a party to a particular arbitration may, upon the consent of such person and all the parties to such arbitration, participate in such arbitration as a claimant or be allowed to participate therein as a respondent.

2. If the participation in the arbitration provided for in the preceding Paragraph occurs before the establishment of the arbitral tribunal, the arbitrators shall be appointed subject to the provisions of Rule 26 and, if such participation occurs after the establishment of the arbitral tribunal, the composition thereof shall not be affected.

3. Notwithstanding that the consent provided for in Paragraph 1 has been given, the arbitral tribunal may deny participation in the arbitration if the arbitral tribunal determines that such participation will delay the arbitral proceedings or for any other proper reason.

4. The provisions of Rule 12 shall apply *mutatis mutandis* to an application for participation in the arbitration; provided that the administrative fee mentioned in Rule 12, Paragraph 4 shall be repaid if such participation is denied.

Rule 41 – Examination of Multiple Requests for Arbitration in the Same Proceedings

1. If the Association or the arbitral tribunal determines that it is necessary to consolidate multiple requests for arbitration that contain claims that are essentially mutually related, the arbitral tribunal, after obtaining the written consent of all the relevant parties, may examine such cases together in the same proceedings; provided that, if multiple requests for arbitration arise out of the same arbitration agreement, no consent of the parties is necessary.

2. If it is determined, pursuant to the provisions of the preceding Paragraph, that multiple requests for arbitration are to be disposed of in the same proceedings, the provisions of Paragraph 2 of the preceding Rule shall apply *mutatis mutandis* to the appointment of arbitrators.

Rule 42 – Closed Proceedings, Obligation of Confidentiality

1. Arbitral proceedings and records thereof shall be closed to the public.

2. The arbitrators, the staff of the Association, the parties and their representatives or assistants shall not disclose facts related to arbitration cases or facts learned through arbitration cases; provided that disclosure may be made subject to the conditions provided in a consent of the arbitral tribunal.

Rule 43 – Record of Hearings and Making a Stenographic Transcript

1. The clerk in charge may, subject to the consent of the arbitral tribunal, make tape-recordings or video-recordings of hearings.

2. The clerk in charge shall, when the arbitral tribunal has so ordered or a party has so requested, arrange for the making of a stenographic transcript. Such order or request shall, in principle, be made not less than three (3) weeks before the date of the hearing at which stenography is required.

3. The cost of making a stenographic transcript shall, if ordered by the arbitral tribunal, be borne equally by each party or, if ordered at a party's request, be borne by the requesting party; provided that the arbitral tribunal may, in view of the circumstances, allocate such cost among the parties.

Rule 44 – Interpretation and Translation

1. The clerk in charge shall, when the arbitral tribunal has so ordered or a party has so requested, arrange for interpreting. Such order or request shall, in principle, be made not less than three (3) weeks before the date when interpreting is required.

2. The provisions of Paragraph 3 of the preceding Rule shall apply *mutatis mutandis* to the cost of interpreting.

3. The provisions of the preceding two (2) Paragraphs shall apply *mutatis mutandis* to the translation of documents.

Rule 45 – Conclusion and Reopening of Examination Proceedings

1. The arbitral tribunal may decide to conclude the examination upon determining that the proceedings have matured enough for the arbitral tribunal to render an arbitral award or that the proceedings should be terminated because it is impossible to continue. If such decision is made other than at a hearing, an appropriate period of time for advance notice shall be provided.

2. The arbitral tribunal shall declare the proceedings closed upon determining that the proceedings should be terminated and concluding the examination. The provisions applied to arbitral awards shall apply *mutatis mutandis* to such declaration.

3. The arbitral tribunal may, if it deems it necessary, reopen the examination. The arbitral tribunal shall, if it decides to reopen the examination, promptly notify the parties in writing of such decision and the reasons therefor.

4. An examination shall, in principle, not be reopened after the lapse of three (3) weeks from the date of the decision to conclude the examination.

Rule 46 – Right to Object

A party who knows or ought to know that the arbitral proceedings have not been conducted properly and who fails to object without delay, shall be deemed to have waived its right to object; provided that no party shall be deemed to have waived any right that it cannot waive.

Rule 47 – Examination Proceedings only on Documents

1. The parties may, at any time, by written agreement, request examination based only on documents. If the parties make such a request, the proceedings already conducted shall remain valid.

2. If it is a violation of the spirit of the provisions of these Rules to apply them to examination proceedings based only on documents, the arbitral tribunal's determination shall prevail.

SECTION II – ARBITRAL AWARD

Rule 48 – Time of Arbitral Award

1. Once the arbitral tribunal has determined that the proceedings have matured enough for it to render an arbitral award and concluded the examination, the arbitral tribunal shall make an arbitral award within five (5) weeks from the date of such conclusion; provided that the arbitral tribunal may, if it deems it necessary in view of the complexities of the case or for any other reason, extend such period of time to an appropriate period of not more than eight (8) weeks.

2. The arbitral tribunal shall, upon conclusion of the examination pursuant to the preceding Paragraph, notify the parties of the period of time during which it shall make an arbitral award.

Rule 49 – Aritral Award

1. The arbitral award shall state the following and bear the signature and seal of each arbitrator; provided that the statement of Item (4) below shall be omitted if the parties have agreed that no statement is necessary and in the case provided for in the following Paragraph and the reason for such omission shall be set forth in the arbitral award:

(1) the full personal or corporate names of the parties and their addresses;

(2) if a party is represented by an agent, the name and address of such agent;

(3) the text of the award;

(4) the reason for the award; and

(5) the date of the award.

2. If the arbitral tribunal deems it appropriate, it may, at the request of the parties reaching a settlement during the course of the arbitral proceedings, set forth the contents of any such settlement in its arbitral award.

3. The arbitral tribunal shall set forth in the text of its arbitral award the total amount and the allocation of the administrative fee, the hearing fee, the necessary expenses incurred during the proceedings and the arbitrators' remuneration and shall, if there is a party who has deposited an amount of money less than the amount allocated in the text of the arbitral award, set forth an order to the effect that the balance shall be paid to the other party.

4. If there are more than one arbitrator and an arbitrator fails to sign and affix its seal to the arbitral award, the arbitral tribunal shall set forth the reasons for such failure in the arbitral award.

Rule 50 – Service and Deposit of Arbitral Award

1. The clerk in charge shall serve an authenticated copy of the arbitral award on each party by hand delivery, by delivery-certified registered mail or any other method proving receipt.

2. Service under the preceding Paragraph shall occur after the fees, the necessary expenses incurred during the proceedings and the arbitrators' remuneration have been fully paid to the Association.

3. After serving authenticated copies of the arbitral award, the clerk in charge shall, without delay, deposit the original text of the arbitral award with a court of appropriate jurisdiction together with certificates of service.

Rule 51 – Interlocutory Award

The arbitral tribunal may, when it deems it appropriate, make an interlocutory award to decide a dispute arising during the course of the arbitral proceedings. The provisions of Rule 49, Paragraph 1 and Rule 50, Paragraph 1 shall apply *mutatis mutandis* to such interlocutory award; provided that the statement of a reason for the interlocutory award may be dispensed with.

CHAPTER V – EXPEDITED PROCEDURES

Rule 52 – Application of Expedited Procedures

1. In any case where the amount and economic value of the claimant's claim are not more than ¥20,000,000, arbitration shall be conducted under the provisions set forth in this Chapter; provided that the provisions set forth in this Chapter shall not apply to either of the following cases:

(1) if the parties notify the Association, within two (2) weeks from the Basic Date provided for in Rule 54, of their agreement that they shall not submit their dispute to the Expedited Procedures;

(2) if the parties notify the Association, within two (2) weeks from the Basic Date provided for in Rule 54, of their agreement that the number of arbitrators shall be more than one (1); or

(3) if a counterclaim is submitted pursuant to the provisions set forth in Rule 55 and the amount and/or economic value of such counterclaim exceed ¥20,000,000.

2. The amount of interest and other fruits, compensation for damages, penalty for breach of contract and expenses incidental to a principal claim shall not be included in either the amount or the economic value of the claim provided for in the preceding Paragraph.

3. Where the economic value of a claim cannot be calculated or its calculation is extremely difficult, or where there is a dispute between the parties concerning such economic value, the economic value provided for in Paragraph 1 shall be deemed to exceed ¥20,000,000.

Rule 53 – Provisions applied to Expedited Procedures

1. The Expedited Procedures shall be conducted as provided for in Rules 54 through 61.

2. For matters not provided for in this Chapter, the provisions of the other Chapters shall apply.

Rule 54 – Basic Date

Notwithstanding the provisions of Rule 10, Paragraph 1, "Basic Date" shall, under this Chapter, be the date after the lapse of one (1) week from the date on which the Association sends a notice of acceptance of the request for arbitration provided for in Rule 13, Paragraph 1; provided that, if the respondent proves that it received such notice of acceptance after such date, the date on which the respondent received such notice shall be the Basic Date.

Rule 55 – Time Limit of Couterclaim

If the amount and economic value of the claimant's claim provided for in Rule 52 are not more than ¥20,000,000, the respondent may, only within two (2) weeks from the Basic Date provided for in Rule 54, submit its counterclaim provided for in Rule 16.

Rule 56 – Prohibition against Amendments to Claims or Counterclaims

Neither the claimant nor the counterclaimant may amend or supplement its claim and counterclaim.

Rule 57 – Appointment of Arbitrators

1. The arbitral tribunal shall consist of a sole arbitrator.

2. The parties shall agree upon and appoint an arbitrator within four (4) weeks from the Basic Date provided for in Rule 54.

3. If the parties fail to notify the Association of the appointment of an arbitrator within the period of time provided for in the preceding Paragraph, the Association shall appoint such arbitrator.

4. If the Association is to appoint an arbitrator pursuant to the provisions of the preceding Paragraph, the Association shall give due consideration to a written request, submitted by either party within five (5) weeks from the Basic Date provided for in Rule 54, that a person of a different nationality from those of the parties be appointed as such arbitrator.

5. The provisions of Rules 21 through 26 shall not apply to the Expedited Procedures.

Rule 58 – Restriction against Hearings

The arbitral tribunal may hold a hearing for one (1) day only; provided that an additional one (1) day may be provided if unavoidable.

Rule 59 – Time Limit of Arbitral Award

1. The arbitral tribunal shall make an arbitral award within three (3) months after the establishment of the arbitral tribunal.

2. Notwithstanding the provisions of the preceding Paragraph, the Association may extend such time limit if the arbitrator and all the parties so agree or if the Association

determines that the arbitrator is unable to make an arbitral award within the time limit for its mental and/or physical troubles or other reason for which the arbitrator is incompetent to perform the arbitrator's duties; provided that, in either case, the extension of the time limit by the Association shall be limited to a maximum of an additional three (3) months.

Rule 60 – Exclusion of Application of Provisions concerning Participation in Proceedings and Consolidated Examination

The provisions of Rules 40 and 41 shall not apply to the Expedited Procedures.

Rule 61 – Replacement of Words

If Rule 14, Paragraph 1 and Rule 19, Paragraph 1 apply, the words "three (3) weeks" provided for in Rule 14, Paragraph 1 and "thirty (30) days" provided for in Rule 19, Paragraph 1 shall be replaced by the words "four (4) weeks" and "ten (10) days", respectively.

CHAPTER VI – SUPPLEMENTARY RULES

Rule 62 – Language

1. The language or languages to be used in arbitral proceedings shall be Japanese or English or both. The arbitral tribunal shall, except where the parties have agreed on one or both of such languages, determine, without delay, the language or languages to be used. The arbitral tribunal shall, in so determining, take into consideration whether interpreting or translating will be required and how the cost thereof should be allocated.

2. Arbitral proceedings conducted, prior to the determination of language or languages pursuant to the preceding Paragraph, in a language other than the language or languages so determined shall remain valid. The Association may, if such language is one other than Japanese or English, require the submission of Japanese or English translations.

3. If it is determined that both Japanese and English are to be the languages used during arbitral proceedings, either Japanese or English may be, at a party's option, used during all arbitral proceedings, including hearings; provided that the arbitral award shall be written in Japanese and English, both versions of which shall be official, and if a discrepancy in interpretation arises between the two (2) versions, the interpretation of the Japanese version shall prevail.

Rule 63 – Extension of Period of Time

1. The parties may, by written agreement, extend any period of time provided for in these Rules, except for the period of time provided for in Rule 10, Paragraph 1, Rule 15, Paragraph 1, Rule 16, Paragraph 1, Rule 19, Paragraph 1 and Rule 24, Paragraph 3 (including the application *mutatis mutandis* of the provisions or such Paragraph under the provisions of Rule 25, Paragraph 5). In the event of such an extension, the parties shall, without delay, notify the arbitral tribunal (or, hereinafter, for purposes of this Rule, the Association if the arbitral tribunal has not been established) thereof.

2. The arbitral tribunal may, if deemed necessary, extend any period of time provided for in these Rules (including a period of time determined by the arbitral tribunal) except for the period of time provided for in Rule 59. In the event of such an extension, the arbitral tribunal shall, without delay, notify the parties thereof.

Rule 64 – Obligation to Pay Fees, etc.

1. The parties shall be jointly and severally liable for payment to the Association of the fees provided for in the Arbitration Fee Regulations, necessary expenses incurred during the proceedings and the arbitrators' remuneration.

2. Any dispute arising between the Association and the parties with respect to the payments provided for in the preceding Paragraph shall be determined by the arbitral tribunal established to determine the dispute between the parties.

Rule 65 – Allocation of Fees and Expenses

1. In addition to the expenses provided for in Rule 28, Paragraphs 1 and 2, Rule 38 and Rule 43, Paragraph 3 (including the application *mutatis mutandis* of the provisions of such Paragraph under the provisions of Rule 44, Paragraphs 2 and 3), the parties shall bear, in the manner provided below, the fees provided for in the Arbitration Fee Regulations and the necessary expenses incurred during the proceedings:

(1) the request fee shall be borne by the party requesting the initiation of arbitral proceedings;

(2) the administrative fee, hearing fee and necessary expenses incurred during the proceedings shall be borne subject to the allocation determined by the arbitral tribunal and set forth in the arbitral award; and

(3) the hearing schedule alteration fee shall be borne, if the alteration is requested by one of the parties, by such party, and, in any other case, equally by both parties.

Rule 66 – Allocation of Remuneration for Arbitrators

The parties shall bear equally the cost of the remuneration fixed by the Association for the arbitrators; provided that the arbitral tribunal may, in view of the circumstances, allocate such cost in any other manner.

Rule 67 – Payment to the Association

1. The parties shall pay to the Association, in the manner and within the period of time determined by the arbitral tribunal, a sum of money fixed by it to cover the hearing fee, the hearing schedule alteration fee, the arbitrators' remuneration and necessary expenses incurred during the proceedings.

2. If a party fails to make payment as provided for in the preceding Paragraph, the arbitral tribunal may suspend or terminate the arbitral proceedings unless the other party makes such payment on behalf of the first party.

3. If, subsequent to termination of the arbitral proceedings, the total sum of money paid under the provisions of Paragraph 1 exceeds the total sum of the administrative fee and other fees and expenses determined by the arbitral tribunal under the provisions of Rule 49, Paragraph 3 and the hearing schedule alteration fee, the Association shall refund the difference to either or both of the parties.

Rule 68 – Official Version of these Rules

These Rules have been prepared in Japanese and in English and both versions are official; provided that, in the event that a discrepancy in interpretation arises between the two versions, the interpretation of the Japanese version shall prevail.

THE KOREAN COMMERCIAL ARBITRATION BOARD ("KCAB") ARBITRATION RULES

Effective as of April 27, 2000

KCAB ARBITRATION RULES

CHAPTER I – GENERAL PROVISIONS

Article 1 – Purpose

The purpose of these Rules is to provide for procedures by The Korean Commercial Arbitration Board (hereinafter referred to as the "KCAB") to expedite fair commercial arbitration under the Arbitration Law.

Article 2 – Types of Arbitration

Commercial arbitration mentioned in Article 1 (hereinafter referred to as "Arbitration") shall be divided into Domestic Arbitration and International Arbitration. Domestic Arbitration refers to arbitrations in which the parties have their principal offices or permanent residences in the Republic of Korea, and International Arbitration refers to all arbitrations other than Domestic Arbitration as defined above.

Article 3 – Secretariat

(1) The KCAB shall establish the Secretariat at its main office or branch offices to conduct business in connection with arbitration.

(2) Matters concerned with system, function and operation of the Secretariat shall be separately determined by the KCAB.

Article 4 – Panel of Arbitrators

The KCAB shall prepare and maintain a Panel of Arbitrators. The arbitrators, if they are to be appointed by the Secretariat, shall be appointed from among those in the Panel of Arbitrators in accordance with the provisions of these Rules.

Article 5 – Arbitration Tribunal

(1) For the purpose of settlement of dispute between the parties, one or more arbitrators appointed under the provisions of these Rules, shall constitute an Arbitration Tribunal (hereinafter referred to as "Tribunal").

(2) The office of the Tribunal shall be set up in the main office or branch offices of the KCAB.

Article 6 – Tribunal Clerk

(1) The KCAB shall designate one or more Tribunal Clerks (hereinafter referred to as "Clerk") from among the employees of the Secretariat so as to carry out the administrative affairs concerning each dispute for arbitration.

(2) The Clerk shall execute the duties prescribed in these Rules with respect to the designated arbitration case.

Article 7 – Representation

Any party may, in taking proceedings under these Rules, be represented by a counsel or such other person as shall be recognized to be proper. However, the Tribunal reserves the right to prohibit such representation when it is deemed to be improper.

Article 8 – Closed Proceedings

The proceedings of the arbitration shall be kept confidential.

CHAPTER II – AGREEMENT OF PARTIES

Article 9 – Agreement of Parties

The parties shall be deemed to have made the provisions of the arbitration procedures of these Rules a part of their agreement whenever, in the submission of existing disputes or in a contract containing an arbitration clause, they have provided for arbitration by the KCAB or under these Rules.

CHAPTER III – STATEMENT OF CLAIM

Article 10 – Claim

(1) A person desiring to file a claim with the KCAB under these Rules shall submit the following documents to the Secretariat accompanied by the arbitration costs as provided in Chapter IX:

a) A document certifying agreement on arbitration;

b) A power of attorney, in case the claim is made by an agent.

(2) The following matters shall be stated in the statement of claim:

a) The full names of the parties and their addresses (in case of corporations, the full names and addresses of the representatives shall also be stated);

b) In case the Claimant is represented by an agent, the full name and address of the agent;

c) The purport of the claim;

d) The grounds for the claim and the method of proof.

Article 11 – Acceptance and Notification of Statement of Claim

(1) The Secretariat shall, upon submission of a statement of claim, examine whether such claim is in conformity with the provisions of Article 10 and accept it upon confirmation of its conformity.

(2) The Secretariat shall, upon acceptance of the statement of claim, give such notice to both parties. In this case, a copy of the statement of claim shall be served on the Respondent accompanied by such notice.

Article 12 – Defence

(1) The Respondent may, within 15 days in case of Domestic Arbitration and within 30 days in case of International Arbitration from the date of receipt of the notice in accordance with Paragraph (2) of Article 11 (hereinafter referred to as "Basic Date"), file a defence with the same Secretariat by submitting the following documents:

a) A statement of defence;

b) The original or reproduced copy of documentary evidence, if any, proving the grounds stated in the said defence;

c) A power of attorney, in case the said defence is made by an agent.

(2) The following matters shall be stated in the statement of defence provided in a) of Paragraph (1):

a) The full names of the parties and their addresses (in case of corporations, the full names and their addresses including the full names of representatives and their addresses shall also be stated);

b) In case the Respondent is represented by an agent, the full name and address of the agent;

c) The purport of the defence;

d) The grounds for the defence and the method of proof.

(3) The Secretariat shall, upon receipt of the statement of defence, examine whether such defence is in conformity with the provision of Paragraph (2) of this Article, and upon confirmation of its conformity, accept it.

(4) The Secretariat shall, upon acceptance of the statement of defence, give notice to the same effect to both parties. In this case, a copy of the said defence shall be served on the Claimant.

(5) If no statement of defence is filed within the period provided in Paragraph (1) hereinabove, the Respondent is considered to have dismissed the claim.

Article 13 – Number of Copies of Documents to be Submitted

The number of copies of the documents to be submitted under the provisions of Paragraph (1) of Article 10, and Paragraph (1) of Article 12 (inclusive of the case where these provisions apply *mutatis mutandis* in Paragraph (3) of Article 14 and Paragraph (3) of Article 16) shall, except in case where such document is a power of attorney, be 5 (including the original when it is so submitted); provided, however, that the Secretariat may, if it is deemed necessary, increase or decrease the number of copies of documents to be submitted.

Article 14 – Counterclaim

(1) The Respondent may submit a counterclaim at any time during the arbitral proceeding. However, if a counterclaim is filed late in the proceeding and has an undue effect on the other party or delays the completion of the proceeding, then the Tribunal may, pursuant to the other party's request or at its own discretion, deny filing of such counterclaim.

(2) The proceedings of the Respondent's counterclaim shall be annexed to the Claimant's request for arbitration.

(3) The provisions of Article 10 through Article 13 shall apply *mutatis mutandis* to the acceptance of a counterclaim, its notice and the answer thereto.

Article 15 – Request by Tribunal for Filing of Counterclaim

When the Tribunal decides that the Respondent's defence includes the grounds as well as the purport of a counterclaim, the Tribunal may request to the Respondent that a clarification be made as to whether such counterclaim would be filed as provided in Article 14.

Article 16 – Amendment and Supplement of Claim and Defence

(1) A party or parties desiring, after filing of a statement of claim or defence, to amend or supplement the said statement, shall file such a request with the Secretariat in writing.

(2) During the course of the arbitral proceedings, any amendments or supplement to claims shall be subject to the approval of the Tribunal. However, if the said amendments or supplement are filed late in the proceeding and have an undue effect on the other party or delay the completion of the proceeding, then the Tribunal may, pursuant to the other party's request or at its own discretion, deny filing of such amendments or supplement.

(3) The provisions of Article 10 through Article 13 shall apply *mutatis mutandis* to the amendments provided in Paragraph (1).

Article 17 – Fixing of Locale

The place of arbitration, in the absence of an agreement by the parties, shall be determined by the Secretariat considering the convenience of the parties and access to documentary evidence.

Article 18 – Settlement by Conciliation

(1) The Secretariat shall, upon the receipt of a conciliation request from both parties within 15 days in case of Domestic Arbitration and within 30 days in case of International Arbitration from the Basic Date, conduct conciliation proceedings before the dispute is presented for arbitration.

(2) The conciliation proceedings shall be followed by the appointment of one or three conciliators by the Secretariat from among those in the Panel of Arbitrators. The Conciliator(s) shall have the discretion to determine the conduct and manner of the conciliation proceeding.

(3) If the conciliation succeeds in settling the dispute, the conciliator shall be regarded as the arbitrator appointed under the agreement of the parties; and the result of the conciliation shall be treated in the same manner as such award as to be given and rendered upon settlement by compromise under the provision of Article 53, and shall have the same effect as an award.

(4) When the conciliation fails to settle the dispute within 30 days after the appointment of conciliator(s), the conciliation procedure shall come to an end and the arbitration procedure under these Rules, inclusive of appointment of arbitrator(s), shall commence immediately. However, the parties may extend the above period by mutual agreement.

(5) The parties to the conciliation proceeding, in the absence of an agreement, shall each bear the conciliation costs.

(6) Provisions of Arbitration Costs provided in Chapter IX shall be applied *mutatis mutandis* to the case of conciliation and when arbitral proceeding is commenced pursuant to Paragraph (4) of this Article, the conciliation costs shall be deemed part of the arbitration costs.

CHAPTER IV – APPOINTMENT OF ARBITRATORS

Article 19 – Qualifications of Arbitrator

No person shall serve as an arbitrator if he has any legal or financial interest in the outcome of the arbitration, provided, however, that the parties can appoint such person as an arbitrator notwithstanding their knowledge of disqualification by mutual agreement in writing.

Article 20 – Appointment by Agreement of Parties

(1) If, in the agreement of the parties, mention is specifically made of the names of the arbitrators or the method of appointment thereof (inclusive of a presiding arbitrator who shall act as chairman, also inclusive thereof as provided in the following provisions), the arbitrator(s) shall be appointed in accordance therewith.

(2) If the arbitrators are to be appointed pursuant to the agreement of the parties provided in Paragraph (2) of Article 12, it shall be done in accordance with the following subparagraphs:

a) When the parties have directly appointed arbitrator(s), a document stating the full name(s), address(es) and occupation(s) of the arbitrator(s) together with his/their written acceptance of assuming appointment shall be submitted to the Secretariat within 15 days from the Basic Date in case of Domestic Arbitration and within 30 days from the Basic Date in case of International Arbitration;

b) The Secretariat shall, upon the request of any appointing party, submit a Panel of Arbitrators of the KCAB;

c) If the agreement of the parties specifies a period of time within which arbitrator(s) shall be appointed, and any party fails to make the appointment thereunder within the fixed period, the Secretariat shall appoint the arbitrator(s);

d) If a time period for appointing arbitrator(s) is not specified in the agreement, the Secretariat shall immediately notify the parties to make the appointment of arbitrator(s), and if within 15 days in case of Domestic Arbitration and within 30 days in case of International Arbitration thereafter such arbitrator has not been appointed thereunder, the Secretariat shall appoint the arbitrator(s);

e) In case arbitrators appointed by the parties in accordance with parties' mutual agreement are mandated to appoint the other arbitrator(s), and the parties do not fix the period of appointment for the other arbitrator or arbitrators do not appoint the other arbitrator within the period of appointment, the Secretariat shall notify arbitrators appointed by the parties to make an appointment of the other arbitrator and if within 15 days in case of Domestic Arbitration and within 30 days in case of International Arbitration thereafter such arbitrator has not been appointed thereunder, the Secretariat shall appoint such arbitrator.

(3) If the parties have not appointed arbitrator(s) or have not provided the method of appointment as provided in Paragraph (1) of this Article, or if the Secretariat appoints an arbitrator(s) in accordance with c) and d) of Paragraph (2) of this Article, an arbitrator(s) shall be appointed by the Secretariat applying Article 21 *mutatis mutandis*.

Article 21 – Appointment by Secretariat

(1) If, after the acceptance of a claim, there is no hope of settlement by conciliation or such conciliation proves unsuccessful as provided in Article 18, the Secretariat shall without delay furnish both parties with a list of several candidate arbitrators by choosing from among the Panel of Arbitrators.

(2) Within 15 days from the date of receipt of the list in case of Domestic Arbitration, and within 30 days from the date of receipt of the list in case of International Arbitration, each party shall return to the Secretariat the list of such candidates as provided in Paragraph (1) after marking by number the order of his preference of the names of the

candidates in the respective columns of the said list for a presiding arbitrator and the other arbitrators. If a party or parties fail to return the list within the above period, all of the candidates shall be deemed to be of the same preference and if more than two candidates are marked on the same order of preference or no particular order of preference is marked on candidate(s) or if the name(s) to which each party objects has been deleted, then the KCAB shall adjust the order of preference giving due consideration to the opponent's order of preference. The remaining names on the list shall be given the following order of preference: more than two candidates who have been marked on the same order of preference; candidate(s) for whom no particular order of preference is marked; and candidates who have been deleted.

(3) The Secretariat shall select the arbitrators in accordance with the designated order of the candidates provided in Paragraph (2) and shall invite the written acceptance of each such arbitrator to serve. However, in the event that there are two or more candidates occupying the same place in the designated order, the Secretariat shall appoint the arbitrators from among the candidates.

(4) If the candidates acceptable to both parties refuse to serve or are unable to perform their duties for any reasons, then candidates on the next order of preference on the candidate's list shall be appointed. If the list of candidates has been fully exhausted, then a new arbitrator shall be appointed pursuant to this Article.

(5) When the Secretariat requests an acceptance to serve as arbitrator(s), it invites his/their attention to the requirements provided in Article 25 of these Rules and enclose a copy of these Rules.

Article 22 – Restriction on Appointment of Arbitrators

In regards to arbitrator(s) to be appointed by the Secretariat, if the parties are nationals of different countries and/or are domiciled in different countries, the sole arbitrator or the presiding arbitrator shall, upon the request of either party, be appointed from among the nationals of a country other than that of any of the parties. However, the request for appointment of arbitrators provided in this Article shall be filed with the Secretariat no later than the return of the list of candidates provided in Paragraph (2) of Article 21.

Article 23 – Number of Arbitrators

If the number of arbitrators is specified in the arbitration agreement, the disputes shall be heard and determined by the same number of arbitrators as so specified; if, however, there has been no agreement as such, the number of the arbitrators shall be determined as 1 or 3 by the Secretariat.

Article 24 – Notice of Appointment of Arbitrators

If the arbitrators have been appointed pursuant to these Rules, the Secretariat shall without delay notify in writing all the arbitrator(s) and both parties of the full name(s), address(es) and occupation(s) of all the arbitrator(s).

Article 25 – Disclosure by Arbitrator of Disqualifications

(1) Upon being notified of his appointment as an arbitrator, he shall immediately disclose in writing to the Secretariat any and all circumstances which might cause reasonable question about his fairness or independence.

(2) Upon receipt of such disclosure of information as prescribed in Paragraph (1), the Secretariat shall immediately disclose it to both the Tribunal and the parties. If either party wishes to raise any objection to the appointment of such arbitrator(s), he or she shall make the challenge within 15 days from the date of the establishment of the Tribunal or from the date when the party making the challenge was informed of those circumstances provided in Paragraph (1) of this Article. But, if either party does not submit any objection within the above period, he can not submit any objection to the qualification of such arbitrator(s) on the same grounds.

(3) If either party submits an objection to the appointment of such questioned arbitrator(s) on the ground of notified reason, the vacancy thus created shall be filled in the same method as provided in Article 26.

Article 26 – Vacancy of Arbitrator

(1) If an arbitrator must resign from the appointed Tribunal because of resignation, death or other causes, the party which appointed the arbitrator shall appoint and notify thereof accordingly, a new arbitrator to take his place in the same manner of appointment as for the vacating arbitrator concerned. If the arbitrator was an appointee of the Secretariat, then the appointment shall be made, and duly notified, pursuant to Paragraphs (3) and (4) of Article 21.

(2) In case of Paragraph (1), unless the parties have agreed otherwise, if both parties submit the conclusions of the previous hearing to the new arbitrator(s) and the new arbitrator(s) do not raise objections thereto, the proceeding shall continue. However, if the parties request a new hearing with regard to a witness from a previous hearing, the arbitrators must conduct the hearing.

CHAPTER V – PROCEEDINGS OF HEARING

Article 27 – Time, Date and Place

(1) The Tribunal shall determine the time, date, place and manner of each arbitration hearing.

(2) The Secretariat shall notify each party of decision provided in Paragraph (1) 10 days prior to the opening date of the hearing for Domestic Arbitration, and 20 days prior to the opening date of the hearing for International Arbitration unless the terms thereof have been modified by mutual agreement.

(3) In determining the manner of hearings under the provisions of Paragraph (1) hereinabove, the Tribunal shall give sufficient consideration in order to prevent a delay of the proceedings through such ways as an intensive hearing, etc.

Article 28 – Stenographic Record, etc.

(1) The Secretariat shall make necessary arrangements for the taking of a stenographic or tape record of statements by either party and/or testimony whenever such record is requested by one or both parties.

(2) The requesting party or parties shall make an advance payment to the Secretariat of the expenses involved in such services referred to in Paragraph (1).

(3) The expenses involved in the services provided in Paragraph (1) herein by order of the Tribunal shall be paid from the deposits made in advance by the party under Article 65.

Article 29 – Presentation of Translation

Parties shall, upon request, present to the Secretariat or the Tribunal, translations of the written statements and evidentiary documents and/or other written materials which are requested by the Secretariat or the Tribunal.

Article 30 – Interpretation or Translation

(1) The Secretariat shall make necessary arrangements for the services of interpretation or translation upon the request of one or both parties or by order of the Tribunal.

(2) The requesting party shall deposit an advance payment to the Secretariat of the expenses involved in such services described in Paragraph (1).

(3) The expenses involved in the services provided in Paragraph (1) herein by order of the Tribunal shall be paid from the deposits made in advance by the party under Article 65.

Article 31 – Attendance at Hearings

(1) Parties are entitled to attend the hearing.

(2) Persons not privy to arbitration, but who have an interest in the outcome of the arbitration award, may submit prima facie evidence of such interest to the Tribunal, and, subject to approval from the Tribunal, may attend the hearing.

(3) The Tribunal may order any witness to retire during the testimony of another witness.

Article 32 – Adjournments or Continuations

The Tribunal may, on justifiable grounds, take adjournments or change the date of hearing upon the request of both parties or on its own motion. However, the adjournment should be made within 15 days in case of Domestic Arbitration and within 30 days in case of International Arbitration, not subject to renewal of second adjournment.

Article 33 – Decisions of Tribunal

Whenever there is more than one arbitrator, simple majority rule shall apply for all decisions, including that of the arbitral awards, unless parties agree otherwise. However, if no majority rule is reached with regard to a procedural matter, then the presiding arbitrator shall decide.

Article 34 – Hearing

(1) Statements and statements of defence containing the statements of claim and the form of presenting evidence may be submitted so that the hearing may be conducted by the Tribunal in a manner that will most expeditiously and accurately permit full presentation of the evidence and arguments of the parties.

(2) The Tribunal, of its own motion or upon the request of the parties, may submit the summarized text of the statements and statements of defence submitted by the parties or summarize the text and present it to the parties for confirmation. In such case, the Tribunal may hear and award only such summarized issues.

Article 35 – Proceedings of Hearing

(1) A hearing shall commence with the announcement of a case and both parties' names.

(2) The Clerk shall keep and provide minutes of the proceedings, containing the following records:

a) Date and place of the hearing;

b) The names of the arbitrator(s), the parties and their agents, and if witnesses are used, their names and addresses;

c) The statements of the parties or their agents, or a summary of each hearing. However, unless otherwise instructed by the Tribunal with regard to the results of the examination of evidence, a recording may be used as a substitute.

(3) The Tribunal may, at the beginning of the hearing, ask for statements clarifying issues involved in the dispute.

(4) The party requesting arbitration shall present his statement on the purport and grounds of the claims, and introduce documentary evidence and his witnesses. The Respondent shall present his defence, and introduce documentary evidence and his witnesses.

(5) Exhibits, when produced by either party, may be accepted as evidence by the Tribunal, and the exhibits so accepted shall be filed in their numerical order by the Clerk and shall be made a part of the record.

(6) The Tribunal may vary the procedure when it may be deemed necessary but the Tribunal shall afford full and equal opportunity to both parties for the presentation of any materials or relevant evidence.

(7) If the parties repeatedly submit a series of statements to show cause of action or as legal defence as to cause undue confusion, the Tribunal may order the presentation of a summary of statements prior to the conclusion of the hearing.

Article 36 – Parties' Lack of Care

If the party requesting arbitration fails to state a specific claim or present a reason or documentary evidence, which unduly hinders the arbitration proceeding, the Tribunal may close the hearings. The Tribunal may also close the hearings if the parties show lack of care in stating claims or presenting evidence, and it is deemed improper to proceed with the hearing.

Article 37 – Arbitration in the Absence of Parties

(1) The arbitration may proceed in the absence of either party who, after due notice, fails to be present, and even if present, does not participate in the hearing.

(2) In case of Paragraph (1), the documents or other evidence produced by the absent party or otherwise not participating in the hearing shall be deemed to have been orally stated or submitted thereat and the hearing necessary for making an award may proceed with a party present.

(3) If the parties have been properly notified of the hearing but fail to attend the hearings two or more times, or even if the parties attend but fail to participate in the hearing, the Tribunal may declare a suspension of the arbitration proceedings.

Article 38 – Withdrawal of Request for Arbitration

(1) The party requesting arbitration may withdraw, in part or in whole, the request for arbitration at any time prior to the arbitration decision.

(2) Withdrawal of a request for arbitration shall not have effect if the other party has already submitted an answer or has made a statement during hearing.

(3) Withdrawal of a request for arbitration shall be in writing. A written withdrawal of a request for arbitration must be dispatched after the other party has been notified of an acceptance of a request for arbitration. However, such request for withdrawal may be made orally during the hearing. However, if the other party does not attend the hearing at the designated date, then a duplicate copy of the hearing record must be dispatched to that party.

(4) If a withdrawal of a request for arbitration is made pursuant to Paragraph (3) above, then the other party is deemed to consent to such withdrawal if no objection is raised within 15 days for Domestic Arbitration and 30 days for International Arbitration after either a written withdrawal has been submitted or when a duplicate copy of the hearing record has been duly dispatched.

Article 39 – Filing of Statements and Other Documents

(1) The statements and other documents not filed with the Tribunal at the hearing, but arranged for filing at the hearings or subsequently by mutual agreement of the parties or at the request of the Tribunal shall be filed with the Secretariat, which, in turn, shall deliver them to the Tribunal. In such case, both parties shall be afforded opportunity to examine such documents.

(2) The Tribunal may, at its discretion, continue with the hearing even if the statements and other documents were not filed by the designated date.

Article 40 – Inspection or Investigation

Should the Tribunal deem it necessary to make an inspection or investigation, it shall, prior to making such inspection or investigation, direct the Secretariat to notify the parties of the purpose, time, date and place for such inspection or investigation. Any party who so desires, may present himself at such inspection or investigation.

Article 41 – Interim Measure

(1) The Tribunal, with the application of any party, may issue to any party such orders as may be deemed necessary to safeguard the property which is the subject matter of the dispute without prejudice to the right of the parties or to the final determination of the dispute.

(2) The Tribunal may, at its discretion, order any party applying for the interim measure to provide a proper security.

Article 42 – Evidence

(1) The parties may offer any evidence they so desire to support their contention or request that any witness or expert witness voluntarily appear at the hearings. However, the Tribunal may refuse to investigate such evidence by finding there exists no relevancy between the evidence so produced and the contention of the parties concerned.

(2) The Tribunal may, where it is deemed necessary, request the production of evidence or the voluntary appearance of a witness or an expert witness at the hearings. However, the Tribunal may, at its discretion, proceed with the hearing even if evidence has not been submitted and/or neither a witness nor an expert witness has appeared within the designated time.

(3) In the event that the Tribunal is unable by itself to examine the evidence necessary for an arbitration award, the Tribunal may file an application with the competent court upon its own initiative or upon the request of any party.

(4) All evidence shall be submitted and examined in the presence of all the parties, and sole arbitrator or the majority of the arbitrators, except where any of the parties is absent without sufficient reason or has waived his right to be present.

(5) The Tribunal shall decide at his own discretion the relevancy and materiality of the evidence offered.

Article 43 – Closing of Hearings

(1) The Tribunal shall, when it believes that all contentions and evidence of the parties have been put forth, declare the hearings closed.

(2) It is required that a summary of statements be submitted, the hearings shall be deemed to be closed as of the final date set by the Tribunal for the submission of the aforementioned documents.

Article 44 – Reopening of Hearings

(1) The hearing may be reopened by the Tribunal on its own discretion, or upon application of a party for good cause, at any time before an award is rendered.

(2) If the reopening of the hearing provided in Paragraph (1) would prevent the making of the award within the specific time agreed upon by the parties in the arbitration agreement, the hearings may not be reopened unless the parties agree upon the extension of such time limit.

(3) When hearings are reopened, the closing date of the hearings shall be the date on which the proceedings of the reopened hearings were concluded.

Article 45 – Arbitration without Oral Hearings

(1) The parties may, by written agreement, submit their dispute to arbitration to be conducted by means of documentary examination without oral hearings.

(2) In case the parties have not agreed otherwise as to procedure, such arbitration shall be conducted under these Rules, except when such provisions are inconsistent with the provisions of this Article.

(3) The Secretariat shall advise the parties to submit documents and evidence necessary for the proceeding of the above arbitration in such manner as provided in the following Paragraphs.

(4) The parties shall submit to the Secretariat their respective contentions in writing, including a statement of facts and causes of action accompanied by evidence. These statements and proofs may be accompanied by briefs.

(5) All the documents shall be filed within 15 days in case of Domestic Arbitration and within 30 days in case of International Arbitration from the date of notice to submit such statement and evidence, in the number of copies requested by the Secretariat.

(6) The Secretariat shall serve on each party a copy of the statement and evidence submitted by the other party. Each party may reply or explain his opinion to the other's statement

and evidence. Any party who fails to make such a reply or explain his opinion within 15 days in case of Domestic Arbitration and within 30 days in case of International Arbitration after the mailing date of such documents to him, shall be deemed to have waived the right to reply or explain his opinion.

(7) The Secretariat shall transmit all the evidence and documents to the Tribunal, which shall have been constituted in any manner provided for in Chapter 4. The Tribunal may request a party or parties to produce additional evidence within 10 days from the date of their delivery to it. The Secretariat shall notify the parties of such request and the party or parties shall submit such additional evidence within 15 days in case of Domestic Arbitration, and within 30 days in case of International Arbitration from the date of such notice.

(8) The Secretariat shall transmit to each party a copy of the additional statement and evidence submitted by the other party. Each party may reply or explain one's opinions to such statement and evidence. Any party who fails to make such a reply or explain his opinion within 15 days in case of Domestic Arbitration and within 30 days in case of International Arbitration after the mailing of such documents to him, shall be deemed to have waived the right to reply or explain one's own opinions.

(9) Upon delivery to the Tribunal of all documents submitted as provided in the preceding Paragraphs, the order of proceeding shall be deemed concluded.

CHAPTER VI – SPECIAL PROVISIONS

Article 46 – Waiver of the Right to Protest

Any party who proceeds with the arbitration, with knowledge or being able to have known that any provision or requirement of these Rules has not been complied with, shall be deemed to have lost his right to object unless he states objection thereto without delay.

Article 47 – Extensions of Period

The parties may modify any period prescribed under these Rules by a mutual agreement in writing. The Tribunal for good cause may extend any period established by these Rules except the period for making an award. The Tribunal shall notify the parties through the Secretariat of any such extension and reasons therefor.

CHAPTER VII – AWARD

Article 48 – Arbitral Award

(1) The award shall be rendered promptly unless otherwise agreed by the parties or specified by law, not later than 30 days from the date of closing the hearings.

(2) Where the Tribunal is composed of more than one arbitrator and less than a majority of arbitrators refuse to partake in the arbitration decision or do not participate in the

arbitration decision without just cause, the award shall be made by the remaining majority of arbitrators.

(3) The Secretariat may, without affecting the arbitral award, present to the Tribunal its opinions on the form of the arbitral award.

Article 49 – Form of Award

(1) The arbitral award shall be made in writing, stating the following particulars and shall be signed by the arbitrator:

a) The full personal or corporate names of the parties and their addresses. In case a party is represented by an agent, the full name and address of the agent;

b) Principal and Reason upon which the award is based;

c) Date of award;

d) Place of arbitration.

(2) If an award is to be made by more than one arbitrator and less than a majority of the arbitrators refuse or fail to sign the award, the remaining arbitrators must specify the reasons on it and sign thereon.

Article 50 – Language

The Korean language shall be used in the arbitral proceedings unless otherwise agreed by the parties. In case there has been a request submitted by one of the parties or both, or there is among the arbitrators a person of nationality other than that of Korea, the arbitral award may be written in both Korean and English languages and both versions shall be the duly authenticated arbitral award. However, when a discrepancy in interpretation has arisen between the two versions, interpretation by the Korean language shall prevail.

Article 51 – Interpretation and Application of Rules

(1) The Tribunal in charge of the case shall interpret and apply these Rules insofar as they relate to the specific case.

(2) In case of Paragraph (1), a difference arising among the arbitrators who are composing the Tribunal shall be decided by a majority rule.

Article 52 – Scope of Award

(1) The Tribunal may not only order the specific performance of a contract but may also grant any remedy and relief which is deemed just and equitable within the scope of the arbitration agreement of the parties.

(2) The Tribunal shall assess the arbitration costs provided in Chapter IX to the party or parties responsible.

Article 53 – Arbitral Award based on Settlement

If the parties reach a settlement during the course of the arbitral proceedings, the Tribunal may, upon their request, record the agreed settlement in the form of an Award.

Article 54 – Correction or Interpretation of Award and Additional Award

(1) The Tribunal may correct, by its decision, any error in computation, any clerical or typographical error, or any other obvious error of a similar nature in the arbitral award. In case such error can not be corrected by the Tribunal concerned, the Secretariat may correct that error.

(2) If the parties request the interpretation of a specific point or any part of the award within the 30 days of receipt of the duly authenticated arbitral award, the Tribunal shall, if so agreed by the parties, decide on it within 30 days of receipt of the request.

(3) The Tribunal shall make an additional award as to claims presented in the arbitral proceedings but omitted from the award within 60 days of receipt of the request by the parties.

(4) All of the corrections, interpretations and the additional awards as provided in this Article shall form part of the award.

Article 55 – Delivery of Arbitral Award

(1) The Secretariat shall deliver a duly authenticated arbitral award to each party or his agent in ways provided in Paragraph (1) through (3) of Article 4 of the Act. The original arbitral award shall be delivered to the competent court, enclosed with a document certifying the delivery.

(2) Service under the provisions of Paragraph (1) may be conducted after all the arbitration costs provided in Chapter IX have been paid in full by the responsible party or parties to the Secretariat unless other circumstances arise.

CHAPTER VIII – EXPEDITED PROCEDURE

Article 56 – Scope of Application

The Expedited Procedure shall be applied to an arbitration case where both parties have agreed to follow the procedures provided in this Chapter in a separate agreement or to a Domestic Arbitration case of which the claim amount is less than 20,000,000 won in the Korean currency. In case of Domestic Arbitration of which the claim amount is less than 20,000,000 won, the increase of the claim amount after the Basic Date shall not be considered.

Article 57 – Appointment of Arbitrator

The Secretariat shall appoint one arbitrator from among the Panel of Arbitrators without recourse to Article 21 of these Rules unless otherwise agreed by the parties.

Article 58 – Proceedings of Hearing

(1) The Tribunal shall fix the time, date and place of the hearing, and the Secretariat shall notify each party of the above decision 3 days prior to the opening date of the hearing by person, by telephone, by letter or by any other appropriate method.

(2) The hearing will be held in principle once. However, provided that it is deemed necessary, the Tribunal may reopen the hearing.

(3) The Tribunal, in case of parties' mutual consent, may direct the Clerk to keep the record without the contents of hearing for the speediness of the procedure.

(4) The Respondent may submit a counterclaim at any time up to the closing of the hearing.

Article 59 – Award

(1) The Tribunal shall render the award not later than 10 days from the date of closing the hearings.

(2) The Tribunal may, upon both parties' consent, omit writing the reasons in the award of Paragraph (1).

Article 60 – Adaptation

The matters which are not prescribed in this Chapter shall be applied by other provisions of these Rules *mutatis mutandis.*

CHAPTER IX – ARBITRATION COSTS

Article 61 – Costs of Arbitration

(1) The costs of arbitration comprise the fees, the expenses and the allowances as prescribed in Article 62 through Article 64 of these Rules.

(2) The costs of arbitration prescribed in Paragraph (1) shall be borne by the parties in accordance with the apportionment fixed in the award. However, such arbitration costs shall be borne equally by the parties unless the award assesses such costs of arbitration or any part thereof against any specified party in the award.

(3) Even where the proceedings shall be conducted only on the basis of the documents under Article 45, the provisions of this Article through Article 65 shall apply to the costs of arbitration.

(4) Any interest incurred pursuant to the advance payment of the arbitration costs need not be refunded.

Article 62 – Fees

(1) The fees shall be deposited in advance by the Claimant and divided into the administrative fee and the hearing date rescheduling fee; provided the Tribunal changes the date of hearing on its own initiative, the hearing date rescheduling fee will not be assessed.

(2) In case the amount of claim is reduced by the change in the claim according to the provisions of Article 16, any differences in the administrative fee shall not be refunded.

(3) The actual rate and the method of deposit, or the ratio and the method of refunds, for the fees shall be determined by the attached Fee Schedule. Fees not specified in the attached Fee Schedule shall be decided by the KCAB.

Article 63 – Expenses

(1) All the expenses required for arbitration including the expenses of the arbitrators and Clerk, the expenses of any proofs produced, the expenses of witness or expert witness, the expenses of inspection, interpretation or translation, tape record, stenographic record or all transcripts thereof shall be deposited in advance by the party ordering such services.

(2) The expenses in Paragraph (1) if they accrued from such services as requested by the Tribunal, shall be deposited in advance by the Claimant unless otherwise specified.

Article 64 – Allowances for Arbitrators

The allowances for the arbitrators fixed by the KCAB shall be deposited in advance by the Claimant.

Article 65 – Method of Deposits, etc.

(1) The Claimant shall deposit in advance to the Secretariat at the time of the request the specified costs of arbitration provided in Article 62 through Article 64 in such currency as the Secretariat deems necessary.

(2) In case such sums of advance payment provided in Paragraph (1) are deemed insufficient, the Secretariat may demand of the Claimant any additional sums of deposit. If the Claimant fails to pay in advance such deposits as provided in Paragraph (1) and (2) herein or the Respondent does not pay in lieu of the Claimant, the Tribunal may terminate the proceedings on its own decision.

(3) The Secretariat shall prepare an Accounting Statement of the deposits when the hearing is closed, and the Balance Statement when the arbitral award is made. After delivery of the arbitral award enclosed with the Balance Statement, the Secretariat shall refund any balance to the parties concerned.

THE SINGAPORE INTERNATIONAL ARBITRATION CENTRE ("SIAC") ARBITRATION RULES

Effective as of October 22, 1997

SIAC ARBITRATION RULES

Rule 1 – Scope of Application and Interpretation

1.1 These Rules shall govern the arbitration save that, where any of these Rules is in conflict with a provision of the applicable law of the arbitration from which the parties cannot derogate, that provision shall prevail.

1.2 In these Rules –

"Centre" means Singapore International Arbitration Centre, a company incorporated under the Companies Act of the Republic of Singapore as a company limited by guarantee;

"Chairman" means the Chairman of the Centre;

"Registrar" means the Registrar of the Centre;

"Tribunal" includes a sole arbitrator or all the arbitrators where more than one is appointed.

Rule 2 – Notice, Calculation of Periods of Time

2.1 For the purposes of these Rules, any notice, including a notification, communication or proposal, shall be in writing and is deemed to have been received if it is physically delivered to the addressee or if it is delivered at his habitual residence, place of business or mailing address, or, if none of these can be found after making reasonable inquiry, then at the addressee's last-known residence or place of business. The notice shall be deemed to have been received on the day it is so delivered.

2.2 For the purposes of calculating any period of time under these Rules, such period shall begin to run on the day following the day when a notice, notification, communication or proposal is received. If the last day of such period is an official holiday at the residence or place of business of the addressee, the period is extended until the first business day which follows. Official holidays occurring during the running of the period of time are included in calculating the period.

2.3 Any written communication may be made by way of any form of electronic transmission effected to a business address of a party or to a facsimile number or e-mail address indicated in a party's letterhead and is deemed to have been received if it is so transmitted on the day of transmission.

2.4 The parties shall file with the Registrar a copy of any notice, including a notification, communication or proposal concerning the arbitral proceedings.

Rule 3 – Request for or Notification of Arbitration

3.1 The party wishing to commence an arbitration under these Rules (hereinafter called the "Claimant") shall give to the other party (hereinafter called the "Respondent") a Notice of Arbitration which shall include or be accompanied by the following:

(a) a demand that the dispute be referred to arbitration;

(b) the names and addresses of the parties to the arbitration;

(c) a reference to the arbitration clause or the separate arbitration agreement that is invoked;

(d) a reference to the contract out of or in relation to which the dispute arises;

(e) a brief statement describing the nature and circumstances of the dispute and specifying the relief claimed; and

(f) a statement of any matters on which the parties have previously agreed as to the conduct of the arbitration or with respect to which the Claimant wishes to make a proposal.

3.2 The Notice of Arbitration may also include:

(a) the proposals for the appointment of a sole arbitrator and an appointing authority referred to in Rules 7.1 and 7.2 respectively

(b) the notification of appointment of an arbitrator referred to in Rule 8; and

(c) the Statement of Case referred to in Rule 18.2

3.3 The date of receipt of the Notice of Arbitration by the Registrar of the Centre shall be deemed to be the date on which the arbitration has commenced.

3.4 The Claimant shall file with the Registrar a copy of the Notice of Arbitration served on the Respondent.

3.5 If the parties have agreed on an appointing authority other than the Chairman, they shall inform the Registrar of the name of that authority.

Rule 4 – Response by Respondent

4.1 For the purpose of facilitating the appointment of arbitrators, within fourteen (14) days of receipt of the Notice of Arbitration, the Respondent may send to the Claimant a Response, in which case, it shall contain:

(a) a confirmation or denial of all or part of the claims;

(b) a brief statement of the nature and circumstances of any envisaged counterclaims; and

(c) a comment in response to any statements contained in the Notice of Arbitration, as called for under Rule 3.1 paragraph (f), on matters relating to the conduct of the arbitration.

4.2 The Response may also include -

(a) a comment in response to any proposal for the appointments of a sole arbitrator and for an appointing authority; and

(b) the notification of the appointment of an arbitrator referred to in Rule 8.

4.3 The Respondent shall send a copy of any Response to the Registrar and shall confirm to the Registrar that copies have been served on the other party.

4.4 Failure to send a Response shall not preclude the Respondent from denying the claim or from setting out a counterclaim in its Statement of Defence.

Rule 5 – Centre to Provide Assistance

The Registrar shall, at the request of the Tribunal or either party, make available, or arrange for, such facilities and assistance for the conduct of arbitration proceedings as may be required, including suitable accommodation for sittings of the Tribunal, secretarial assistance and interpretation facilities.

Rule 6 – Number of Arbitrators

6.1 A sole arbitrator shall be appointed unless the parties have agreed otherwise.

Rule 7 – Appointment of Sole Arbitrator

7.1 If a sole arbitrator is to be appointed, either party may propose to the other, the names of one or more persons, one of whom would serve as the sole arbitrator.

7.2 If within twenty-one (21) days after receipt by a party of a proposal made in accordance with Rule 7.1 the parties have not reached agreement on the choice of a sole arbitrator, the sole arbitrator shall be appointed by the appointing authority agreed upon by the parties, and if no appointing authority has been agreed upon by the parties, or if the appointing authority agreed upon refuses to act or fails to appoint the arbitrator within twenty-one (21) days of the receipt of a party's request thereof, the Chairman shall appoint the arbitrator as soon as practicable.

7.3 If either party does not wish to propose the names of one or more persons to serve as the sole arbitrator, either party may request the Chairman to appoint the sole arbitrator. The Chairman shall as soon as practicable appoint the sole arbitrator upon the receipt of such a request.

7.4 A decision on a matter entrusted by Rule 7.2 and 7.3 to the Chairman shall not be subject to appeal.

Rule 8 – Appointment of Three Arbitrators

8.1 If three arbitrators are to be appointed, each party shall appoint one arbitrator. The two arbitrators thus appointed shall choose the third arbitrator who will act as the presiding arbitrator of the tribunal.

8.2 If within twenty-one (21) days after the receipt of a party's notification of the appointment of an arbitrator, the other party has not notified the first party of the arbitrator he has appointed:

(a) the first party may request the appointing authority previously designated by the parties to appoint the arbitrator; or

(b) if no such authority has been previously designated by the parties, or if the appointing authority previously designated refuses to act or fails to appoint the arbitrator within twenty-one (21) days after receipt of a party's request thereof, the first party may request the Chairman to appoint the second arbitrator.

8.3 If within twenty-one (21) days after the appointment of the second arbitrator the two arbitrators have not agreed on the choice of the presiding arbitrator, the presiding arbitrator shall be appointed by an appointing authority or by the Chairman if no appointing authority has been previously designated by the parties or, if the appointing authority previously designated refuses to act within the prescribed time, in the same way as a sole arbitrator would be appointed under Rule 7.

8.4 A decision on a matter entrusted by Rule 8.2 or 8.3 to the Chairman shall not be subject to appeal.

Rule 9 – Multi-party Appointment of Arbitrator(s)

9.1 If there are three or more parties in the arbitration, the parties shall endeavour to agree on the procedure for appointing the arbitrator(s) and if within twenty-one (21) days of the receipt of the Notice of Arbitration, the parties have not reached an agreement on the procedure for appointing the arbitrator(s), the arbitrator(s) shall be appointed by the Chairman as soon as practicable after the receipt of a party's request to the Chairman.

9.2 A decision on a matter entrusted by Rule 9.1 to the Chairman shall not be subject to appeal.

Rule 10 – Information to be Furnished to the Appointing Authority

10.1 When an appointing authority is requested to appoint an arbitrator pursuant to Rule 7 or 8, the party which makes the request shall send to the appointing authority a copy of the Notice of Arbitration, a copy of the contract out of or in relation to which the dispute has arisen and a copy of the arbitration agreement if it is not contained in the contract. The appointing authority may require from either party such information as it deems necessary to fulfill its function.

10.2 Where the names of one or more persons are proposed for appointment as arbitrators, their full names, addresses and nationalities shall be indicated, together with a description of their qualifications.

Rule 11 – Independence and Impartiality of Arbitrators

11.1 In making an appointment under these Rules, the Chairman shall have due regard to any qualifications required of the arbitrator by the agreement of the parties and to such considerations as are likely to secure the appointment of an independent and impartial arbitrator and where the parties are of different nationalities, shall also take into account the advisability of appointing an arbitrator of a nationality other than those of the parties.

11.2 Any arbitrator (whether or not appointed by the parties) conducting an arbitration under these Rules shall be and remain at all times independent and impartial, and shall not act as advocate for any party.

11.3 A prospective arbitrator shall disclose to those who approach him in connection with his possible appointment, any circumstances likely to give rise to justifiable doubts as to his impartiality or independence.

11.4 An arbitrator, once appointed or chose, shall disclose any such circumstance (referred to in Rule 11.3 above) to all parties, not already informed by him, of these circumstances.

Rule 12 – Challenge of Arbitrators

12.1 Any arbitrator may be challenged if circumstances exist that give rise to justifiable doubts as to the arbitrator's impartiality or independence.

12.2 A party may challenge the arbitrator appointed by him only for reasons of which he becomes aware after the appointment has been made.

Rule 13 – Notice of Challenge

13.1 A party who intends to challenge an arbitrator shall send notice of his challenge within fourteen (14) days after the appointment of the challenged arbitrator has been notified to the challenging party or within fourteen (14) days after the circumstances mentioned in Rule 12.1 or 12.2 became known to that party.

13.2 The challenge shall be notified to the other party, the arbitrator who is challenged and the other members of the Tribunal. The notification shall be in writing and shall state the reasons for the challenge. Upon receiving the notification of challenge by the Registrar, the arbitration shall be suspended until the challenge is resolved or decided upon.

13.3 When an arbitrator has been challenged by one party, the other party may agree to the challenge. The arbitrator may also, after the challenge, withdraw from his office. In neither case does this imply acceptance of the validity of the grounds for the challenge. In both cases, the procedure provided in Rule 7, 8 or 9 shall be used in full for the appointment of the substitute arbitrator, even if during the process of appointing the challenged arbitrator, a party had failed to exercise his right to appoint or to participate in the appointment.

Rule 14 – Decision on Challenge

14.1 If the other party does not agree to the challenge and the challenged arbitrator does not withdraw, the decision on the challenge will be made:

(a) when the initial appointment was made by an appointing authority, by that authority; and

(b) in all other cases, by the Chairman whose decision shall be final and not be subject to appeal.

14.2 If the appointing authority or the Chairman, as the case may be, sustains the challenge, a substitute arbitrator shall be appointed or chosen pursuant to the procedure applicable to the appointment or choice of an arbitrator as provided in Rules 6 to 9 except that, when this procedure would call for the designation of an appointing authority, the appointment of the arbitrator shall be made by the appointing authority which decided on the challenge.

Rule 15 – Replacement of An Arbitrator

15.1 In the event of the death or resignation of an arbitrator during the course of the arbitral proceedings, a substitute arbitrator shall be appointed or chosen pursuant to the procedure provided for in Rules 7 to 11 that was applicable to the appointment or choice of the arbitrator being replaced.

15.2 In the event that an arbitrator refuses or fails to act or in the event of the *de jure* or *de facto* impossibility of his performing functions, the procedure in respect of the challenge and replacement of an arbitrator as provided in Rules 12 to 14 and 15.1 shall apply.

Rule 16 – Repetition of Hearings in the Event of the Replacement of an Arbitrator

If under Rules 13 to 15 the sole or presiding arbitrator is replaced, any hearings held previously shall be repeated unless otherwise agreed to by the parties. If any other arbitrator is replaced, such prior hearings may be repeated at the discretion of the Tribunal.

Rule 17 – Conduct of the Proceedings

17.1 The parties may agree on the arbitral procedure, and are encouraged to do so.

17.2 In the absence of procedural rules agreed by the parties or contained herein, the Tribunal shall have the widest discretion allowed under such law as may be applicable to ensure the just, expeditious, economical, and final determination of the dispute.

17.3 In the case of a three-member Tribunal, the presiding arbitrator may, after consulting the other arbitrators, make procedural rulings alone.

Rule 18 – Submission of Written Statements and Documents

18.1 The Tribunal may determine the periods of time within which the parties shall submit their written statements. If no specific periods of time are determined by the Tribunal the parties shall proceed as set out in this Rule 18.

18.2 Within thirty (30) days of receipt of notification from the Registrar that the Tribunal has been constituted, the Claimant shall, if it has not done so, send to the Respondent a Statement of Case setting out in full detail the facts and any contention of law on which it relies, and the relief claimed.

18.3 Within thirty (30) days of receipt of the Statement of Case by the Respondent, or, where the Statement of Case was served with the Notice of Arbitration, the notification referred to in Rule 18.2, the Respondent shall send to the Claimant, a Statement of Defence stating in full detail which of the facts and contentions of law in the Statement of Case it admits or denies, on what grounds, and on what other facts and contentions of law it relies. Any counterclaims shall be submitted with the Statement of Defence in the same manner as claims are set out in the Statement of Case.

18.4 The Tribunal shall decide which further written statements, in addition to the Statement of Case and the Statement of Defence, shall be required from the parties or may be presented by them and shall fix the periods of time for communicating such statements.

18.5 The periods of time fixed by the Tribunal for the submission of written statements (including the Statement of Case and Statement of Defence) shall not exceed forty-five (45) days. However the Tribunal may extend the time-limits on such terms as it may deem appropriate.

18.6 All statements referred to in this Rule shall be accompanied by copies (or, if they are especially voluminous, lists) of all essential documents on which the party concerned relies and which have not previously been submitted by any party, and (where appropriate) by any relevant samples.

18.7 Copies of all statements referred to in this Rule shall be served on the Tribunal and the Registrar.

18.8 As soon as practicable following completion of the submission of the statements specified in this Rule, the Tribunal shall proceed in such manner as has been agreed by the parties, or pursuant to its authority under these Rules.

18.9 If the Claimant fails within the time specified under these Rules or as may be fixed by the Tribunal, to submit its Statement of Case, the Tribunal may issue an order for the termination of the arbitral proceedings or make such other directions as may be appropriate in the circumstances. If the Respondent fails to submit a Statement of Defence, or if at any point any party fails to avail itself of the opportunity to present its case in the manner directed by the Tribunal, the Tribunal may nevertheless proceed with the arbitration and make the award.

Rule 19 – Place of Arbitration

19.1 The parties may choose the place of arbitration. Failing such a choice, the place of arbitration shall be Singapore, unless the Tribunal determines in view of all the circumstances of the case that another place is more appropriate.

19.2 The Tribunal may hold hearings and meetings anywhere convenient, subject to the provisions of Rule 22.2 and provided that the award shall be made at the place of arbitration.

Rule 20 – Language of Arbitration

20.1 Subject to any agreement by the parties, the Tribunal shall, promptly after its appointment, determine the language or languages to be used in the proceedings. This determination shall apply to the Statement of Case, the Statement of Defence, and any further written statements or other communications and, if oral hearings take place, to the language or languages to be used in such hearings.

20.2 If a document is drawn up in a language other than the language(s) of the arbitration, and no translation of such document is submitted by the party producing the document, the Tribunal, or if the Tribunal has not been established, the Registrar, may order that party to submit a translation in a form to be determined by the Tribunal or the Registrar.

Rule 21 – Party Representatives

Any party may be represented by legal practitioners or any other representatives, subject to such proof of authority as the Tribunal may require.

Rule 22 – Hearings

22.1 Unless the parties have agreed on documents-only arbitration, the Tribunal shall, if either party so requests, hold a hearing for the presentation of evidence by witnesses, including expert witnesses, or for oral submissions.

22.2 The Tribunal shall fix the date, time and place of any meeting and hearing in the arbitration, and the sole or presiding arbitrator shall give the parties reasonable notice thereof.

22.3 If any party to the proceedings fails to appear at a hearing, without showing sufficient cause for such failure, the Tribunal may proceed with the arbitration and may make the award on the evidence before it.

22.4 The Tribunal may in advance of hearings, submit to the parties, a list of questions which it wishes them to treat with special attention.

22.5 All meetings and hearings shall be in private unless the parties agree otherwise.

22.6 The Tribunal may declare the hearings closed if it is satisfied that the parties have no further proof to offer or witnesses to be heard or submissions to make. The Tribunal may on its own motion or upon application of a party but before any award is made, reopen the hearings.

22.7 All statements, documents or other information supplied to the Tribunal by one party shall be communicated to the other party. Also, any expert report or evidentiary document on which the Tribunal may rely in making its decision shall be communicated to the parties.

Rule 23 – Witnesses

23.1 Before any hearing, the Tribunal may require any party to give notice of the identity of witnesses it wishes to call, as well as the subject matter of their testimony and its relevance to the issues.

23.2 The Tribunal has discretion to allow, refuse, or limit the appearance of witnesses, whether witnesses of fact or expert witnesses.

23.3 Any witness who gives oral evidence may be questioned by each of the parties or their representatives, under the control of the Tribunal. The Tribunal may put questions at any stage of the examination of the witnesses.

23.4 Subject to such order or direction which the Tribunal may make, the testimony of witnesses may be presented in written form, either as signed statements or by duly sworn affidavits. Subject to Rule 23.2, any party may request that such a witness should attend for oral examination at a hearing. If he fails to attend, the Tribunal may place such weight on the written testimony as it thinks fit, or exclude it altogether.

23.5 Subject to the mandatory provisions of any applicable law, it shall be proper for any party or its representatives to interview any witness or potential witness prior to his appearance at any hearing.

Rule 24 – Experts Appointed by the Tribunal

24.1 Unless otherwise agreed by the parties, the Tribunal:

(a) may appoint one or more experts to report to the Tribunal on specific issues;

(b) may require a party to give any such expert(s) any relevant information or to produce, or to provide access to any relevant documents, goods or property for inspection by the expert(s).

24.2 Unless otherwise agreed by the parties, if a party so requests or if the Tribunal considers it necessary, any expert shall, after delivery of his written or oral report, participate in a hearing at which the parties shall have the opportunity to question him, and to present expert witnesses in order to testify on the points at issue.

Rule 25 – Additional Powers of the Tribunal

Unless the parties at any time agree otherwise, and subject to any mandatory limitations of any applicable law, the Tribunal shall have the power, on the application of any party or of its own motion, but in either case only after giving the parties a proper opportunity to state their views, to:

(a) order the correction of any such contract or arbitration agreement, but only to the extent required to rectify any mistake which it determines to be common to all the parties and then only if and to the extent to which the rules of law governing or applicable to the contract permit such correction;

(b) allow other parties to be joined in the arbitration with their express consent, and make a single final award determining all disputes between them;

(c) allow any party, upon such terms (as to costs and otherwise) as it shall determine, to amend any pleading or submissions;

(d) extend or abbreviate any time limits provided by these Rules or by its directions;

(e) conduct such enquiries as may appear to the Tribunal to be necessary or expedient;

(f) order the parties to make any property or thing available for inspection, in their presence, by the Tribunal or any expert;

(g) order the preservation, storage, sale or other disposal of any property or thing which is the subject-matter of the dispute;

(h) order any party to produce to the Tribunal, and to the other parties for inspection, and to supply copies of, any documents or classes of documents in their possession or power which the Tribunal determines to be relevant;

(i) to make orders or give directions to any party for interrogatories;

(j) to make orders or give directions to any party for an interim injunction or any other interim measure;

(k) to make orders or give directions to any party for giving of evidence by affidavit;

(l) to make orders or give directions to any party for ensuring that any award which may be made in the arbitral proceedings is not rendered ineffectual by the dissipation of assets by a party; and

(m) to make orders or give directions to any party to stay any of the Tribunal's awards previously made.

Rule 26 – Jurisdiction of The Tribunal

26.1 The Tribunal shall have the power to rule on its own jurisdiction, including any objections with respect to the existence, termination or validity of the arbitration agreement. For that purpose, an arbitration agreement which forms part of a contract shall be treated as an agreement independent of the other terms of the contract. A decision by the Tribunal that the contract is null and void shall not entail *ipso jure* the invalidity of the arbitration agreement.

26.2 A plea that the Tribunal does not have jurisdiction shall be raised not later than in the Statement of Defence. A plea that the Tribunal is exceeding the scope of its authority shall be raised promptly after the Tribunal has indicated its intention to decide on the matter alleged to be beyond the scope of its authority. In either case the Tribunal may nevertheless admit a late plea under this Rule if it considers the delay justified. A party is not precluded from raising such a plea by the fact that he has appointed, or participated in the appointment of an arbitrator.

26.3 In addition to the jurisdiction to exercise the powers defined elsewhere in these Rules, the Tribunal shall have jurisdiction to determine any question of law arising in the arbitration; proceed with the arbitration notwithstanding the failure or refusal of any party to comply with these Rules or with the Tribunal's orders or directions, or to attend any meeting or hearing, but only after giving that party written notice that it intends to do so; and to receive and take into account such written or oral evidence as it shall determine to be relevant, whether or not strictly admissible in law.

26.4 The Tribunal may rule on a plea referred to in Rule 26.2 above either as a preliminary question or in an award on the merits.

Rule 27 – Deposits and Security

27.1 The Registrar or the Tribunal (at any time after it has been constituted) may direct each party to deposit an equal amount with the Centre as an advance of the costs referred to in Rule 30.

27.2 During the course of the arbitration proceedings the Registrar or the Tribunal may request supplementary deposits from the parties.

27.3 The Tribunal shall have the power to order any party to provide security for the legal or other costs of any other party by way of deposit or bank guarantee or in any other manner the Tribunal thinks fit.

27.4 Without prejudice to the right of any party to apply to a competent court for pre-award conservatory measures, the Tribunal shall also have the power to order any party to provide security for all or part of any amount in dispute in the arbitration.

27.5 In the event that orders under Rules 27.1, 27.2, 27.3 or 27.4 are not complied with, the Tribunal may refuse to hear the claims or counterclaims by the non-complying party, although it may proceed to determine claims or counterclaims by complying parties.

Rule 28 – The Award

28.1 Unless all parties agree otherwise, the Tribunal shall make its award in writing within forty-five (45) days from the date on which the hearings are closed and shall state the reasons upon which its award is based. The award shall state its date and shall be signed by the arbitrator or arbitrators.

28.2 If any arbitrator refuses or fails to comply with the mandatory provisions of any applicable law relating to the making of the award, having been given a reasonable opportunity to do so, the remaining arbitrators shall proceed in his absence.

28.3 Where there is more than one arbitrator and they fail to agree on any issue, they shall decide by a majority. Failing a majority decision on any issue, the presiding arbitrator of the Tribunal shall make the award alone as if he were sole arbitrator. If an arbitrator refuses or fails to sign the award, the signatures of the majority shall be sufficient, provided that the reasons for the omitted signature is stated.

28.4 The sole arbitrator or presiding arbitrator shall be responsible for delivering the award to the Registrar, who shall transmit certified copies to the parties provided that the costs of the arbitration have been paid to the Centre in accordance with Rule 30.

28.5 The Tribunal may award simple or compound interest on any sum which is the subject of the reference at such rates as the Tribunal determines to be appropriate, in respect of any period which the Tribunal determines to be appropriate ending not later than the date upon which the award is complied with.

28.6 The Tribunal may make separate final awards on different issues at different times, which shall be subject to correction under the procedure specified in Rule 29. Unless otherwise stated by the Tribunal, such awards shall be individually enforceable as soon as they are made.

28.7 In the event of a settlement, the Tribunal may render a consent award recording the settlement if any party so requests. If the parties do not require a consent award, then on confirmation in writing by the parties to the Registrar that a settlement has been reached, the Tribunal shall be discharged and the reference to arbitration concluded, subject to payment by the parties of any outstanding costs of the arbitration in accordance with Rule 30.

28.8 By agreeing to have an arbitration under these Rules, the parties undertake to carry out the award without delay. Awards shall be final and binding on the parties from the date they are made.

Rule 29 – Correction of Awards and Additional Awards

29.1 Within thirty (30) days of receipt of the award, unless another period of time has been agreed upon by the parties, a party may by notice to the Registrar request the Tribunal to correct in the award any error in computation, any clerical or typographical error or any error of a similar nature. If the Tribunal considers the request to be justified, it shall make the correction(s) within thirty (30) days of receipt of the request. Any correction, which shall take the form of a separate memorandum, shall become part of the award.

29.2 The Tribunal may correct any error of the type referred to in Rule 29.1 on its own initiative within thirty (30) days of the date of the award.

29.3 Unless otherwise agreed by the parties, a party may, within thirty (30) days of receipt of the award, and with notice to the other party or parties, by notice to the Registrar request the Tribunal to make an additional award as to claims presented in the arbitral proceedings but not dealt with in the award. If the Tribunal considers the request to be justified, it shall make the additional award within forty-five (45) days of receipt of the request.

29.4 The provisions of Rule 28 shall apply *mutatis mutandis* to a correction of the award and to any additional award.

Rule 30 – Costs

30.1 The costs of the arbitration shall be taxed by the Registrar or fixed by the Tribunal in its award. The term "costs of the arbitration" includes:

(a) the fees of the Tribunal;

(b) the travel and other expenses incurred by the arbitrators;

(c) the costs of expert advice and of other assistance required by the Tribunal;

(d) any fees and expenses of the appointing authority, if applicable; and

(e) expenses reasonably incurred by the Centre in connection with the arbitration as well as its administrative charges, but shall not include the legal or other costs incurred by the parties themselves.

30.2 The Tribunal shall specify in the award, the total amount of the costs of the arbitration. Unless the parties shall agree otherwise, the Tribunal shall determine the proportions in which the parties shall pay all or part of them to the Centre. If the Tribunal has determined that all or any part of the costs of the arbitration shall be paid by any party other than a party which has already paid them to the Centre, the latter shall have the right to recover the appropriate amount from the former.

30.3 The Tribunal shall have the authority to order in its award that all or a part of the legal or other costs of a party (apart from the costs of the arbitration) be paid by another party. Such costs shall, unless the award otherwise directs, be taxable by the Registrar.

30.4 If the arbitration is abandoned, suspended or concluded, by agreement or otherwise, before the final award is made, the parties shall be jointly and severally liable to pay the costs of the arbitration as determined by the Tribunal. In the event that the costs so determined are less than the deposits made, there shall be a refund in such proportions as the parties may agree, or failing agreement, in the same proportions as the deposits were made.

30.5 A certificate signed by the Registrar on the amount of costs or fees taxed shall form part of the award of the Tribunal.

Rule 31 – Amount of Tribunal's Fees

31.1 The fees of the Tribunal shall be reasonable in amount, taking into account the amount in dispute, the complexity of the subject-matter, the time spent by the arbitrators and any other relevant circumstances of the case.

31.2 If an appointing authority has been agreed upon by the parties or designated by the Chairman, and if that authority has issued a schedule of fees for arbitrators in international cases which it administers, the Tribunal in fixing its fees shall take that schedule of fees into account to the extent that it considers appropriate in the circumstances of the case.

31.3 If such appointing authority has not issued a schedule of fees for arbitrators in international cases, and if the parties fail to agree, an appropriate rate shall be determined by the Registrar and communicated in writing to the parties.

31.4 In all cases when a party so requests, the Tribunal shall fix its fees only after consultation with the Registrar who may advise the Tribunal concerning the fees.

Rule 32 – Law of the Arbitration

If the place of arbitration is Singapore, the parties agree that the International Arbitration Act (Cap 143A) as amended from time to time is applicable.

Rule 33 – Exclusion of Liability

33.1 Neither the Centre, any of its officers, employees or agents, nor any arbitrator shall be liable for:

(a) negligence in respect of anything done or omitted to be done in the capacity of arbitrator or in connection with any arbitration conducted under these Rules; and

(b) any mistake in law, fact or procedure made in the course of arbitral proceedings or in the making of an arbitral award.

33.2 Neither the Centre, any of its officers, employees or agents, nor any arbitrator shall be under any obligation to make any statement to any person about any matter concerning the arbitration, nor shall any party seek to make any arbitrator or any officer, member, servant or agent of the Centre, a witness in any legal proceedings arising out of the arbitration whether before, during or after the arbitration.

Rule 34 – General Provisions

34.1 A party who knows that any provision of, or requirement under, these Rules has not been complied with and yet proceeds with the arbitration without promptly stating its objection to such non-compliance, shall be deemed to have waived its right to object.

34.2 The provisions in these Rules shall insofar as they relate to the powers and functions of the Tribunal be interpreted by the Tribunal.

34.3 In all matters not expressly provided for in these Rules, the Chairman, the Registrar and the Tribunal shall act in the spirit of these Rules and shall make every reasonable effort to ensure that the award is legally enforceable.

34.4 Notwithstanding any provision by the parties in any contract for an appointing authority to appoint a sole arbitrator or arbitrators, such provision shall be deemed to be completely and irrevocably waived upon the appointment by the Chairman of the sole arbitrator or any arbitrator pursuant to these Rules, and thereafter all powers and functions of the appointing authority whether in such contract or in the Rules shall vest in the Chairman, in addition to and without derogation to the powers of the Chairman set out in these Rules.

34.5 Subject to Rule 34.4, in the event of conflict between these Rules and the terms of any contract entered into between the parties, the terms of the said contract shall prevail, save that where the parties have acted pursuant to or in accordance with any Rule in conflict with any term of the said contract, that Rule shall prevail, and any right vested in any party pursuant to that term in the said contract shall be deemed to be completely and irrevocably waived.

34.6 The parties and the Tribunal shall at all times treat all matters relating to the proceedings (including the existence of the proceedings) and the award as confidential. A party or any arbitrator shall not, without the prior written consent of the other party or the parties, as the case may be, disclose to a third party any such matter except:

(a) for the purpose of making an application to any competent court;

(b) for the purpose of making an application to the courts of any State to enforce the award;

(c) pursuant to the order of a court of competent jurisdiction;

(d) in compliance with the provisions of the laws of any State which is binding on the party making the disclosure; or

(e) in compliance with the request or requirement of any regulatory body or other authority which, if not binding, nonetheless would be observed customarily by the party making the disclosure.

THE UNITED NATIONS COMMISSION ON INTERNATIONAL TRADE LAW ("UNCITRAL")

Effective as of December 15, 1976

UNCITRAL ARBITRATION RULES

SECTION I – INTRODUCTORY RULES

Article 1 – Scope of Application

1. Where the parties to a contract have agreed in writing that disputes in relation to that contract shall be referred to arbitration under the UNCITRAL Arbitration Rules, then such disputes shall be settled in accordance with these Rules subject to such modification as the parties may agree in writing.

2. These Rules shall govern the arbitration except that where any of these Rules is in conflict with a provision of the law applicable to the arbitration from which the parties cannot derogate, that provision shall prevail.

Article 2 – Notice, Calculation of Periods of Time

1. For the purposes of these Rules, any notice, including a notification, communication or proposal, is deemed to have been received if it is physically delivered to the addressee or if it is delivered at his habitual residence, place of business or mailing address, or, if none of these can be found after making reasonable inquiry, then at the addressee's last-known residence or place of business. Notice shall be deemed to have been received on the day it is so delivered.

2. For the purposes of calculating a period of time under these Rules, such period shall begin to run on the day following the day when a notice, notification, communication or proposal is received. If the last day of such period is an official holiday or a non-business day at the residence or place of business of the addressee, the period is extended until the first business day which follows. Official holidays or non-business days occurring during the running of the period of time are included in calculating the period.

Article 3 – Notice of Arbitration

1. The party initiating recourse to arbitration (hereinafter called the "claimant") shall give to the other party (hereinafter called the "respondent") a notice of arbitration.

2. Arbitral proceedings shall be deemed to commence on the date on which the notice of arbitration is received by the respondent.

3. The notice of arbitration shall include the following:

(a) A demand that the dispute be referred to arbitration;

(b) The names and addresses of the parties;

(c) A reference to the arbitration clause or the separate arbitration agreement that is invoked;

(d) A reference to the contract out of or in relation to which the dispute arises;

(e) The general nature of the claim and an indication of the amount involved, if any;

(f) The relief or remedy sought;

(g) A proposal as to the number of arbitrators (i.e. one or three), if the parties have not previously agreed thereon.

4. The notice of arbitration may also include:

(a) The proposals for the appointments of a sole arbitrator and an appointing authority referred to in article 6, paragraph 1;

(b) The notification of the appointment of an arbitrator referred to in article 7;

(c) The statement of claim referred to in article 18.

Article 4 – Representation and Assistance

The parties may be represented or assisted by persons of their choice. The names and addresses of such persons must be communicated in writing to the other party; such communication must specify whether the appointment is being made for purposes of representation or assistance.

SECTION II – COMPOSITION OF THE ARBITRAL TRIBUNAL

Article 5 – Number of Arbitrators

If the parties have not previously agreed on the number of arbitrators (i.e. one or three), and if within fifteen days after the receipt by the respondent of the notice of arbitration the parties have not agreed that there shall be only one arbitrator, three arbitrators shall be appointed.

Article 6 – Appointment of Arbitrators (Articles 6 to 8)

1. If a sole arbitrator is to be appointed, either party may propose to the other:

(a) The names of one or more persons, one of whom would serve as the sole arbitrator; and

(b) If no appointing authority has been agreed upon by the parties, the name or names of one or more institutions or persons, one of whom would serve as appointing authority.

2. If within thirty days after receipt by a party of a proposal made in accordance with paragraph 1 the parties have not reached agreement on the choice of a sole arbitrator, the sole arbitrator shall be appointed by the appointing authority agreed upon by the parties. If no appointing authority has been agreed upon by the parties, or if the appointing authority agreed upon refuses to act or fails to appoint the arbitrator within sixty days of the receipt of a party's request therefor, either party may request the Secretary-General of the Permanent Court of Arbitration at The Hague to designate an appointing authority.

3. The appointing authority shall, at the request of one of the parties, appoint the sole arbitrator as promptly as possible. In making the appointment the appointing authority

shall use the following list-procedure, unless both parties agree that the list-procedure should not be used or unless the appointing authority determines in its discretion that the use of the list-procedure is not appropriate for the case:

(a) At the request of one of the parties the appointing authority shall communicate to both parties an identical list containing at least three names;

(b) Within fifteen days after the receipt of this list, each party may return the list to the appointing authority after having deleted the name or names to which he objects and numbered the remaining names on the list in the order of his preference;

(c) After the expiration of the above period of time the appointing authority shall appoint the sole arbitrator from among the names approved on the lists returned to it and in accordance with the order of preference indicated by the parties;

(d) If for any reason the appointment cannot be made according to this procedure, the appointing authority may exercise its discretion in appointing the sole arbitrator.

4. In making the appointment, the appointing authority shall have regard to such considerations as are likely to secure the appointment of an independent and impartial arbitrator and shall take into account as well the advisability of appointing an arbitrator of a nationality other than the nationalities of the parties.

Article 7

1. If three arbitrators are to be appointed, each party shall appoint one arbitrator. The two arbitrators thus appointed shall choose the third arbitrator who will act as the presiding arbitrator of the tribunal.

2. If within thirty days after the receipt of a party's notification of the appointment of an arbitrator the other party has not notified the first party of the arbitrator he has appointed:

(a) The first party may request the appointing authority previously designated by the parties to appoint the second arbitrator; or

(b) If no such authority has been previously designated by the parties, or if the appointing authority previously designated refuses to act or fails to appoint the arbitrator within thirty days after receipt of a party's request therefor, the first party may request the Secretary-General of the Permanent Court of Arbitration at The Hague to designate the appointing authority. The first party may then request the appointing authority so designated to appoint the second arbitrator. In either case, the appointing authority may exercise its discretion in appointing the arbitrator.

3. If within thirty days after the appointment of the second arbitrator the two arbitrators have not agreed on the choice of the presiding arbitrator, the presiding arbitrator shall be appointed by an appointing authority in the same way as a sole arbitrator would be appointed under article 6.

Article 8

1. When an appointing authority is requested to appoint an arbitrator pursuant to article 6 or article 7, the party which makes the request shall send to the appointing authority a copy of the notice of arbitration, a copy of the contract out of or in relation to which the dispute has arisen and a copy of the arbitration agreement if it is not contained in the contract. The appointing authority may require from either party such information as it deems necessary to fulfil its function.

2. Where the names of one or more persons are proposed for appointment as arbitrators, their full names, addresses and nationalities shall be indicated, together with a description of their qualifications.

Article 9 – Challenge of Arbitrators (Articles 9 to 12)

A prospective arbitrator shall disclose to those who approach him in connexion with his possible appointment any circumstances likely to give rise to justifiable doubts as to his impartiality or independence. An arbitrator, once appointed or chosen, shall disclose such circumstances to the parties unless they have already been informed by him of these circumstances.

Article 10

1. Any arbitrator may be challenged if circumstances exist that give rise to justifiable doubts as to the arbitrator's impartiality or independence.

2. A party may challenge the arbitrator appointed by him only for reasons of which he becomes aware after the appointment has been made.

Article 11

1. A party who intends to challenge an arbitrator shall send notice of his challenge within fifteen days after the appointment of the challenged arbitrator has been notified to the challenging party or within fifteen days after the circumstances mentioned in articles 9 and 10 became known to that party.

2. The challenge shall be notified to the other party, to the arbitrator who is challenged and to the other members of the arbitral tribunal. The notification shall be in writing and shall state the reasons for the challenge.

3. When an arbitrator has been challenged by one party, the other party may agree to the challenge. The arbitrator may also, after the challenge, withdraw from his office. In neither case does this imply acceptance of the validity of the grounds for the challenge. In both cases the procedure provided in article 6 or 7 shall be used in full for the appointment of the substitute arbitrator, even if during the process of appointing the challenged arbitrator a party had failed to exercise his right to appoint or to participate in the appointment.

Article 12

1. If the other party does not agree to the challenge and the challenged arbitrator does not withdraw, the decision on the challenge will be made:

(a) When the initial appointment was made by an appointing authority, by that authority;

(b) When the initial appointment was not made by an appointing authority, but an appointing authority has been previously designated, by that authority;

(c) In all other cases, by the appointing authority to be designated in accordance with the procedure for designating an appointing authority as provided for in article 6.

2. If the appointing authority sustains the challenge, a substitute arbitrator shall be appointed or chosen pursuant to the procedure applicable to the appointment or choice of an arbitrator as provided in articles 6 to 9 except that, when this procedure would call for the designation of an appointing authority, the appointment of the arbitrator shall be made by the appointing authority which decided on the challenge.

Article 13 – Replacement of an Arbitrator

1. In the event of the death or resignation of an arbitrator during the course of the arbitral proceedings, a substitute arbitrator shall be appointed or chosen pursuant to the procedure provided for in articles 6 to 9 that was applicable to the appointment or choice of the arbitrator being replaced.

2. In the event that an arbitrator fails to act or in the event of the *de jure* or *de facto* impossibility of his performing his functions, the procedure in respect of the challenge and replacement of an arbitrator as provided in the preceding articles shall apply.

Article 14 – Repetition of Hearings in the Event of the Replacement of an Arbitrator

If under articles 11 to 13 the sole or presiding arbitrator is replaced, any hearings held previously shall be repeated; if any other arbitrator is replaced, such prior hearings may be repeated at the discretion of the arbitral tribunal.

SECTION III – ARBITRAL PROCEEDINGS

Article 15 – General Provisions

1. Subject to these Rules, the arbitral tribunal may conduct the arbitration in such manner as it considers appropriate, provided that the parties are treated with equality and that at any stage of the proceedings each party is given a full opportunity of presenting his case.

2. If either party so requests at any stage of the proceedings, the arbitral tribunal shall hold hearings for the presentation of evidence by witnesses, including expert witnesses, or for oral argument. In the absence of such a request, the arbitral tribunal shall decide whether

to hold such hearings or whether the proceedings shall be conducted on the basis of documents and other materials.

3. All documents or information supplied to the arbitral tribunal by one party shall at the same time be communicated by that party to the other party.

Article 16 – Place of Arbitration

1. Unless the parties have agreed upon the place where the arbitration is to be held, such place shall be determined by the arbitral tribunal, having regard to the circumstances of the arbitration.

2. The arbitral tribunal may determine the locale of the arbitration within the country agreed upon by the parties. It may hear witnesses and hold meetings for consultation among its members at any place it deems appropriate, having regard to the circumstances of the arbitration.

3. The arbitral tribunal may meet at any place it deems appropriate for the inspection of goods, other property or documents. The parties shall be given sufficient notice to enable them to be present at such inspection.

4. The award shall be made at the place of arbitration.

Article 17 – Language

1. Subject to an agreement by the parties, the arbitral tribunal shall, promptly after its appointment, determine the language or languages to be used in the proceedings. This determination shall apply to the statement of claim, the statement of defence, and any further written statements and, if oral hearings take place, to the language or languages to be used in such hearings.

2. The arbitral tribunal may order that any documents annexed to the statement of claim or statement of defence, and any supplementary documents or exhibits submitted in the course of the proceedings, delivered in their original language, shall be accompanied by a translation into the language or languages agreed upon by the parties or determined by the arbitral tribunal.

Article 18 – Statement of Claim

1. Unless the statement of claim was contained in the notice of arbitration, within a period of time to be determined by the arbitral tribunal, the claimant shall communicate his statement of claim in writing to the respondent and to each of the arbitrators. A copy of the contract, and of the arbitration agreement if not contained in the contract, shall be annexed thereto.

2. The statement of claim shall include the following particulars:

(a) The names and addresses of the parties;

(b) A statement of the facts supporting the claim;

(c) The points at issue;

(d) The relief or remedy sought.

The claimant may annex to his statement of claim all documents he deems relevant or may add a reference to the documents or other evidence he will submit.

Article 19 – Statement of Defence

1. Within a period of time to be determined by the arbitral tribunal, the respondent shall communicate his statement of defence in writing to the claimant and to each of the arbitrators.

2. The statement of defence shall reply to the particulars *(b)*, *(c)* and *(d)* of the statement of claim (article 18, para. 2). The respondent may annex to his statement the documents on which he relies for his defence or may add a reference to the documents or other evidence he will submit.

3. In his statement of defence, or at a later stage in the arbitral proceedings if the arbitral tribunal decides that the delay was justified under the circumstances, the respondent may make a counter-claim arising out of the same contract or rely on a claim arising out of the same contract for the purpose of a set-off.

4. The provisions of article 18, paragraph 2, shall apply to a counter-claim and a claim relied on for the purpose of a set-off.

Article 20 – Amendments to the Claim or Defence

During the course of the arbitral proceedings either party may amend or supplement his claim or defence unless the arbitral tribunal considers it inappropriate to allow such amendment having regard to the delay in making it or prejudice to the other party or any other circumstances. However, a claim may not be amended in such a manner that the amended claim falls outside the scope of the arbitration clause or separate arbitration agreement.

Article 21 – Pleas as to the Jurisdiction of the Arbitral Tribunal

1. The arbitral tribunal shall have the power to rule on objections that it has no jurisdiction, including any objections with respect to the existence or validity of the arbitration clause or of the separate arbitration agreement.

2. The arbitral tribunal shall have the power to determine the existence or the validity of the contract of which an arbitration clause forms a part. For the purposes of article 21, an arbitration clause which forms part of a contract and which provides for arbitration under these Rules shall be treated as an agreement independent of the other terms of the

contract. A decision by the arbitral tribunal that the contract is null and void shall not entail *ipso jure* the invalidity of the arbitration clause.

3. A plea that the arbitral tribunal does not have jurisdiction shall be raised not later than in the statement of defence or, with respect to a counter-claim, in the reply to the counter-claim.

4. In general, the arbitral tribunal should rule on a plea concerning its jurisdiction as a preliminary question. However, the arbitral tribunal may proceed with the arbitration and rule on such a plea in their final award.

Article 22 – Further Written Statements

The arbitral tribunal shall decide which further written statements, in addition to the statement of claim and the statement of defence, shall be required from the parties or may be presented by them and shall fix the periods of time for communicating such statements.

Article 23 – Periods of Time

The periods of time fixed by the arbitral tribunal for the communication of written statements (including the statement of claim and statement of defence) should not exceed forty-five days. However, the arbitral tribunal may extend the time-limits if it concludes that an extension is justified.

Article 24 – Evidence and Hearings (Articles 24 and 25)

1. Each party shall have the burden of proving the facts relied on to support his claim or defence.

2. The arbitral tribunal may, if it considers it appropriate, require a party to deliver to the tribunal and to the other party, within such a period of time as the arbitral tribunal shall decide, a summary of the documents and other evidence which that party intends to present in support of the facts in issue set out in his statement of claim or statement of defence.

3. At any time during the arbitral proceedings the arbitral tribunal may require the parties to produce documents, exhibits or other evidence within such a period of time as the tribunal shall determine.

Article 25

1. In the event of an oral hearing, the arbitral tribunal shall give the parties adequate advance notice of the date, time and place thereof.

2. If witnesses are to be heard, at least fifteen days before the hearing each party shall communicate to the arbitral tribunal and to the other party the names and addresses of the witnesses he intends to present, the subject upon and the languages in which such witnesses will give their testimony.

3. The arbitral tribunal shall make arrangements for the translation of oral statements made at a hearing and for a record of the hearing if either is deemed necessary by the tribunal under the circumstances of the case, or if the parties have agreed thereto and have communicated such agreement to the tribunal at least fifteen days before the hearing.

4. Hearings shall be held *in camera* unless the parties agree otherwise. The arbitral tribunal may require the retirement of any witness or witnesses during the testimony of other witnesses. The arbitral tribunal is free to determine the manner in which witnesses are examined.

5. Evidence of witnesses may also be presented in the form of written statements signed by them.

6. The arbitral tribunal shall determine the admissibility, relevance, materiality and weight of the evidence offered.

Article 26 – Interim Measures of Protection

1. At the request of either party, the arbitral tribunal may take any interim measures it deems necessary in respect of the subject-matter of the dispute, including measures for the conservation of the goods forming the subject-matter in dispute, such as ordering their deposit with a third person or the sale of perishable goods.

2. Such interim measures may be established in the form of an interim award. The arbitral tribunal shall be entitled to require security for the costs of such measures.

3. A request for interim measures addressed by any party to a judicial authority shall not be deemed incompatible with the agreement to arbitrate, or as a waiver of that agreement.

Article 27 – Experts

1. The arbitral tribunal may appoint one or more experts to report to it, in writing, on specific issues to be determined by the tribunal. A copy of the expert's terms of reference, established by the arbitral tribunal, shall be communicated to the parties.

2. The parties shall give the expert any relevant information or produce for his inspection any relevant documents or goods that he may require of them. Any dispute between a party and such expert as to the relevance of the required information or production shall be referred to the arbitral tribunal for decision.

3. Upon receipt of the expert's report, the arbitral tribunal shall communicate a copy of the report to the parties who shall be given the opportunity to express, in writing, their opinion on the report. A party shall be entitled to examine any document on which the expert has relied in his report.

4. At the request of either party the expert, after delivery of the report, may be heard at a hearing where the parties shall have the opportunity to be present and to interrogate the

expert. At this hearing either party may present expert witnesses in order to testify on the points at issue. The provisions of article 25 shall be applicable to such proceedings.

Article 28 – Default

1. If, within the period of time fixed by the arbitral tribunal, the claimant has failed to communicate his claim without showing sufficient cause for such failure, the arbitral tribunal shall issue an order for the termination of the arbitral proceedings. If, within the period of time fixed by the arbitral tribunal, the respondent has failed to communicate his statement of defence without showing sufficient cause for such failure, the arbitral tribunal shall order that the proceedings continue.

2. If one of the parties, duly notified under these Rules, fails to appear at a hearing, without showing sufficient cause for such failure, the arbitral tribunal may proceed with the arbitration.

3. If one of the parties, duly invited to produce documentary evidence, fails to do so within the established period of time, without showing sufficient cause for such failure, the arbitral tribunal may make the award on the evidence before it.

Article 29 – Closure of Hearings

1. The arbitral tribunal may inquire of the parties if they have any further proof to offer or witnesses to be heard or submissions to make and, if there are none, it may declare the hearings closed.

2. The arbitral tribunal may, if it considers it necessary owing to exceptional circumstances, decide, on its own motion or upon application of a party, to reopen the hearings at any time before the award is made.

Article 30 – Waiver of Rules

A party who knows that any provision of, or requirement under, these Rules has not been complied with and yet proceeds with the arbitration without promptly stating his objection to such non-compliance, shall be deemed to have waived his right to object.

SECTION IV – THE AWARD

Article 31 – Decisions

1. When there are three arbitrators, any award or other decision of the arbitral tribunal shall be made by a majority of the arbitrators.

2. In the case of questions of procedure, when there is no majority or when the arbitral tribunal so authorizes, the presiding arbitrator may decide on his own, subject to revision, if any, by the arbitral tribunal.

Article 32 – Form and Effect of the Award

1. In addition to making a final award, the arbitral tribunal shall be entitled to make interim, interlocutory, or partial awards.

2. The award shall be made in writing and shall be final and binding on the parties. The parties undertake to carry out the award without delay.

3. The arbitral tribunal shall state the reasons upon which the award is based, unless the parties have agreed that no reasons are to be given.

4. An award shall be signed by the arbitrators and it shall contain the date on which and the place where the award was made. Where there are three arbitrators and one of them fails to sign, the award shall state the reason for the absence of the signature.

5. The award may be made public only with the consent of both parties.

6. Copies of the award signed by the arbitrators shall be communicated to the parties by the arbitral tribunal.

7. If the arbitration law of the country where the award is made requires that the award be filed or registered by the arbitral tribunal, the tribunal shall comply with this requirement within the period of time required by law.

Article 33 – Applicable Law, *Amiable Compositeur*

1. The arbitral tribunal shall apply the law designated by the parties as applicable to the substance of the dispute. Failing such designation by the parties, the arbitral tribunal shall apply the law determined by the conflict of laws rules which it considers applicable.

2. The arbitral tribunal shall decide as *amiable compositeur* or *ex aequo et bono* only if the parties have expressly authorized the arbitral tribunal to do so and if the law applicable to the arbitral procedure permits such arbitration.

3. In all cases, the arbitral tribunal shall decide in accordance with the terms of the contract and shall take into account the usages of the trade applicable to the transaction.

Article 34 – Settlement or Other Grounds for Termination

1. If, before the award is made, the parties agree on a settlement of the dispute, the arbitral tribunal shall either issue an order for the termination of the arbitral proceedings or, if requested by both parties and accepted by the tribunal, record the settlement in the form of an arbitral award on agreed terms. The arbitral tribunal is not obliged to give reasons for such an award.

2. If, before the award is made, the continuation of the arbitral proceedings becomes unnecessary or impossible for any reason not mentioned in paragraph 1, the arbitral tribunal shall inform the parties of its intention to issue an order for the termination of the

proceedings. The arbitral tribunal shall have the power to issue such an order unless a party raises justifiable grounds for objection.

3. Copies of the order for termination of the arbitral proceedings or of the arbitral award on agreed terms, signed by the arbitrators, shall be communicated by the arbitral tribunal to the parties. Where an arbitral award on agreed terms is made, the provisions of article 32, paragraphs 2 and 4 to 7, shall apply.

Article 35 – Interpretation of the Award

1. Within thirty days after the receipt of the award, either party, with notice to the other party, may request that the arbitral tribunal give an interpretation of the award.

2. The interpretation shall be given in writing within forty-five days after the receipt of the request. The interpretation shall form part of the award and the provisions of article 32, paragraphs 2 to 7, shall apply.

Article 36 – Correction of the Award

1. Within thirty days after the receipt of the award, either party, with notice to the other party, may request the arbitral tribunal to correct in the award any errors in computation, any clerical or typographical errors, or any errors of similar nature. The arbitral tribunal may within thirty days after the communication of the award make such corrections on its own initiative.

2. Such corrections shall be in writing, and the provisions of article 32, paragraphs 2 to 7, shall apply.

Article 37 – Additional Award

1. Within thirty days after the receipt of the award, either party, with notice to the other party, may request the arbitral tribunal to make an additional award as to claims presented in the arbitral proceedings but omitted from the award.

2. If the arbitral tribunal considers the request for an additional award to be justified and considers that the omission can be rectified without any further hearings or evidence, it shall complete its award within sixty days after the receipt of the request.

3. When an additional award is made, the provisions of article 32, paragraphs 2 to 7, shall apply.

Article 38 – Costs (articles 38 to 40)

The arbitral tribunal shall fix the costs of arbitration in its award. The term "costs" includes only:

(a) The fees of the arbitral tribunal to be stated separately as to each arbitrator and to be fixed by the tribunal itself in accordance with article 39;

(b) The travel and other expenses incurred by the arbitrators;

(c) The costs of expert advice and of other assistance required by the arbitral tribunal;

(d) The travel and other expenses of witnesses to the extent such expenses are approved by the arbitral tribunal;

(e) The costs for legal representation and assistance of the successful party if such costs were claimed during the arbitral proceedings, and only to the extent that the arbitral tribunal determines that the amount of such costs is reasonable;

(f) Any fees and expenses of the appointing authority as well as the expenses of the Secretary-General of the Permanent Court of Arbitration at The Hague.

Article 39

1. The fees of the arbitral tribunal shall be reasonable in amount, taking into account the amount in dispute, the complexity of the subject-matter, the time spent by the arbitrators and any other relevant circumstances of the case.

2. If an appointing authority has been agreed upon by the parties or designated by the Secretary-General of the Permanent Court of Arbitration at The Hague, and if that authority has issued a schedule of fees for arbitrators in international cases which it administers, the arbitral tribunal in fixing its fees shall take that schedule of fees into account to the extent that it considers appropriate in the circumstances of the case.

3. If such appointing authority has not issued a schedule of fees for arbitrators in international cases, any party may at any time request the appointing authority to furnish a statement setting forth the basis for establishing fees which is customarily followed in international cases in which the authority appoints arbitrators. If the appointing authority consents to provide such a statement, the arbitral tribunal in fixing its fees shall take such information into account to the extent that it considers appropriate in the circumstances of the case.

4. In cases referred to in paragraphs 2 and 3, when a party so requests and the appointing authority consents to perform the function, the arbitral tribunal shall fix its fees only after consultation with the appointing authority which may make any comment it deems appropriate to the arbitral tribunal concerning the fees.

Article 40

1. Except as provided in paragraph 2, the costs of arbitration shall in principle be borne by the unsuccessful party. However, the arbitral tribunal may apportion each of such costs between the parties if it determines that apportionment is reasonable, taking into account the circumstances of the case.

2. With respect to the costs of legal representation and assistance referred to in article 38, paragraph *(e)*, the arbitral tribunal, taking into account the circumstances of the case,

shall be free to determine which party shall bear such costs or may apportion such costs between the parties if it determines that apportionment is reasonable.

3. When the arbitral tribunal issues an order for the termination of the arbitral proceedings or makes an award on agreed terms, it shall fix the costs of arbitration referred to in article 38 and article 39, paragraph 1, in the text of that order or award.

4. No additional fees may be charged by an arbitral tribunal for interpretation or correction or completion of its award under articles 35 to 37.

Article 41 – Deposit of Costs

1. The arbitral tribunal, on its establishment, may request each party to deposit an equal amount as an advance for the costs referred to in article 38, paragraphs *(a), (b)* and *(c).*

2. During the course of the arbitral proceedings the arbitral tribunal may request supplementary deposits from the parties.

3. If an appointing authority has been agreed upon by the parties or designated by the Secretary-General of the Permanent Court of Arbitration at The Hague, and when a party so requests and the appointing authority consents to perform the function, the arbitral tribunal shall fix the amounts of any deposits or supplementary deposits only after consultation with the appointing authority which may make any comments to the arbitral tribunal which it deems appropriate concerning the amount of such deposits and supplementary deposits.

4. If the required deposits are not paid in full within thirty days after the receipt of the request, the arbitral tribunal shall so inform the parties in order that one or another of them may make the required payment. If such payment is not made, the arbitral tribunal may order the suspension or termination of the arbitral proceedings.

5. After the award has been made, the arbitral tribunal shall render an accounting to the parties of the deposits received and return any unexpended balance to the parties.